Sport's
Most Bizarre Moments

Sport's
Most Bizarre Moments

John Griffiths, Geoff Tibballs
and Andrew Ward

ROBSON BOOKS

This edition first published in Great Britain in 2004
by Robson Books, an imprint of Chrysalis Books Group
Exclusively for Marks and Spencer p.l.c., PO Box 3339, Chester CH99 9QS

www.marksandspencer.com

British Library Cataloguing in Publication Data
A catalogue record for this title is available from the British Library.

ISBN 1 86105 758 X

Printed in Great Britain

Front-cover picture credits
Left: Mary Evans Picture Library; centre: Hulton|Getty Images; right: Mirrorpix.

Contents

FOOTBALL

by Andrew Ward

The One-Man Team

Burnley, December 1891

Snow was falling heavily and it was one of the coldest weeks of the year. No one felt much like playing football. Certainly none of the Blackburn Rovers players did; but, being mainly professionals, they came out of the pavilion to take on Burnley.

Conceding three goals in the first 25 minutes did nothing to raise their spirits. Already it was a tetchy game. Two players squared up to each other in a bid to keep warm and settle a quarrel in the cold. When half-time arrived everybody was pleased.

The ten-minute interval passed. Burnley were on the field but there was no sign of Blackburn Rovers. The referee was the notorious J C Clegg from Sheffield, a high-ranking FA official and a man to stand no nonsense. Nor did he like waiting in the cold. He warned the teams that he would start in two minutes. In fact he waited four. Even then not all the Rovers players had returned to the pitch.

Soon tempers rose again. The two feuding players came to blows and were sent off. But what followed next was extraordinary. All the Blackburn players except goalkeeper Herby Arthur left the field. The referee, aware that he had done the correct thing by starting the game when there were more than six players, simply carried on. It was Burnley against the opposing goalkeeper.

Herby Arthur was nearing the end of his tremendous career with Blackburn Rovers. He had joined the club as a right-half in 1880, then volunteered to keep goal in the reserve team when a vacancy occurred with no obvious replacement. He played in Rovers' hat trick of FA Cup Final wins in the mid-1880s and became an established England international. Unlike most of the Rovers' players, he remained an amateur.

This was his biggest test. Burnley restarted the game and bore down on his goal.

'Offside,' yelled Herby Arthur.

It was given.

There followed an eternal period of time-wasting. Herby Arthur, with no one to pass the ball to, dallied as long as he could. Eventually the referee gave up and abandoned the game.

Blackburn Rovers later apologised, saying that their players were numb with cold and couldn't continue. Two days later Herby Arthur was given a benefit when Rovers played Sunderland.

The Game of Three Halves
Sunderland, September 1894

On the first day of the 1894–5 soccer season Sunderland were at home to Derby County. The official referee, Mr Kirkham, was late. The game started with a deputy in charge, later named as John Conqueror of Southwick. The two teams played for 45 minutes and then Mr Kirkham arrived. What should he do?

Mr Kirkham made an incredible decision. He offered Derby County, who were losing 3–0, the option of starting again. Naturally they took it. Two more halves followed, and the game became known as 'the game of three halves'.

Derby were captained by England international John Goodall, who lost the toss twice. Derby were forced to kick against a strong gale for the first two halves. But the biggest panic was among the pressmen present at the game. They had already despatched messages all over the country to the effect that Sunderland were winning 3–0 at half-time. Fortunately, Derby obliged by conceding three more goals during the second first half.

Perversely, the decision to start the game *de novo* probably favoured Sunderland more than Derby. After kicking against the wind for 90 minutes the visiting players were, to say the least, weary. Sunderland scored five more in the third half. The result was recorded as an 8–0 win although Sunderland had scored 11 goals during the three halves. A pattern was set for the season. Sunderland sailed to their third Football League

Championship, while Derby were fortunate to hang on to their First Division status.

The 'game of three halves' assumed a legendary place among the folklore of Derby County players, none more than England-international goalkeeper Jack Robinson, who conceded eleven goals that afternoon. Robinson had previously boasted that he would never concede ten goals in a game (adding as a joke that he would come out of goal when the opposition reached nine) and his team-mates debated whether the Sunderland game counted as eight or eleven. Robinson explained the débâcle by his failure to eat rice pudding before the match at Sunderland – the only time he missed with his superstition. 'No pudding, no points,' Robinson would tell his team-mates, who would go to great lengths to indulge their temperamental goal-keeper. One day at Burnley, when a hotel waitress announced the rice pudding was 'off', John Goodall went searching for an hour before he came up with a plate of something which would pass for the same dish. Derby County won at Burnley that day, and they played just two halves.

Not One Shot at Goal

Stoke, April 1898

Modern-day soccer may have its highly developed defensive strategies and across-the-field build-up, but the strangest shot-shy game of all took place more than 90 years ago, when Stoke City and Burnley engineered a goalless draw to save their places in the First Division.

Stoke and Burnley were engaged with two other teams (Newcastle and Blackburn) in a series of test matches to decide promotion and relegation between the two divisions. On the morning of the final round of matches, Stoke and Burnley were joint top of the mini-league. A draw would suit them both, but it didn't suit the 4,000 people who braved torrential rain and strong wind to attend the game at Stoke's Victoria Ground.

It was a fiasco. The goalkeepers hardly touched the ball, passes went to opponents when either team looked well placed to attack, and, if a forward did by chance find himself in a shooting position he would aim at the corner-flag. Players' kit remained surprisingly clean in the atrocious conditions, and the best chance of a goal was a tame backpass.

The crowd quickly realised what was happening. They booed and jeered, or, for variation, cheered sarcastically. They shouted kind words of advice.

'Come off the field, we're doing more than you!'

'Play the game!'

'Them goal-nets were invented for a reason.'

As the second half progressed, still no goals, still no shots at goal, the crowd on the Boothen Road side of the ground began to make their own entertainment. When the ball was kicked into their small wooden stand, they hung on to it. To their utter disgust another ball appeared. Undaunted, however, they tried again, and again, and again. This small section of the crowd spent most of the second half trying to stop the game by keeping all the footballs. They put one on top of the grandstand and another in the River Trent. Five balls were used altogether, but the game continued to its bitter goalless end.

The crowd's game within a game did lead to the day's best action. A linesman sprinted along the touchline in a bid to catch a ball before it went into the crowd. A perambulating policeman had his eye on the same ball. The linesman collided with the policeman and they lay spreadeagled across the track. The crowd roared, but only with laughter.

The result was never in doubt. Stoke City retained their First Division status and Burnley were promoted from Division Two. Poor Newcastle United, whose players were showing much more effort in defeating Blackburn, finished third in the mini-league, a point behind Stoke and Burnley.

Perhaps one interesting question is how the goalless draw was arranged in such a way that the players trusted one another. Among the participants were experienced Jimmy Ross, who played in five successive test-match series (for Preston, Liverpool and Burnley), and most interestingly, Jack 'Happy Jack' Hillman, the burly and brilliant Burnley goalkeeper whose career was always within a whisker of controversy and comedy.

Hillman, a Devonian by birth, played for Burnley and Everton before a two-season spell with Dundee. During his second season with the Scottish club Hillman was suspended for not trying, which was why he came to Burnley for £130 in time to help them into the First

Division. Hillman was then in his late twenties, but much was still to happen to him. He played a game for England, and was twice suspended by the FA – for a season (1900–01) after allegedly bribing Nottingham Forest players to lose to Burnley, and for eight months (1906–07) for receiving illegal payments as a Manchester City player.

Jack Hillman had once won a bet that he could keep goal in a charity match with one hand tied behind his back and not concede a goal. At Stoke, on that farcical goalless afternoon, he had no need to handle the ball at all. Indeed, he had already bet someone that he would not concede four goals in Burnley's four test matches. He had let in three before the Stoke stroll and there was no chance of a fourth going past him that afternoon.

The Stoke–Burnley game goes down in history on two counts. The authority's disgust at the players' actions led to the curtailing of test matches in favour of automatic promotion and relegation, and, secondly, as far as I am aware, it is the only game without a shot at goal played at the highest levels. There have been games where teams have settled for a result by mutual consent, notably West Germany's 1–0 win over Austria, which enabled both countries to progress to the next group of the 1982 World Cup Finals, and the relegation-escaping 2–2 draw between Coventry and Bristol City in 1977; and there have always been goalless games that tested spectators' patience. When Chelsea met Portsmouth in an end-of-season goalless bore in 1932, the highlight of the game was when the ball burst. 'The ball's packed up,' shouted one spectator. 'Why don't you do the same?'

Any survivors from the Stoke–Burnley pantomime would have sympathised.

Completed – Fifteen Weeks Later
Sheffield, November 1898, March 1899

At half-time on a drab November Saturday, Argus-Jud, a Birmingham pressman, bet a Sheffield reporter a cigar and a cognac that the game wouldn't be completed. He won his bet – the game was abandoned ten minutes from time – but the Sheffield man might have felt he had cause for a refund when he heard the Football League's decision. In the 1890s each abandoned game was treated on its merits rather than automatically replayed. For some, the score was allowed to stand. For others, as in the case of this Sheffield Wednesday–Aston Villa game, the game had to be completed at a later date.

The problems started when the match referee, Aaron Scragg, a Crewe fuel agent and FA councillor, missed his Manchester train connection by ten seconds. He telegraphed to the Sheffield Wednesday offices, but these were some distance from Wednesday's ground. By kick-off time (2.30 p.m.) no one knew where the referee was.

The game started seven minutes late. A local Football League referee, Fred Bye, took charge until Aaron Scragg arrived at half-time. About 17,000 were present, a good-sized crowd considering Wednesday were on the slide and the weather was dire. It had rained all morning and a keen, piercing wind blew towards the Heeley end. The ground was heavy and the ball fell dead at times. It was also very, very gloomy.

Wednesday took the lead after 20 minutes, Crawshaw's shot hitting the legs of three or four defenders and zig-zagging into the net. Aston Villa equalised a minute later. Frank Bedingfield, a late replacement at centre-forward, hooked Smith's centre into the net. It was the only Football League goal Bedingfield would ever score. Three years later he collapsed after playing an FA Cup-tie for Portsmouth and he died of consumption in South Africa not long afterwards.

A goal by Dryburgh gave Wednesday a 2–1 half-time lead. The next goal – Hemmingfield's header giving Wednesday a 3–1 lead – was awarded by match-referee Aaron Scragg, who had finally found his way to the ground. But Scragg's difficulties continued. The pitch was in semi-darkness. Players tried to spot the white shorts or striped shirts that weren't too muddy. Spectators listened for the sounds of players shouting. Some could see the ball only when it was punted above the level of the stands.

There were just over ten minutes left to play when protests by Devey of Aston Villa led to Aaron Scragg consulting a linesman. The game was abandoned and the debate began. Wednesday claimed that their 3–1 lead was the springboard for almost certain victory and they should be awarded the game. Reporters agreed that, from what they could see, Villa looked very unlikely to recover. On the other hand, Villa claimed Wednesday were to blame for arranging such a late kick-off; they should have known November days were gloomy, and therefore the whole match should be replayed.

The Football League, in their wisdom, compromised. They decided the extra ten-and-a-bit minutes should be played on a convenient date. So the game continued . . . fifteen weeks later.

One conundrum was how to start the game. Would Aaron Scragg remember where the ball was when he abandoned the game, so that he could drop it from the right place?

A second conundrum was the eligibility of players. Would the same 22 men be forced to resume their places?

A third problem was the likely low attendance. Who would turn out to watch the last ten minutes of a game when the result was cut and dried?

The Football League ruled that play would start in the usual manner – tossing a coin for choice of ends and then a place-kick – and that any registered player could take part. In the event, Villa used 13 players and Wednesday 16. No doubt the club secretary needed an abacus to decide how the win bonus would be divided.

Someone had a bright idea to entice the crowd. After the ten-minute farce, the two teams would play a 90-minute friendly (provided the light held good). The proceeds of the friendly would go to Wednesday's Harry Davis, whose benefit match a few weeks before was very badly attended. (On this occasion 3,000 people turned up and Wednesday beat Villa 2–0.)

For fifteen weeks Wednesday had desperately needed the two points held in abeyance. Relegation was probable, whereas Villa were favourites for the League Championship. During the infamous 630 seconds of the replay, Wednesday added a further goal to make it a 4–1 victory, but it didn't keep them in the First Division. Villa won the Championship.

This was not the only Football League game to be completed at a later date – Stoke were once ordered to Wolverhampton to play five minutes, and Walsall and Newton Heath completed on a second day – but it proved to be the last. Such was the adverse publicity that the Football League changed its rules over abandoned matches.

In recent years, however, there have been at least two similar events in Spain. A 1989 match between Osasuna and Real Madrid was abandoned after 43 minutes, and the remaining 47 minutes were played just before the end of the season. Osasuna led 1–0 after 43 minutes but Hugo Sanchez equalised three months later. The second example was the 1995 Spanish Cup final between Deportivo La Coruna and Valencia. The first attempt was abandoned after 79 minutes, so the two teams returned two days later and played the remaining eleven minutes.

Soccer Sickness

Liverpool, January 1902

The Stoke City management made a serious tactical error before the game at Liverpool – they allowed all the players to eat plaice for lunch. After the half-time interval in the game, only seven Stoke players were fit to resume. The Stoke secretary, Mr Austerberry, was very sympathetic. He was as sick as any of them.

Stoke goalkeeper Dick Roose was in distress before the game started. Roose, a Welsh international, was known as an adventurous goalkeeper whose tactics of wandering all over the field were not curbed until the 1912 change of law. On this day Roose could think only of wandering *off* the field . . . as quickly as possible. He lasted just ten minutes, by which time Stoke were a goal behind.

'Who wants to go in goal, lads? Come on, someone will have to go in.'

Meredith was the unlucky Stoke player appointed as deputy goalkeeper. For the rest of the first half, during which time he conceded three goals, Meredith made frantic gestures to indicate he would be happier out of goal. His captain, Johnstone, merely flashed back encouraging smiles.

At half-time the busiest man in the dressing-room was Dr Moody, a Stoke director, who examined most of the players and detected signs of lead poisoning. Moody had made his own way to the ground and had therefore escaped the midday meal.

Roose and Ashworth were the most afflicted of the Stoke players, and it was apparent that they would take no further part in the match. Dr Moody also recommended that Watkins and Whitehouse remain in the dressing-room. The only two people in the Stoke party seemingly unaffected were the two trainers, who had passed over the fish at lunch-time.

Dr Moody was left in no doubt about the seriousness of the illnesses. He said later: 'In fact the dressing-room resembled the cabin of a cross-Channel steamer in bad weather, and smelt like it . . . only more so.'

Stoke started the second half with seven players. They played with a goalkeeper – still Meredith – one back, two halves and three forwards. And did quite well too. There was a short spell when Liverpool failed to score.

While people were beginning to debate at what point the game might be abandoned, the two missing forwards, Watkins and Whitehouse, gallantly reappeared against doctor's orders. Goalkeeper Roose, meanwhile, who had a pulse rate of 148 per minute when he left the field, would need a few hours' rest to recover.

In his absence Liverpool scored some soft goals. Not until the sixth went in did Meredith have his wish granted; Clarke took over in goal.

The final total was seven. Not Stoke's favourite number. They had seven fit men, conceded seven goals . . . and lost the next seven games.

Under the Scorching Sun

Manchester, September 1906

At half-time Manchester City players could talk only of the sun, those who could still talk. Outside it was more than 90 degrees Fahrenheit in the shade – too hot for sunbathing. There had been no forewarning of the unbearable heat for the newcomers to the City team, especially the Scottish imports, and it was virtually a new-look team because seventeen City players and ex-players had recently been suspended by the FA. On the first day of the season, City were sunshocked and shellshocked.

Harry Newbould was the new secretary-manager of Manchester City – several officials had also been suspended after the FA inquiry into financial affairs – and he must have been desolate when he saw the dressing-room scene at half-time. City were 2–0 down to Woolwich Arsenal, three players looked incapable of continuing and it was 60 years before the use of substitutes. Thornley and Grieve were flat on their backs, too ill with sunstroke to do any more work that day. Little Jimmy Conlin, who had sensibly taken the field with a handkerchief tied over his head, had been forced to take refuge in the dressing-room a few minutes before half-time. City were down to eight men.

In Harry Newbould's day, managers were not the strategic conjurors and media magic-men that they are today. Their role was mainly to sign players, pin up team sheets and ensure the players were all in the right railway carriage.

Newbould was one of the more enterprising of his ilk, and at half-time he might have had some say about tactics on that scorching day. Translated into more modern managerial hype, the message conveyed to the City players would have been something like this: 'Right, lads, I know it was a bad toss to lose, and it's not the best of conditions, but we'll have the sun on our backs this second half and it'll be the same for them. It's only eleven of them against eight of us. No, Bill, it won't be like this every week in Manchester. OK, lads, we're two down, and we've only got eight men, but we can go out and take the game to them. I want us to play a 1–3–3 formation this half. That's one full-back, three half-backs and three forwards. And we'll try to catch them offside. Yes, I know you don't know each other very well and only a couple of you have played for City before, but look at it this way, it'll be easier to get to know seven others than ten others. This is a great chance for a good start to the season. And, remember, if you hear the crowd cheering, they're cheering for you, not because they've seen the sun in Manchester.'

Whatever Newbould or anybody else actually said at half-time, it certainly did the trick. Even though City had lost three forwards with sunstroke, they pushed a defender into the forward line and played a 1–3–3 formation. In the 50th minute Jimmy Conlin returned to the field and the crowd cheered as if they'd seen the sun for the first time.

Taking his position in what was now a 1–3–4 formation, Conlin made a goal for Dorsett, and City, only 2–1 down, were back in the game. But that was as far as it went. Dorsett collapsed soon afterwards, the heat struck down Kelso and Buchan, and City were down to five fit men plus the plucky Conlin.

The referee spoke to his linesmen, but they agreed that there was no just cause for abandoning the game. The Woolwich Arsenal players, meanwhile, were far less affected. They scored two more goals, taking the score to

4–1, but sportingly didn't cash in too much when they faced five fit men in the closing stages of the game.

It took City some time to recover from this setback – two days later they lost 9–1 at Everton – but the new-look team pulled together sufficiently to keep the club in the First Division.

Triumph of the 'Fair Leather Booters'

New Bedford, Mass., October 1922

During the inter-war period, Dick-Kerr's factory team from Preston was the Huddersfield Town and Arsenal of women's soccer. The team toured Britain, Europe and the United States, playing in aid of charity and winning almost all their games. In their heyday, Dick-Kerr's would attract five-figure attendances. They once packed over 50,000 into Goodison Park (with many more left in the streets outside) and one game in Paris was abandoned five minutes from the end after spectators had burst on to the field to protest about a corner-kick decision.

Dick-Kerr's were a team to get excited about. Unless, of course, you happened to be a council member of the men's FA. In 1921, a consultative committee of the council claimed that women's teams were showbiz outfits exploiting football and not always devoting sufficient funds to charity. The FA therefore banned women's soccer from major football stadiums.

Fortunately, as often happens, such restrictions led to greater innovation. Take, for example, the novel 1924 floodlit match when Dick-Kerr's played Bradford Ladies and the lights were so bright it was claimed you could read the match programme in the centre of the field; or the 1922 tour of the United States, when the girls from

Preston received star billing for games against a dozen American teams.

What an attraction Dick-Kerr's were that 1921–2 season. They turned up for matches (sometimes two a week) clad in frills and furbelows, carrying cases and parcels which contained all the essential gear – boots, shinpads, powder puffs, hairpins, etc. The team's playing kit was black-and-white striped shirts, black or blue knickers (the pre-war name for shorts) and black-and-white knitted hats. Some players, opting to play bare-headed, pinned their hair into bobs.

And what a team they were. They had a French international goalkeeper, Carmen Pomies, who had been a champion javelin thrower before she came across the Channel to work at the Dick-Kerr's factory (now the General Electric Company). There was a consistent defence, with players such as Lily Lee and Alice Kell, both of whom were to play for years. And, most dramatically, there was a forward line which was averaging around six goals a game. The star centre-forward, Florrie Radford, scored prolifically (about two a game); and, as in all great teams of the era, there were two entertaining wingers, Jenny Harris and Lily Parr. If Arsenal's Cliff Bastin could be dubbed 'Boy' Bastin in recognition of his early achievements, then Lily deserved to be 'Girl' Parr. After celebrating her winning goal against St Helens' Ladies at Wrexham by turning a gymnastic Catherine wheel (much to the crowd's amusement), there were typical letters to the local newspaper suggesting it was time Wrexham gave her a chance in Division Three (North).

It was from this atmosphere of adulation and heroine-worship that the girls (all unmarried and most in their very early twenties) set sail for the United States. They were on the same ship as French boxer Georges Carpentier, heavyweight and light-heavyweight champion of Europe. The girls thought Carpentier gorgeous, but they were lucky not to see him a week after his arrival in the United States, by which time he had been pulped and knocked out.

The girls, meanwhile, concentrated on the more gentle pastime of soccer. They set their standards in the first minute of the tour when, playing against the men of Paterson, Alice Woods brought down McGuire, described as a 'noted one-armed forward from Brooklyn'. Dick-Kerr's lost that game 6–3 in front of 5,000 people.

The New Bedford game was the fifth of the tour. Two had been drawn and two lost. Pre-match preparation included a sing-song in the YWCA where they were staying. The two wingers played their mouth organs, but there was to be no more play for Lily Parr that week. She had damaged a knee playing basketball and would miss the big soccer game.

The promoters of the game had guaranteed £1,000 so they were all smiles when the biggest soccer crowd in New Bedford history turned out to see the women of England take on the local all-male team. Despite a hefty police presence (twelve men), there was little chance that passions would erupt.

Dick-Kerr's were twice behind early in the game. Each time Molly Walker equalised. Then Florrie Radford chipped in with two goals, and the women led 4–2.

Late in the game, the men pressed hard. They pulled back a goal. Then another. The scores were level with time running out. Then, in the dying minutes, Florrie Radford took a penalty kick. Her shot was saved. No matter. A minute later Jenny Harris, the smallest player on the field, scored for the women, and they won 5–4.

There were some indications that the men had played within themselves, and that the second half had gone on a long time, but there was no disputing the final result. The Preston women, described in the American press as the 'fair leather booters', had beaten the American men.

Wilfred Minter's Goal-scoring Feat

Dulwich, November 1922

Never has one man made such a strange goal-scoring impact on a game than Wilfred Minter did that dark Wednesday afternoon in Dulwich. The occasion was an FA Cup replay in the fourth round of the qualifying stage of the competition. In the original game, the previous Saturday, St Albans City and Dulwich Hamlet had drawn 1–1 in controversial circumstances. There was major debate as to whether Redvers Miller's corner kick had touched any other player before it entered the net – not until 1924 were goals direct from corner kicks permitted – but referee Rolfe decided it had and St Albans had their late equaliser.

Wilf Minter had been St Albans's outstanding forward in the first game between these two teams of amateurs. He was a local lad, having attended the Hatfield Road school and received football tuition from J Dickinson, a former St Albans City captain. Minter entered the army when war broke out. While serving overseas he developed his fitness and football talents, and, after demobilisation, played for his school old boys' team, helping them to win the 1919–20 Aubrey Cup competition. He joined St Albans City in February 1921 and soon became a goal-scoring phenomenon for club and county. Representative honours followed, but he turned down professional offers to enter his father's business and remain as an amateur with St Albans.

He was to create a record which no professional has ever matched.

The game was played at Champion Hill, Dulwich, where both the home team and St Albans were forced to field deputy goalkeepers after injuries on the Saturday. No doubt this contributed to the afternoon's entertainment. Alf Fearn, a half-back from St Albans Gasworks, was never likely to be a genius at handling corner kicks and crosses.

Inside fifteen minutes Dulwich were a goal ahead. Then Wilf Minter took over. He scored from a crossbar rebound, headed in a Pierce centre and added a third after exchanging passes with H S Miller.

After half an hour the score was clear cut: Dulwich 1 (Kail), St Albans 3 (Minter 3).

During the next half-hour Alf Fearn's lack of goal-keeping experience was exposed. Dulwich scored four times.

After 60 minutes, therefore, the score conveyed a different message: Dulwich Hamlet 5 (Davis 3, Kail 2), St Albans City 3 (Minter 3).

All over? Not quite. When Harold Figg's shot hit a goalpost, Minter followed up to pull back a goal, then he shot two more to give St Albans the lead.

Seventy minutes played, and again the score was transformed: Dulwich Hamlet 5 (Davis 3, Kail 2), St Albans City 6 (Minter 6).

In these earlier days of soccer, people would dispute what was a real hat trick. To conform with the cricketing model – three wickets in three consecutive balls – soccer goals really needed to be three in a row rather than three in a game. But here there was no dispute. Minter had done it twice in one game – three in a row in twelve first-half minutes and three in a row again in ten second-half minutes. Astonishing.

And there was more to come. Five minutes from the end Dulwich put the ball in the St Albans net. The referee reversed his original decision and gave a goal, much to the dismay of the St Albans players. It meant the scores were level at 6–6 after 90 minutes. Extra time of fifteen minutes each way began in fading light.

After 100 minutes Kail sprinted from the halfway line and gave Dulwich Hamlet a 7–6 lead. In the gathering gloom, at the other end, Minter was tackled clumsily in the penalty area. Appeals for a penalty were turned down. Too dark for the referee to see, some argued.

With just four minutes to play Redvers Miller took a corner kick for St Albans City. This time there was no doubt that someone touched the ball before it hit the net – Wilfred Minter.

Imagine the mood of the man now. Seven goals each and he has scored all his team's goals. The referee is set to blow his whistle as the 120 minutes are just about played. Then the linesman flags and the referee awards a dubious free kick to Dulwich. Over comes the cross, Davis heads a goal for the London side. The game ends.

Dulwich Hamlet 8 (Davis 4, Kail 3, Nicol 1), St Albans City 7 (Minter 7).

For an individual to score seven goals is not all that uncommon, but to score *all* his team's goals including *two* hat tricks, and for the *losing* team – that was unique. The next Saturday Wilfred Minter was made captain and the band played 'For he's a jolly good fellow' when he went to the centre of the field for the coin-tossing ritual.

Whether it would have been better to win 1–0 than lose 8–7, we will leave for the modern-day managers to discuss.

Strikers Against Police
Plymouth, May 1926

It seems strange that striking trade-unionists would play the police at soccer on the day of their most intense conflict in history, yet such a match occurred in Plymouth during the 1926 General Strike. A crowd of over 10,000 saw the strikers win by two goals to one. The policemen had their work cut out – on and off the field.

Industrial unrest among northern coal-miners had spread to other industries and services. The effects reached Plymouth later than most towns, but the outcome was devastating. At the end of the first week in May the General Strike was a week old, and the *Western Morning News and Mercury* was talking of a state bordering on civil war: 'Football is all very well in normal circumstances, and there is no reason why policemen and workmen should not play it. But conditions today are not normal, and a match between policemen and strikers is, at least, strange.'

The events of the Saturday confirmed some people's worst fears. Tramway employers tempted fate by resuming a modified service using volunteers and inspectors to replace the 800 workers who were on strike. Confrontation and chaos were the result. During the morning crowds gathered in the town centre to prevent tramcars passing.

By 11.30 that Saturday morning there were around 4,000 people doing their best to block the trams. Amid the jostling a few stones smashed tramcar windows. About 20 or 30 policemen charged the crowd, wielding batons, but it did not prevent the continued harassment of the tramcars. Ironically, this happened just before the soccer match was due to start at Home Park. Once again the police and the strikers were on opposite sides.

The tramway team scored midway through the first half, and a wave of enthusiasm greeted this first – dare I say it? – strike.

Another ironic touch came at half-time, when the music was provided by the tramway band – workers at the very heart of the dispute. When the second half started, large sections of the crowd followed the band off the pitch and out of the stadium. By the time the strikers scored their second goal, ten minutes from the end, the tramway band was leading a procession of people, four by four, walking along the tramlines to ensure no cars passed. There were more ugly scenes.

Mounted police were called in to deal with a 20,000 crowd in Old Town Street. Three arrests were made, but the tramcar service was withdrawn and the likelihood of pitched battle averted. The next week the strike was called off, leaving the Plymouth strikers with a 100 per cent record on the soccer pitch. That same month games also took place between the Sheffield Police and strikers at Park Colliery.

Ten Goals at His First Attempt
Luton, April 1936

Easter Monday at Kenilworth Road. The home team, Luton Town, preparing for a Third Division (South) game against Bristol Rovers, discovered that they had two centre-forwards on the injury list. Manager Ned Liddell opted for Joe Payne as a replacement. Payne, a reserve wing-half, had some experience of playing in the forward line but had never appeared there in the Luton first team. Yet Payne made such an impact that his record may never be beaten.

There was no early hint of what was to come. Payne collected a goal in the 23rd minute and Roberts soon made it 2–0 to Luton, but, five minutes before half-time, the game could have gone either way. Then Joe Payne scored nine in 46 minutes, and no one else scored during this incredible period. With three headers and seven shots, Joe Payne had scored ten goals on his first attempt at centre-forward. Martin scored one in the last minute to make the final score 12–0.

The previous individual scoring record was nine, and Joe Payne's record of ten in a Football League game has held ever since. Payne, a former Derbyshire coal-miner, was 22 years old at the time of his baptism at centre-forward. Two years later, in 1938, he went to Chelsea for £2,000, already an England international. During the war he twice broke an ankle, and never added to the one cap he won against Finland, when he scored two goals. After the war he scored

six League goals for West Ham in a spell of nine months –
four goals less than he managed in 63 minutes that
sensational day at Luton.

Taking It at Walking Pace

Derby, May 1937

This was the sixth annual walking match between the Crewe and Derby Railway Veterans Associations. Derby held the Cup, having won 2–0 at Crewe in 1936, and were looking to win it two years running (not that the referee would have allowed that).

All the players were over 65 years old. The oldest, Young (Derby) and Betley (Crewe), were both 73. The venue was the Baseball Ground, home of Derby County, and 1,500 spectators turned out on a fine day. The game was one of the most bizarre ever refereed by Arthur Kingscott, who had officiated in two FA Cup Finals, but he had no difficulty keeping up with play, which, at times, reached the frenzied pace of six miles per hour.

Crewe started well on top and looked set for a walkaway victory. By comparison Derby looked pedestrian, which, of course, they were. But once Derby discovered their wing men, the pattern of play changed. Their left-wing pair of Collier and Briddon walked rings round the Crewe right flank, while Radford, only 67, put in some good walks and centres on the Derby right. Radford had the best chance of the match, only the goalkeeper to beat, but shot five yards wide. The crowd groaned. They felt he could have walked the ball in.

The build-up of both teams was slow, naturally, but there was no holding back by the players. One or two of them received minor knocks but were advised by the trainer to 'walk it off'. There were only two things missing. The occasion deserved a walking commentary from a radio station and it also needed a goal.

The game ended 0–0 and both teams shared the Cup, which was filled to the brim and passed round the players at the end. Crewe were optimistic about their chances the next season, when they would be at home. They had a younger team than Derby – average age 68 as against Derby's 69 – and knew the Derby 'lads' would be a year older when they met again.

The 203-Minute Game

Stockport, March 1946

No one had yet conceived penalty-kick deciders. When the Division Three North wartime Cup-tie between Stockport County and Doncaster Rovers ended in a draw after extra time, the two teams were asked to settle the outcome that day. The first team to score would win. But the scores were still level after 203 minutes when the game was abandoned through bad light.

The players were perhaps fortunate that the game didn't take place a month later. Had the clocks been on summer time, play might have lasted until eight o'clock.

The Cup-tie had two legs. The first, at Doncaster, ended in a 2–2 draw. The second, at Stockport, finished with the same 2–2 scoreline. The competition rules dictated extra time of ten minutes each way. This was played with no scoring. Then the teams played on until the first goal. Referee Baker of Crewe proved a hard taskmaster.

Three times Stockport's Ken Shaw had chances to add to the two goals he had scored in the first 90 minutes. Each time the chance went astray. The game went on and on. Stockport's Les Cocker (later trainer of Leeds United and England) put the ball into the Doncaster net but Mr Baker disallowed the point for an infringement.

There were 13,000 spectators at the game and most stayed until the end. Some went home for their tea and then came back again. The teams toiled on. The sultry heat took its toll.

After 200 minutes Stockport's Rickards tried a shot in the failing light. The ball cannoned off two Doncaster defenders and the goalkeeper. All three Rovers players were left laid out like ninepins. Eventually, after 203 minutes, the referee ended the endurance test. The two teams tossed a coin for choice of ground in the replay. Rovers won the toss and chose their own ground. The following Wednesday they beat Stockport 4–0.

The Invisible Game

Southampton, October 1950

When Southampton pioneered a floodlit exhibition match against neighbours Bournemouth, about 10,000 people took advantage of the offer of free admission, but they only just got their money's worth. It was a mysterious game that no one could see properly.

The idea emerged from Southampton's summer tour of Brazil, where they played several games under artificial light. The Southampton Supporters' club, on hearing the good reports, invested £600 for a firm called B A Corry to install sixteen 1,500-watt arc lamps. Everyone was pleasantly surprised that electricity running costs would be as low as six or seven shillings, so the big question was whether spectators would like it. Here was the big test.

Approaching kick-off time of 6.30 p.m., the crowd began to gather and exchange wisecracks.

'Bring on the shadow teams.'

'Come on Wraith Rovers.'

'Pylon the pressure.'

The spectators had to rely on their own entertainment. Although the lights worked well, visibility was destroyed by a familiar British problem – fog. That evening the whole country was enveloped in a thick mist. At London Airport a BEA Viking airliner crashed, killing all 31 people aboard.

At Southampton's ground, the Dell, the fog wasn't too much of a handicap for the players, who could see the ball reasonably clearly, except when it was kicked high in the air, but the referee couldn't see a hand-ball in front of him, and the spectators were literally in the dark. At times visibility slumped to three or four yards and only nearside play could be seen.

The teams played for an hour, changing straight round without a half-time interval. For the spectators it was an eerie experience. In the damp night air, the Bournemouth players, wearing all-white, were a team of apparitions, flitting about like will-o'-the-wisps. From the stand, for all the crowd knew, the players could have been ghosts of the days when footballers wore moustaches and shin-pads outside socks – except for one two-minute period when the fog temporarily lifted and the outcome was theatrical.

There was a rumour that Southampton came close to scoring – Ken Bird pushed Eric Day's shot on to a goalpost – and the consensus was that the game finished without a goal. This was confirmed later by the players.

'Floodlit play needed infra-red glasses,' shrieked the *Daily Telegraph* headline the next day. Their reporter, Lainson Wood, was dubious about the future prospects of floodlights, saying that no one had made it pay in 20 years of dabbling, and there would always be fog.

Yet several onlookers were impressed.

'There were efforts to introduce floodlight football to this country before the war, but never anything so simple and economical as the installation at the Dell,' wrote Clifford Webb in the *Daily Herald.*

Another observer – if that is the right term for this fog-shrouded night – was Walter Winterbottom, the England team manager. 'This match,' Winterbottom was quoted as saying, 'has proved that even on a foggy night amateur players who cannot train in the daytime can get on to a pitch and have real match practice.'

Here, too, was the crux of Southampton's argument. Their chairman, Penn Barrow, pointed out that the cost of floodlights was far less than the cost of buying players. If they could produce one player from floodlight training it would have paid them.

This game, mysterious though it was to spectators, symbolised a new wave in the floodlighting movement. By the mid-1950s, lights were being used for games as well as for training.

Six in a Row to Stay Up

Lincoln, May 1958

Shortly after the 3–1 home defeat by Barnsley on Easter Monday, when Lincoln City were all but mathematically certain of relegation with six games to play, Lincoln manager Bill Anderson explained to his players how they stood: 'If we win our last six games we'll stay up.'

Ho, ho, very funny. Lincoln had not won for four months and had won only five of their 36 Second Division matches that season. This could only be the talk of a desperate manager. Anderson, who had been in charge of Lincoln for twelve seasons, the last six in the Second Division, was in his toughest spot yet.

The fixture list left Lincoln with three away games and three at home. There were no outstanding teams among the opponents – two or three were also needing points for safety – but all the fixtures were psychologically daunting, including the first of the six, away to Barnsley on Easter Tuesday, the day after suffering that resounding defeat at home to the same team.

The strangest fixture, though, was the last of the season – Cardiff City at home. That one had already been lost. Back in March Cardiff had been winning 3–0 at Lincoln when a blizzard wiped out the play and caused an abandonment. The teams would have to start again, but Cardiff had already won the game once.

Bill Anderson made four changes for the return game at Barnsley, and his new-look team won 3–1. Then Lincoln won 3–1 at second-from-bottom Doncaster and beat Rotherham (2–0) and Bristol City (4–0) at home. They were left needing a win and a draw from their last two games.

The away game at Huddersfield was their most difficult game on paper, but Ron Harbertson's sixth goal in five games brought a 1–0 victory. All that remained was the home game with Cardiff City. Had the game been completed in March, when Cardiff led 3–0, manager Anderson's Easter pep talk wouldn't have made as much sense. Lincoln would have needed to win six of their last five games to escape relegation.

The whole city had caught the spirit of Lincoln's five-match run. It was as though it was a Cup run which had taken them to the final. Inside-forward George Hannah described the tension before the Cardiff game, when over 18,000 people packed into the tiny Sincil Bank stadium, as worse than when he played at Wembley with Newcastle United.

Just after half-time Cliff Nugent scored for Cardiff. Lincoln, playing edgily, looked doomed to Division Three. For the second time that season Cardiff appeared to have an away game at Lincoln firmly in control.

There were 20 minutes to play when Roy Chapman lunged for a centre and levelled the scores. Chapman, who had regained his place in the team at the start of this run, scored again soon afterwards. Harbertson scored a third from 20 yards, and the crowd roared as if Lincoln City had won the FA Cup. Three goals in ten minutes.

Lincoln, 3–0 down to Cardiff when the game was abandoned in March, 1–0 down after 70 minutes of the replay, beat Cardiff 3–1 and avoided relegation by a point. They had won their last six games, and Bill Anderson had got it exactly right.

The Nightmare Day-trip
Barrow, October 1961

Gillingham thought they could travel to Barrow on the day of the game. The journey from the mouth of Kent's River Medway to the tip of the Furness peninsula in Lancashire (as it was then) was over 300 miles. A train leaving London Euston at 9.05 a.m. seemed a safe bet. The team should arrive over an hour before kick-off, which was at 5.15 p.m. as Barrow had no floodlights.

First came the 35-mile coach trip to Euston. The coach made an early-morning start but ran into heavy traffic. Officials estimated the time-distance equation and grew agitated. The coach arrived at Euston half an hour after the train had left.

The options remaining were not promising. The next train, the 10.25, would arrive one minute after the kick-off. Coach would be far too slow, and cars would be very risky. There was only one possible option – aeroplane. Club officials discovered two suitable scheduled flights – the 10.40 to Manchester and the 11.00 to Newcastle. Both were fully booked.

The next idea was to charter a plane. One was arranged but the company had to fly it from Gatwick to London Airport, where the Gillingham party would be waiting. The cost of the plane was £500 – money in advance.

Gillingham officials also telephoned the Football League. They negotiated a fifteen-minute delay in kick-off time. The players would be asked to forgo their half-time interval. It was a 5.30 p.m. kick-off now.

The next problem was the plane's destination. They decided to head for Squire's Gate Airport at Blackpool, about 70 miles from Barrow. This meant arranging another journey. A coach was hired to meet them at Squire's Gate, but, as time slipped by, officials realised a coach would be too slow. Four cars were hired and a police escort arranged for what would be a hectic last leg of the trip.

The charter flight left London Airport at 2.31, having been delayed in a queue of planes. There were less than three hours before the match.

The plane arrived at Squire's Gate at 3.25 p.m. Within 20 minutes everybody was in cars. They had a 70-mile journey and 105 minutes.

There were no motorways in the north-west in October 1961. The roads around Morecambe Bay were among the country's worst for a late dash by car through driving rain. They reached Holker Street at 5.30 p.m. The players needed to change.

Gillingham, as you can appreciate, were not ideally prepared to play a Fourth Division game. They'd been up early, stuck in traffic on a coach, forced to hang around, shepherded on to a plane (the first time for some), driven rapidly through the countryside and told to change as quickly as they could. By half-time they were five goals down to Barrow.

The problem now was the light. By the 74th minute, when Barrow were leading 6–0, referee Mr Jobling from Morecambe felt it was too dark for football. He allowed an extra couple of minutes under Barrow's training lights – just time for Barrow's seventh goal – but finally abandoned the game shortly after seven o'clock.

The Football League ruled that the 7–0 scoreline should stand as a result. Gillingham's next away game was an even longer trip – Carlisle United. They set off in good time and won 2–1.

The Referee's Winning Goal

Barrow, November 1968

Barrow 0 Plymouth Argyle 0. Thirteen minutes to play. Then came a goal to settle this Division Three game, scored by the most unlikely person on the pitch – referee Ivan Robinson.

Barrow won a corner kick. The ball was cleared out. George McLean shot hard from outside the penalty area and the ball was going well wide. Referee Robinson, perhaps fifteen yards from goal, was in the ball's path. He jumped up to avoid the ball but it hit him on the inside of his left foot and flew off at an angle. Plymouth goalkeeper Pat Dunne was completely deceived by the deflection. Having moved to cover McLean's shot, Dunne was stranded as the ball shot past him into the net. Barrow 1 (The Referee) Plymouth 0.

The rules are quite clear. The ball is in play if it rebounds off either the referee or linesmen when they are in the field of play. Ivan Robinson knew that. He pointed meekly to the centre-circle to confirm his goal. Plymouth players looked stunned and shocked.

The incident spurred Plymouth into a frenzied late rally. Barrow hung on to win 1–0 and the referee had to try to avoid congratulatory pats on the back from Barrow supporters as he ran off the field.

Barrow took their unbeaten home run to 18 games and moved into second place in Division Three, probably the highest position they ever reached in the Football League. Diplomatically, they credited the goal to McLean.

Plymouth were left with a long, disconsolate journey home, hardly assuaged by Mr Robinson's subsequent apology.

The Endless Cup-tie

Alvechurch, Oxford and Birmingham, November 1971

When Alvechurch of the Midland Combination and Oxford City of the Isthmian League played out their final qualifying round FA Cup-tie, people began to joke that the Cup Final might have to be delayed. It took six games and 660 playing minutes to decide the tie. Finally, Bobby Hope's 588th-minute headed goal divided the teams and champagne flowed in both dressing-rooms.

The marathon started and finished on treacherous pitches. The Cup-tie moved from Alvechurch's Lye Meadow (with its corner-to-corner slope) to Aston Villa's Villa Park, calling on the way at Oxford City's White House, Birmingham City's St Andrews and Oxford United's Manor Stadium (where two games were played).

At Alvechurch, the home team led 2–0 but Oxford clawed back into the game to force the first draw. Had Oxford City goalkeeper Peter Harris not dived bravely at the feet of Bobby Hope (not the Scottish international) late in the game, a lot of travelling might have been avoided.

The Cup-tie was chronicled excellently by *Oxford Mail* reporter Jim Rosenthal, who covered five of the six games. His only mistake was to suggest that Alvechurch might have missed their best chance. 'In this competition,' Rosenthal wrote, 'you only get one bite at the cherry, and Oxford will want to emphasise that point at the White House tomorrow night.'

In fact, Alvechurch had another five bites at the cherry, something neither Rosenthal nor anyone else could have predicted. By the time of the first replay, the two teams knew the winners would play Aldershot (away) in the first round of the FA Cup proper. Aldershot manager Jimmy Melia turned up to watch his future opponents without realising that he would have four more opportunities to see them play. By the end of the saga Melia might have reconsidered how best to use his time.

The first replay, the most rugged of the six games, had two first-half goals, shared of course. By the end of extra time the two teams were exhausted, but Alvechurch maintained their season's unbeaten away record.

The next game was in Birmingham – almost a home game for Alvechurch – and the 3,600 crowd was the highest attendance of the six. Having drawn a league game on the Saturday, Oxford City extended their sequence with an equaliser just after half-time of this second replay. But that was the last goal the Cup-tie produced for about 330 minutes.

There was enough action. Another fine save from Harris (after 324 minutes) kept the third match alive, while City's Andy Mitchell cleared from the goal-line (365 minutes) and Tommy Eales twice hit the crossbar (388 minutes and 449 minutes) in the goalless fourth game.

It became an endurance test. Alvechurch midfielder Derek Davis, a car-worker on nights, had to be rested from the fourth game. City's Eric Metcalfe, a schoolteacher, received a hairline fibula fracture in the fifth game. The trainers became experts on cramp.

The *Oxford Mail*'s Bill Beckett, deputising for Jim Rosenthal at the fourth game, reported that someone in the crowd suggested an annual reunion for those who had thus far watched all four games. Unfortunately, a few minutes after the fifth game (one of three in Oxford), an elderly Alvechurch supporter collapsed and died.

By the sixth game, at Villa Park, there was little new for coaches John Fisher (Oxford City) and Rhys Davies (Alvechurch) to try. The two teams knew each other very well. Fisher was forced to make changes, however, as the Army couldn't release two of his men and two other key players were injured. Then came Bobby Hope's goal in the eighteenth minute of the sixth game. The winners were Alvechurch.

For the record, the six games were as follows: Sat. 6 Nov. (Alvechurch) Alvechurch 2 (Horne, Allner), Oxford City 2 (McCrae, Metcalfe)

Tues. 9 Nov. (Oxford) Oxford City 1 (Eales) Alvechurch 1 (Allner)

Mon. 15 Nov. (Birmingham) Alvechurch 1 (Alner) Oxford City 1 (Goucher)

Wed. 17 Nov. (Oxford) Alvechurch 0 Oxford City 0

Sat. 20 Nov. (Oxford) Alvechurch 0 Oxford City 0

Mon. 22 Nov. (Villa Park) Alvechurch 1 (Hope) Oxford City 0

(All except the first and last went to extra time.)

The first round game against Aldershot was delayed, but only by four days. Alvechurch, playing their ninth game in eighteen days, went down 4–2 and were out of the competition.

When the draw for the FA Amateur Cup was made a week later you can almost imagine a wag going into the Oxford City dressing-room: 'Heard the draw, lads? Alvechurch away.' Fortunately, it didn't happen.

'We didn't know the Oxford players at the start but we were on first-name terms at the end,' says Graham Alner who played for Alvechurch in all six matches. 'We were turning up as if long-lost mates – the same teams, the same players, the same result. It was a big experience for me. It was character hardening. Tactics went out of the window. We just carried on playing the same way. Before every game, Rhys Davis used to say, "Go out and give it some tonk and bottle." That was his favourite phrase at the time.'

Referee Who Forgot the Rules

Lisbon, November 1971

One of the most embarrassing refereeing errors of recent years came when Dutchman van Ravens got the rules wrong during the second leg of a second-round European Cup-winners' Cup-tie between Sporting Lisbon and Glasgow Rangers.

All referees make mistakes occasionally. Such errors usually result from the officials' inability to see everything from every angle and make the correct split-second decision. This gives rise to a spate of jokes and stories about 'blindness' ('I agreed to escort the referee to the railway station,' said the policeman, 'because I always like to take care of the handicapped') and 'bias' ('We were playing against twelve men'). Those familiar with refereeing history are probably aware that many contemporary referees are often compared with the much-respected official in the 1878 FA Cup Final, Mr Segar Bastard.

Most major refereeing howlers occurred in the early days of soccer. There was the referee who ordered off a dumb man for abusive language (the decision was later reversed), the referee who headed a goal (he apologised but had to let the goal stand) and the referee who stood in a dressing-room washbowl and broke it.

In the post-war era a referee at Sunderland in 1954 started the second half before realising that only one linesman was in place. In front of 43,000 people, his face was as red as the missing flag.

At Wimbledon, in 1983, a referee wrongly awarded Millwall a goal after Wimbledon full-back Wally Downes chipped a direct free-kick over goalkeeper Dave Beasant's head and into his own net. The correct decision here is a corner kick; the early rule-makers sensibly decided that a team scoring in its own net from a direct free-kick shouldn't be punished more heavily than if it had done so from an indirect free-kick, as the offence being punished was obviously more serious in the first instance.

Refereeing can give rise to all manner of wild questions about soccer oddities and offbeat features of the game. For example, a penalty kick is taken, the ball bursts as it is kicked, the casing flies over the crossbar, the lace spins out and wraps itself around the goalkeeper's neck, hindering him from saving the bladder as it sails into the net – what is the correct decision?

That incident, as far as I am aware, never happened, even in the days when balls had laces. But the events in Lisbon in 1971 showed that one referee had not been tested on the rules of the competition.

Rangers had won the first leg at Ibrox Park 3–2 after being 2–0 ahead at one stage. Now they had a difficult game in Lisbon. Sporting Lisbon twice took the lead. Each time Colin Stein equalised. Then Rangers' Scottish international centre-half Ron McKinnon fractured a leg, and Sporting took the lead again with 25 minutes to play. Somehow Rangers hung on to take the tie into extra time.

During this period both teams scored once. Thereupon, referee van Ravens ordered each team to take five penalties to decide the tie. Rangers qualified for some sort of record by missing all five kicks. In fact, Tommy McLean missed twice as the Sporting goalkeeper moved too quickly for the first. Sporting won 3–0 on penalties and were through to the next round. Or were they?

The Scottish journalists were already scratching their heads in bewilderment. Surely, they thought, away goals count double in the event of a tie. At the end of extra time Rangers had scored *three* away goals against Sporting's *two* in Glasgow.

The referee was wrong. Rangers were indeed the winners. The UEFA officials later reversed the referee's decision and suspended the Dutch referee. The rules were very clear. The provision that away goals counted double in the event of a draw also applied to those scored in extra time. That gave rise to an even better sporting question: which team missed all its six penalties during a penalty shoot-out and still won the tie?

That season Glasgow Rangers won the European Cup-winners' Cup.

The 28-Penalty Shoot-out
Hong Kong, June 1975

The Asia Cup semi-final between North Korea and Hong Kong finished 2–2 after 90 minutes and 3–3 after extra time. The ensuing penalty shoot-out had spectators wondering whether it might have been quicker to play another game.

It was an agonising few hours for North Korea coach Pak Du-ik, best remembered in Britain for the goal that beat Italy in the 1966 World Cup Finals. His team led by two goals in the game against Hong Kong, then looked in danger of losing 3–2 when Hong Kong scored with seven minutes of extra time remaining. The penalty shoot-out tested the coach's nerve even more.

Hong Kong took the first penalty and scored. North Korea took the second penalty and scored. Hong Kong took the next and missed. North Korea missed their second too, and then the neck-and-neck competition continued.

Each team scored five of their first six. Lai Sun-cheung took Hong Kong's seventh kick. He missed. It was now 'sudden death'. Up stepped Cha Jung-sok to take North Korea's seventh kick. Hong Kong goalkeeper Chu Kwok-kuen saved it.

It was back to stalemate, each team scoring with alternate kicks. Soon, all the players except the goal-keepers had taken kicks, and they had to start over again.

Wu Kwok-hung took Hong Kong's thirteenth kick and missed.

Pak Jung-hun had the chance to win the game for North Korea but his penalty was saved by Chu Kwok-kuen.

The duel continued.

Hong Kong missed their fourteenth penalty too, so Kim Jungmm was the next potential match-winner for North Korea. He shot left-footed, low to the goalkeeper's right. Chu Kwok-kuen moved the wrong way and the game was over. North Korea had won the penalty shoot-out 11–10 on the 28th penalty. They were very tired when they beat China in the Asia Cup Final a few days later.

The One-Scorer Four-Goal Draw
Leicester, March 1976

Northern Ireland international Chris Nicholl, later manager of Southampton, played 648 Football League games during his long career with Halifax Town, Luton Town, Aston Villa, Southampton and Grimsby Town. None was more bizarre than Aston Villa's away game at Leicester City in March 1976, which goes down in history for Nicholl's remarkable piece of goal-scoring. The tall central defender scored all four goals in a 2–2 draw. Twice he headed own-goals to put Leicester ahead. Twice he equalised with close-range shots.

The game at Leicester was the eighteenth of 21 away games Aston Villa failed to win that season, their first season back in Division One. They started well enough, but Leicester went ahead after fifteen minutes, Nicholl heading Brian Alderson's shot on to a better course for it to find the net. In the 40th minute, however, after Brian Little's header had created confusion in the Leicester penalty area, Nicholl hooked in an equaliser for Villa.

Eight minutes after half-time Chris Nicholl conceded his second own-goal. Leicester's Frank Worthington lobbed the ball into the penalty area and Nicholl, challenging with Bob Lee, sent another fine header past John Burridge. But, once again, he cancelled out his own-goal with one at the other end. Four minutes were left when 'Chico' Hamilton sent over a corner kick. A scramble in the goalmouth gave Nicholl a chance to put boot on ball, and there was his fourth goal of the game, his second for Villa.

Chris Nicholl's amazing feat of two for each side equalled the 'achievement' of Sam Wynne in a 1923 game for Oldham Athletic against Manchester United. Wynne scored a free-kick and a penalty kick for Oldham and two own-goals for Manchester United. Oldham won 3–2. But, in Nicholl's case, all his goals came from open play and they were the only goals of the game.

Also, there were a couple of strange indicators from the previous week. Chris Nicholl had scored an own-goal a week before, diverting a shot from Tottenham Hotspur's Ralph Coates past John Burridge. And, on the same day, Leicester had beaten Middlesbrough, the only goal of the game being an own-goal by tall Middlesbrough central defender Stuart Boam.

One of the strangest things about Nicholl's performance was his two goals for Villa. His goals usually came from his head, but here he was scoring with his feet. It was surprising that Villa never used him as an out-and-out attacker. After all, that day at Leicester he demonstrated that he had the one thing that all natural goal-scorers possess – a beautiful sense of balance.

'We Want Twenty'

Stirling, December 1984

Stirling Albion had some trepidation about their first round Scottish Cup-tie at home to Selkirk. The previous season Stirling were sitting on a huge lead at the top of the Scottish Second Division when they lost 2–1 at home to Inverness Caledonian of the Highland League, the winning goal coming in the last minute of extra time. Stirling's season had gone downhill from there. They missed the chance of a Cup-tie at home to Rangers, and they missed out on promotion. Stirling were still in the Second Division when they were drawn against Selkirk of the Border Amateur League W Division. The prevailing opinion, supported by Stirling manager Alex Smith, was that the game shouldn't be taken lightly. It wouldn't be easy.

Stirling sent chief scout George Rankin to watch Selkirk. He saw them take a 3–0 lead at Leithen Rovers and left before the finish. He didn't see them concede five in the last 20 minutes and go down to a 5–3 defeat.

Stirling Albion, meanwhile, were scoring four in the last fifteen minutes of their match at Albion Rovers. Both sides, unwittingly, were warming up for their next week's Cup match, which would establish a British record for this century.

From the start to the end of the game, Stirling Albion showed no signs of underestimating their amateur opponents. Their five first-half goals were all scored by different players – Irvine (6 mins), Maxwell (12), Ormond (26), Thompson (34) and Dawson (36) – and Walker became the sixth Stirling player on the score-sheet shortly after half-time. Thereafter it was one long procession towards the Selkirk goal.

On another day, Selkirk goalkeeper Richard 'Midge' Taylor might have saved the thirteenth goal, and there was a suspicion of offside about the nineteenth, scored by Neil Watt. Otherwise, Stirling were pretty good value for their 20–0 win, and Taylor made some good saves to restrict the score to a score.

Stirling's second-half goal-scoring was dominated by David Thompson, a £10,000 signing from Stenhousemuir, who scored six in the second half. The 20 goals were shared by eight players – David Thompson (7), Willie Irvine (5), Keith Walker (2), substitute Neil Watt (2), Scott Maxwell (1), Jimmy Ormond (1), Rab Dawson (1) and Gerry McTeague (1).

Selkirk player-manager Jackson Cockburn had the idea that his team might just be able to frustrate Stirling and catch them in the second half. There's no telling what would have happened had one of Selkirk's two shots gone in, or their one corner kick had come to something. Towards the end, though, the dreams had been obliterated. I am reminded of a line in a report of Arbroath's 36–0 win over Bon Accord in 1885: 'After the 20th goal, Bon Accord played like a team with no hope.'

There was a touching moment near the end, when Stirling's score was in the high teens. Selkirk officials on the touch-lines collected as many numbers as they could and held them up to indicate they wanted to substitute them all. It was a pity there weren't more than a few hundred spectators present to laugh at the joke.

Stirling supporters, having chanted 'we want ten' after an hour's play, were able to chant 'we want twenty' in the last few minutes. At the end manager Smith thought his team had scored 19 rather than 20 goals. It was an excusable mistake. It was very easy to miss a goal.

This was Stirling Albion's second record of the 1980s. The other was not so positive. They failed to score a goal in the last thirteen Scottish League games of 1980–1, altogether playing 1,293 minutes between McPhee's goal (31 January 1981) and Torrance's goal on the opening day of the next season (29 August 1981). That was probably the point at which they started saving them up for poor Selkirk.

Stirling Albion could justifiably be proud of their achievement of recording the biggest victory in British soccer this century, but Selkirk, completely outclassed on the day, could also be proud. Theirs had been an incredible achievement to reach the first round of the Scottish Cup for the first time.

A Pooch of a Goal
Stoke-on-Trent, November 1985

To say a dog scored a goal is understating the case. It's almost like saying England scored a fourth in the 1966 World Cup Final when a forward tapped in a pass from a defender. So let's give the dog full credit. This was no everyday goal by a dog. This was supreme opportunism at its best.

David Hall, secretary of Knave of Clubs, recalls the most amazing thing he has ever seen on a football field: 'We were playing Newcastle Town in the Staffordshire Sunday Cup, and I think we were losing 2–0 at the time. One of our players was running down the field with only the goalkeeper to beat. He tried a shot from fifteen yards out and miscued it, so it was going well wide. The dog ran on to the field, jumped up at the ball and headed it. The ball flew into the net.'

The dog, a mongrel, disappeared before either secretary had a chance to sign him. He left behind an argument which will continue for years. Should the referee give a goal? David Hall explains: 'There was quite a crowd at Monks Neil Park. Most were laughing at it, but a lot didn't know what the rules would say. The Newcastle players argued that the referee couldn't allow a goal, but the referee did. Our side rejoiced, but their players weren't too happy.'

Newcastle Town hung on to win the Cup-tie 3–2.

Like star midfield players, dogs can arrive from nowhere and make an impact on games. They are usually good at keeping their eyes on the ball and dribbling it, but not many are as good in the air as the mongrel at Monks Neil Park. Unfortunately, for at least one footballer, dogs can also be strong tacklers. Chic Brodie was keeping goal for Brentford against Colchester in 1970 when a ferocious white mutt ran full pelt into him just as he was collecting a back-pass. The dog hit Brodie's left knee as he twisted and the goalkeeper suffered serious knee-ligament damage, enough to finish his career at Football League level. The nearest the goalkeepers' union came to exacting retribution on wildlife, as far as I'm aware, was a game in Holland. A high kick from the Feyenoord goalkeeper hit a pigeon which fell dead on to the field.

Football For Pigs

Various pig farms in Britain, from June 1990

While the world's football press concentrated on seemingly strange events, like Cameroon's defeat of World Cup holders Argentina, something was stirring at the grassroots of football. More and more pigs were taking up the game.

When Bernard Hoggarth visited the Paris Agricultural Show early in the year, he spotted a Danish product, the Domino Stress Ball, which enabled pigs to play football. Hoggarth bought some balls for his pig business at Cranswick Mill, near Driffield in Yorkshire, and, after successful trials, began marketing Stress Balls in Britain. The manufacturers claim that football-playing pigs are less aggressive and less stressed and therefore happier and more likely to put on weight. You may have heard the same argument applied to human footballers.

The product was publicised around the time of the 1990 World Cup Finals. There were suggestions that an international team of pigs should be managed by Franz Baconbauer, and an English Premier Cut League should include Trotterham Hotspur, Queen's Pork Rangers and Roast Ham United. It would appeal to those football-club groundsmen who claim they've seen dressing-rooms looking like pigsties.

Pigs are intelligent creatures. When bored, they can become aggressive, and bite the tails or ears of other pigs in the pen. Hence the need to amuse them. Traditionally, some pig-keepers have suspended chains or left cans in pens for pigs to chew on. The Stress Ball is a more sophisticated toy. 'They roll it around the sty, shoot it into corners and leap over it on their way to their fodder,' says the promotion literature. In practice, pigs rely more on dribbling with their snouts than kicking the ball.

Stress Balls are indestructible. They are bright red, about eight or nine inches in diameter and made of sturdy plastic. Each one has a ball-bearing in the middle which rattles as the pigs knock the ball around the pen. A Stress Ball needs to be disinfected and cleaned after each batch of pigs, but can be used time and time again.

On his Yorkshire pig farm, Bernard Hoggarth experimented with one ball in a pen of about fifteen pigs. The pigs tended to play with the ball on their own and when one had had enough another took over. No doubt this ability to pass the ball at the right moment can be developed further. Perhaps we will eventually see pigs playing team games, and spectators guaranteed lots of excitement around the pen areas.

It sounds like something out of *Animal Farm*, doesn't it? Those familiar with George Orwell's satirical fable may recall that the pigs learned to read, lead and stand on hind legs, and Animal Farm became a replica of the human society it had replaced. A manager of a soccer team of pigs would be especially vulnerable to the chop.

Stress Balls have also been supplied to breeding stables for racehorses to play with, but a well-hoofed shot could cause damage if it hits a passing spectator. At the time of going to press chickens had yet to be approached: the manufacturers were worried about too many fouls.

'One Team in Tallinn'
Tallinn, Estonia, October 1996

Having beaten Latvia 2–0 in Riga on 5 October, the Scotland party flew to Tallinn in readiness for their next Group 4 World Cup qualifying match – against Estonia on 9 October.

The two countries had a good football relationship: Scottish fans had enjoyed visiting Estonia when the teams met in a 1993 World Cup qualifier and some of them had even returned to see the Estonia–Croatia game; Estonian officials had visited the Scottish Football Association to improve their understanding of football administration; and the SFA had sent equipment for Estonian youngsters. Yes, the two nations had a good rapport . . . until Scottish officials saw the floodlights in the Kadriorg Stadium.

In preparation for the 6.45 p.m. kick-off, Estonian officials had arranged for temporary floodlighting to be brought from Finland. Scotland complained to FIFA that the low-level floodlights, mounted on lorries, would cause problems for goalkeepers when dealing with crosses from one particular side. It was reminiscent of floodlight debates in the fifties.

The next morning, at nine o'clock, FIFA announced that the time of the game would be changed from 6.45 p.m. to 3 p.m. Scottish officials ran round all the locals haunts to spread news to their fans, buses were hired to ferry supporters to the ground and the players' preparations were changed accordingly. However, the Estonian officials pleaded that they had far more to consider – security arrangements in the stadium, consideration of supporters who were working during the day and the location of the players (80 kilometres from the ground). The most important thing, however, was the television contract, which had been arranged for a 6.45 p.m. kick-off.

Scotland manager Craig Brown fully expected Estonia to conform with FIFA's ruling, so he went ahead with the preparations. Just before three o'clock John Collins led out Scotland but the opposition had still not arrived.

'One team in Tallinn,' sang the Scotland supporters. 'There's only one team in Tallinn.'

The Scotland players lined up for the kick-off. The referee, Miroslav Radoman of Yugoslavia, is probably the only referee in history who had to be certain that players couldn't be offside from a kick-off. (They must be inside their own half or the place-kick is retaken.) He blew the whistle and Billy Dodds tapped the ball to Collins.

The referee blew his whistle again.

The match was over.

Tosh McKinlay punched the air and raised his hands to the Scottish fans. Scotland thought they must have won the game by default as a FIFA directive stated that teams would win 3–0 if the opposition failed to turn up.

'Easy, easy, easy,' chanted the supporters.

No caps were awarded but the Scottish players were allowed to keep their shirts. They couldn't very well swap them with the opposition, could they?

As for the two teams:

ESTONIA:
SCOTLAND: Goram, McNamara, Boyd, Calderwood, McKinlay, Burley, Lambert, Collins, McGinlay, Dodds, Jackson.

The Estonia team bus arrived at the Kadriorg Stadium at five o'clock. They were too late for the game, such as it was.

On 7 November the World Cup organising committee met and decided that the Estonia–Scotland tie should be replayed on neutral ground. There was some disquiet about this decision, not least because the chair of the committee, Lennart Johansson, came from Sweden, and Sweden were in the same group as Scotland and Estonia. Scotland felt they (and their fans) were being punished for something that was no fault of their own. On 27 November it was announced that the re-match would take place in Monaco.

The next month the English Premier League had to deal with a similar situation when Middlesbrough failed to turn up for a match at Blackburn Rovers, claiming that 23 players were ill or injured. Middlesbrough were later deducted three points and fined £50,000, even though no formal directive seemed to exist. When that game was re-arranged, the two teams drew 0–0. The two lost points caused Middlesbrough to be relegated.

Estonia finally played Scotland on 4 February 1997. Scottish fans turned up with miners, glasses and special spectacles with torches to mock the floodlight farce in Tallinn. Scotland's only good spell came late in the first half. Duncan Ferguson's header was scrambled off the line, Tom Boyd's shot hit the crossbar, and Estonia goalkeeper Mart Poom made two wonderful saves. The match ended 0–0 but Scotland went on to qualify for France 1998 as the best second-place finishers in the European groups.

RUGBY

by John Griffiths

One-armed Player's Record

Newton Abbot, January 1886

When a player named Wakeham kicked 13 conversions from 13 attempts for Newton Abbot against Plymouth on 30 January 1886 it was claimed as a record for a club match in England.

The mark has long since been overtaken but one astonishing fact regarding Wakeham renders his record remarkable to this day: he had only one arm.

Is a Dog a Spectator?
Portsmouth, November 1886

The early rugby handbooks provide fascinating insights into the laws of the game in a series of space-fillers under the heading of points often inquired about. One such query relates to a match played between Portsmouth Victoria and Southampton Trojans in November 1886.

During the match the ball was kicked into the Trojans' in-goal area where it rebounded off a stray dog. One of the Victoria players gathered it and touched down to claim a try. The Trojans protested, claiming that the referee should have ruled 'dead ball' the ball having struck 'a spectator'.

The objection was later referred to the Rugby Football Union whose committee ruled that the try should stand, as dogs were not classed as spectators.

Rugby Versus Soccer
London, April 1892

Imagine the British Lions taking on the cream of the country's soccer players at a selection of different sports. Jeremy Guscott sprinting 100 metres against Michael Owen perhaps, Scott Quinnell putting the shot against Paul Gascoigne, or Robert Howley contesting the high jump against David Beckham. And then soccer and rugby games between the teams, before rounding off the event with a limited-overs cricket match involving elevens skippered by Martin Johnson and Alan Shearer.

Far-fetched? Maybe. Yet in 1892 precisely such an unusual sporting challenge featuring the nation's leading footballers and rugby players occurred in a charity festival at Queen's Club in West Kensington.

The protagonists in this pioneering version of Super-stars were the Barbarians Rugby Club and the Corinthians Football Club, two sides with such impeccable pedigrees that they were national institutions.

Formed in 1882, the Corinthians were keen to uphold the standards of amateur soccer at a time when the social background of the country's leading footballers was changing. In an earlier incarnation as the Wanderers the team had comprised old boys of the soccer-playing public schools and had won the FA Cup five times. But a tenet of its new constitution prohibited entry to league or cup competition (a rule that was later relaxed). University men and ex-public schools players dominated the club and so gentlemanly were the players that when the Corinthians conceded a penalty their goalkeeper was removed to offer opponents a free shot at goal.

The Barbarians Rugby Club was less exclusive. Founded by an inveterate rugby tourist named Percy Carpmael at an oyster supper in Bradford in 1890, their membership was, in the words of the club's motto: 'for gentlemen in all classes but no bad sportsmen in any class'.

The unique sporting challenge of 1892 was issued by the Corinthians, whose squad included nine players who were or who would become soccer internationals. There were eight established or future rugby caps in the Barbarians' ranks, so it would be fair to conclude that the two codes were pretty well represented when the festival began with an athletics competition followed by a football match on Boat Race Saturday, 9 April.

Despite winning four of the track events the Baa-Baas struggled in the field events, where the matchless talents of one C B Fry were displayed. Charles Fry was arguably the best all-round sportsman who ever lived. An athletics, cricket and soccer Blue at Oxford, he would have added a Rugby Blue but for a leg injury. He played soccer and cricket for England and even found time to set the world long jump record.

On this particular day, playing for the Corinthians, he won both the long jump and high jump comfortably to reduce a commanding Barbarians' lead and the outcome of the athletics was decided in the Corinthians' favour on the final event, the mile.

Fry then excelled for the Corinthians in the soccer match where the famous Walters brothers, Arthur and Percy, who had played together as full-backs for the England XI, were unperturbed by the unusual tactics of the rugby men. The Barbarians amused the crowd by instinctively resorting to the hand-off as a device for parrying opponents. A hat-trick by Tom Lindley helped the Corinthians to an easy 6–0 win, and after the first day of competition the footballers were two up with two to play.

Surely the Barbarians would resume two days later with a win in the rugby contest? For that match their side would be reinforced by several members of the England pack that a month earlier had completed a Triple Crown of victories in the International Championship without conceding a single score.

But they lost. Displaying astonishing ingenuity the dribblers outwitted the handlers. Lindley again showed himself to be a skilful games player, crossing for two tries and impressing the rugby men with his prodigious punting in a 14–12 victory. Newspaper reports of the match suggested that the referee was not fully acquainted with rugby's off-side laws. Even so, the Barbarians were gracious in defeat and many years later one of their committee members recalled, 'the Corinthians were entitled to the glory that follows a fully substantiated challenge.'

The rugby players did salvage some respect when the sides met again late in April for the cricket match. Batting first, the Corinthians were dismissed for 170 with C B Fry, thinly disguised as 'A Fryer' on the scorecards, falling for only 25 runs. Australians would consider Fry's wicket cheap at twice that price in several Ashes Tests in later years.

The Barbarians went on to win by four wickets, thanks mainly to an unbeaten 55 from one John Le Fleming, a former England wing threequarter who was a more than useful performer in the Kent XI. Thus a charming sporting challenge unparalleled in the annals of Britain's two footballing codes ended 3–1 in favour of the soccer players.

The Chief Constable Saves Wales

Cardiff, February 1906

Matches between Wales and Scotland invariably settled the International Championship title in the first decade of the twentieth century. A look at the roll of honour for those years will show the reader that the nations exercised a duopoly over international rugby, either Wales or Scotland finishing top of the table every year from 1900 to 1909.

Wales were reigning champions and recent victors over the All Blacks when the nations met for their annual bash in front of 25,000 at Cardiff in 1906. Scotland had been beaten 12–7 by the New Zealanders in a closely contested match but entered the Welsh game full of optimism.

High social status was attached to attendance at Wales's matches at the turn of the century, and even the Chief Constable of Cardiff felt that he should be seen to be on active duty when international rugby matches were played on his patch. On this particular occasion he turned out in his finery as usual, though little did he realise that he was about to play a part in the evolution of the game's laws.

Early in the match, Scotland were pressing. 'Darky' Bedell-Sivright, a former Lions captain and a strapping wing forward who was renowned for his dribbling powers, led a Scottish rush into the Welsh 25 and a try seemed certain. He toed the ball over the Welsh line but was astonished to see it strike 'the might and majesty of the stalwart Chief Constable' who at that moment was strutting his stuff up and down the Welsh in-goal area.

The Scot reacted quickly, changed direction and managed to touch the ball down to claim a try. But Mr Allen, the Irish referee, ruled 'dead ball' and Scotland's chance of taking the lead was lost. Later in the half, Wales scored tries through Jehoida Hodges and Cliff Pritchard, two of the heroes of their victory over the All Blacks, and finished the match winners by 9–3. Wales went on to retain the International Championship.

But the good Chief Constable later warranted his own footnote to the history of the game's laws. The International Board, the body that frames rugby's rules and regulations, subsequently reflected long and hard on the events at Cardiff and introduced a new clause to ensure that any repeat act should be fairly covered.

The outcome of their deliberations was to rule that in future referees should regard all officials and spectators as offending players on the home side, and that any doubt regarding a point or score arising should be awarded against the side responsible for the ground arrangements.

Selectors' Cock-up

London, December 1906

One can accept that in the early days of international rugby travelling problems or communication difficulties contributed to teams arriving one or perhaps two short for a big match. But surely the mix-up surrounding the selection of the 1906 England team to face the First Springboks was inexcusable.

One of the prominent forwards of the early part of the 1906–7 season was a Liverpool and Lancashire player named Noel Slocock, who was making a reputation as an effective line-out jumper. The main England trial in those days was the North–South match, and he had already given a tidy account of himself in one of those encounters when the England selectors sat down to deliberate over the XV to meet South Africa at the Crystal Palace in December 1906.

Slocock's name was, by all accounts, put forward for the match but when the team was announced his name was omitted owing to a clerical error. Instead, the name of Arnold Alcock appeared in the team lists. Alcock was a medical student at Guy's Hospital and no more than a useful forward in their Hospitals' Cup side. Yet he was to gain his cap at Slocock's expense.

The student doctor played a part in a creditable 3–3 draw but reports of the match do not single him out for praise. He was never invited to take part in a trial and never again played for England. In later life, however, he was the shining example of the past player who puts something back into the game.

He settled in general practice in Gloucester and from 1924 until 1969 served the club as president. He died in 1973, aged 91, and was the last survivor of his one and only England XV.

Noel Slocock scored a try for the Lancashire XV that made the South Africans work hard for victory in their first match after the England Test and, tellingly, came into the England team for their next international. He became a regular member of their pack for two seasons until his playing career ended in 1908, after captaining a losing England side in the Calcutta Cup match. He died young, killed in action in France in 1916.

Seven Brothers Versus Seven Brothers

Carmarthen, April 1909

The credit for devising the seven-a-side version of rugby goes to Ned Haig, a local butcher who arranged the first tournament in Melrose at the end of the 1882–3 season. Within two years there were annual sevens competitions staged at Gala and Hawick and by the turn of the century the abbreviated game had established a unique end-of-season circuit in the Scottish Borders.

Special permission had to be obtained from the Rugby Unions to allow such tournaments to take place and it was not until the 1920s that sevens became a feature of the season in England. Tournaments were long outlawed because they led to the award of prize money, in direct contravention of the laws pertaining to amateurism.

One of the most unusual sevens challenges took place in West Wales at Easter 1909, when a family of seven Williams brothers from Haverfordwest in Pembrokeshire took on the seven Randall brothers of Llanelli. The match was staged on neutral ground at Carmarthen, roughly halfway between the two towns, where more than a thousand of the brothers' travelling supporters turned up to see the 'Family Championship of the United Kingdom'. There was a £100 prize at stake and both sides employed their own trainers to assist with their preparations for a match that was refereed by the ex-Welsh international full-back, Billy Bancroft of Swansea.

The Randalls were brawny steel workers and millmen typical of the working population of Llanelli at the turn of the century. The Haverfordwest boys were sons of the local police superintendent, though none followed their father into the constabulary. Three were hairdressers, three worked as commission agents and the seventh brother was a clerk.

The match itself was a scrappy, ill-tempered affair according to several local press reports. The Williamses lost one of their brothers through injury early on and Mr Bancroft had to intervene several times as the contest frequently threatened to degenerate into a glorified fight. 'It was more like a wrestling match,' Bancroft commented after the Williamses ran out 8–0 winners.

Joe's New Year Cap

Swansea, January 1910

The first ever Five Nations match took place in January 1910 at Swansea, though it is doubtful whether the players who played in the game realised at the time that they were creating a piece of history, by launching what became the jewel in the northern hemisphere's rugby crown. The Five Nations tournament became the byword for European rugby at its best for the rest of the twentieth century.

But back in 1910, the competition came about by accident. France had entered the lists of international rugby on New Year's Day, 1906, with an international against the All Blacks. Later the same year, England crossed the Channel for their first taste of French rugby and two years later Wales hosted the newcomers for the first time. Ireland gave the French an inaugural fixture in 1909 before, the following year, Scotland decided that they, too, would join the *entente cordiale*.

So 1910 is the date from which Five Nations history is reckoned, simply because it was the first time that the round-robin of ten matches involving the nations was completed. The phrase *Tournoi des Cinq Nations* was coined by the French press as early as the 1920s, though its use in the Home Unions did not really catch on until the 1960s.

Could France have made a more inauspicious start to the competition than the events surrounding the departure of their team from Paris for their journey to Wales on New Year's Eve, 1909?

When the players and officials assembled to make their journey to Swansea they discovered that one of their number, a new cap in the forwards named Hélier Tilh, had been forced to withdraw owing to military duties in Bordeaux. The boat train departed with fourteen players aboard, leaving one of the French selectors to search the streets of the capital for someone to make up the pack.

At length, the weary official discovered one Joe Anduran working in a picture gallery on the Rue La Boétie. Anduran thought he was the butt of a practical joke when he was first approached about representing his country. Eventually he was persuaded that his services were genuinely required and he enthusiastically joined the selector in a taxi to gather his kit from home.

Preparations for New Year celebrations were well under way back at the Anduran household and poor Joe had plenty of explaining to do to his wife to excuse himself from the forthcoming family festivities. Nevertheless, despite his wife's displeasure, he set off for Swansea and eventually caught up with the rest of the French team on the morning of the match.

France were overwhelmed 49–14. The Welsh ran rings around their hapless visitors and raced over for ten tries to two in reply. Poor old Joe didn't even warrant a mention in any of the press reports of the match and he never again received an invitation to represent his country.

Even so, Mme Anduran must have forgiven him for his commitment to the game: in 1913, aged nearly 31, Joe turned out for his club, SCUF (a university sports club in Paris), in the final of the French Championship and collected a loser's medal in a side beaten by Bayonne.

The man who played rugby for his country at the drop of a hat in 1910 was just as quick to serve his country in more serious battles four years later. Joe joined the infantry at the outbreak of the First World War and survived barely two months before losing his life in the fighting south-east of Lens in October 1914. He was 32.

The Crowd Oversteps the Mark

Swansea, February 1921

There have been international matches where the crowd rioted after the final whistle, occasions where the referee has had to shepherd crowds back from the touch-lines and there have even been Tests where captains have led their sides off the field temporarily in protest at refereeing decisions. But only once in a major international has the referee had to interrupt play to take the teams off the field because of the antics of spectators.

The occasion was the Wales–Scotland Five Nations match of 1921 played at St Helen's, Swansea. The match started promptly at 3 p.m. despite the problems caused by the record crowd, which resulted in spectators being allowed on to the grass in front of the terraces, bringing them fairly close to the touch-lines.

There was no sign of trouble until six minutes into the game when Wales were awarded a penalty. As Albert Jenkins prepared to take the kick, pandemonium broke out. A mass of spectators got to their feet and swarmed across the pitch, some 'committing disgraceful acts on the field of play'.

The police were unable to contain the crowd and the referee had no alternative but to halt the game. The players retreated to the pavilion for fifteen minutes, during which time mounted police were called to clear the pitch. Wales appeared to be more discomfited by the disturbances than Scotland. When play resumed Jenkins missed his kick and the Scots, despite further stoppages for the referee and officials to persuade the encroaching crowds to retreat, coasted to an eleven-point lead before half-time.

Further crowd disturbances occurred during the interval and in the second half. For Wales, Jenkins landed two dropped goals and the Welsh backs engaged in an aerial bombardment of the Scottish goal, seeking a third which would have brought the home side the lead. (Such goals were valued at four points at this time.) But just as Wales appeared to be gaining the upper hand, the crowd again overstepped the lines and were lapping around the Scottish goal when the referee was again forced to stop play.

With patience the officials persuaded the crowd to settle, but when the game resumed it was Scotland who wrested the initiative from Wales and a late try sealed their first victory on Welsh soil for 29 years.

Never before, nor indeed since, have such disgraceful scenes been witnessed on an international ground.

Trying the High Jump
Twickenham, February 1924

Twickenham has enjoyed its fair share of famous tries: Prince Obolensky in 1936, Peter Jackson in 1958, Richard Sharp in 1963, and Andy Hancock in 1965, to mention four. But a couple of tries scored in the 1924 England–France match stand out as two of the more unusual witnessed at the ground.

England were playing a French XV that had been forced to make disruptive late changes when three of its leading players withdrew at the eleventh hour. The English side went ahead by 2–0, but there was a feeling among the crowd that their team was coasting. The match reports indicated a casualness in the home side's approach to the first half.

Then, just before the interval, came a blind-side England move that at last had the spectators on the edges of their seats. The half-backs, Arthur Young and Edward Myers, opened a gap to work Carston Catcheside clear on the right wing. Catcheside was not one of the fastest wings to play for England but when confronted by the French full-back, Laurent Pardo, a couple of yards from the goal line, he astounded everyone. Seeing his opponent stoop in preparation for a head-on tackle, Catcheside coolly high-jumped over Pardo and grounded the ball for a try as he landed.

At six-foot Pardo was one of the tallest full-backs in the Five Nations. Even the esteemed rugby correspondent of *The Times* was bemused. 'To jump over a big full-back's head – even though the latter be bending to make a low tackle – was an unexpected revelation,' he told his readers. Catcheside's move was catching. Towards the end of the match and with the score 19–4 in England's favour, the French right wing performed the same feat in the same corner of the ground. The second jump-try was scored by new cap Jacques Ballarin after he had cleared Bev Chantrill, the England full-back.

HM King George V was an interested spectator at the match and when introduced to Catcheside on a later Twickenham visit referred to the winger's flying try, adding a royal touch of disapproval at what he believed was a dangerous tactic.

Very dangerous, in fact. In 1899 a former New Zealand representative named Barney Armit had died performing the very same trick that Catcheside had perfected. Armit was playing for Otago against Taranaki when he was tipped over hurdling his opposite number. He landed heavily on the back of his head and broke his neck. Paralysed, he was taken to Dunedin hospital where he died from his injuries nearly eleven weeks later.

Last-Minute Team Change
Cardiff, January 1930

Sam Tucker of Bristol was the outstanding hooker of the 1920s. He was one of the first Englishmen to specialise in the position, it being common up to the First World War for forwards to pack down in scrum formation simply in the order that they arrived: the so-called First Up, First Down arrangement.

Tucker had already won 22 caps and had helped England to a Grand Slam when, at the start of the 1930 Five Nations Championship, he was dropped from the England side to meet Wales in Cardiff. The England selectors were looking for a fast, fit eight to take on the Welsh and named an experimental pack in which five players were new caps.

On the eve of the match, prop Henry Rew stubbed his toe in training at Penarth. On the morning of the game it transpired that his injury was worse than originally diagnosed and he had to withdraw from the side. Faced with several options, the Rugby Football Union's secretary, Sydney Cooper, telephoned Sam Tucker's Bristol office at 12.25 p.m. and, finding the former hooker at his desk, demanded that Tucker get himself to Cardiff pretty damned quick.

Tucker managed to arrange a flight from nearby Filton Aerodrome and, after picking up his kit, took a taxi and boarded a two-seater bi-plane at 1.50. In his own words, Tucker 'was in an open cockpit with what looked to me like a bit of fuselage and a few pieces of wire between me and eternity'. Ten minutes into his maiden flight he was over Cardiff and, after circling around, the pilot landed in a field on the outskirts of the city. Tucker hitched a lift in a coal lorry to the city centre where his next problem was to gain entry to the ground.

A huge crowd had turned up at the gates to see the match. In those days internationals at Cardiff were not all-ticket affairs and it was a matter of first come, first served, as far as admittance to the ground was concerned. Eventually, Tucker managed to talk his way in and arrived in the changing room at 2.40, five minutes before kick-off time. He played hooker with Dave Kendrew, the originally selected hooker, moving to prop. Tucker had a blinder and kept his place in the side for the rest of a season in which England carried off the Five Nations title.

For last-minute call-ups Sam Tucker's adventure was unique. But spare a thought for poor Norman Matthews, the Bath and Bridgwater prop who was an England travelling reserve for that Cardiff game. The England selectors, thinking that Tucker had failed to arrange transport, had decided that Matthews would take Henry Rew's place in the front row. Matthews was actually ready changed into an England jersey when Tucker turned up breathless at the dressing-room door. Matthews never got to wear an England jersey again: a case of so near, so close and so unlucky.

The Wrong Score

Twickenham, January 1933

Wales had already made nine fruitless journeys to the Rugby Football Union's Twickenham headquarters when an experimental side that was a mix of experienced forwards and youthful backs travelled from the Principality to London for the opening match of the 1933 International Championship. Many of Wales's defeats at the ground had been near things and over the years a myth had developed in South Wales that Twickenham was their bogey ground.

High hopes were pinned on a 19-year-old leggy centre from North Wales named Wilf Wooller who was among the seven Welsh newcomers. The teenager enjoyed a successful debut. He was given few opportunities to show his strides in attack but his magnificent side-on tackling, especially in the second half, had the required effect of reducing the danger posed by England's centres.

Even so, England opened the scoring when Don Burland broke through in the first half to send Walter Elliot in for a try. Soon after the interval, however, Wales took the lead when wing threequarter Ronnie Boon dropped a goal from a loose maul 20 yards from the English posts. That put Wales 4–3 ahead with all to play for. The Welsh pack began to exercise a hold on their opponents, though only Wooller's tackle at the corner flag prevented Elliot from restoring England's lead after a 30-yard chase.

Then Ronnie Boon put Wales further ahead with a try that was followed by a most unusual incident. Welsh centre

Claude Davey drew the English full-back perfectly to release Boon on a run that took the wing arcing outside the defence for a try near the posts. Viv Jenkins, making his Welsh debut despite nursing a high fever, lined up the simple kick and sent the ball, so the Welsh supporters and Welsh touch judge thought, straight between the posts. Even the scoreboard operator believed that the kick was good, for he marked up a Welsh lead of 9–3 with time running out. Converted tries were worth only five points at this time, so most of the crowd and probably the players, too, felt that Wales were virtually safe with England having to score twice to win.

That, however, was not so. Only at the end of the match was it made clear by the Irish referee, Tom Bell, that Jenkins's conversion kick from close range had failed. It was true that Mr Llewellyn, the Welsh touch judge, had signalled a goal. He was from Bridgend, Jenkins's home club, and presumably could not believe that the young place kicker would miss a kick from such a good position.

The score had come ten minutes from no-side and the misunderstanding could have had a profound influence on the outcome of the match. The fact was that England only needed another breakaway try and conversion to win the match. Whether or not the English players were aware of the position is not recorded, though it was reported that the Welsh forwards so dominated the closing stages of the match that it was as much as England could do to prevent Wales from increasing their lead.

A similar incident in the Paris international between France and Scotland in 1951 might have had more serious consequences. A French conversion attempt on the stroke of half-time was touched in flight by a Scotsman and therefore disallowed by the referee. But the Stade Colombes scoreboard operator, Jacques Robin, credited his side with the two points after an announcer had given the score as 8–6 to France instead of 6–6.

The second half was a see-saw affair and with five minutes remaining Scotland actually led 12–11 while the scoreboard showed France ahead 13–12. The referee was the well-known English official Tom Pearce, who had earlier communicated the correct score to the marker in the score box. The 30-year-old Monsieur Robin, however, deliberately ignored requests to change the scores, despite pleas from the French officials as well as from the referee.

'I was afraid of trouble from the crowd if I corrected the scoreboard,' he told reporters later. 'I was waiting for the loudspeaker to announce the correction, but it remained silent,' he added.

Fortunately a major incident was avoided when Jean Prat landed what turned out to be France's winning points from a penalty goal only three minutes from time. British journalists attending the match were unanimous in siding with the score-marker's view, noting that the French crowd was the most partisan seen since the war.

Army Forgets Its Drill
Twickenham, April 1950

During the 1950 season, the Army were the unbeaten winners of the annual Inter-Services Triangular tournament and went into the traditional annual match against their French counterparts on All Fools' Day as hot favourites to continue their successful run.

For once, though, the Army forgot its drill in an extraordinary start to the match. As the home side was warming up to go out onto the Twickenham pitch their experienced full-back, Lieut. Roberts, tweaked a leg muscle and had to withdraw from the XV. Normally, one of the reserves would have stepped in, but the Army's reserve players had already left the dressing-rooms and were making their way to seats high in the West Stand.

No contingency plan was in place and there was nothing for it but for the Army to start the match with only fourteen players. Chaos ruled for the next 20 minutes as desperate messages were relayed over the loudspeaker system urging one of the reserves to return to the changing rooms and get stripped to join the action on the field. At length, Captain Scarr of the Hussars emerged to complete the team.

By then fully 25 minutes had passed and the French Army had taken advantage of the situation, taking a six-point lead and playing with their tails up. Although the British Army, fielding six seasoned internationals and playing with the stiff breeze after the interval, did give their opponents a stern test in the second half, the result was a well merited 12–8 win for a visiting side that contained only one international player.

No doubt the Army rugby authorities absorbed the moral of this episode in subsequent seasons: keep your reserves where you know that you can lay your hands on them.

Did the Touch Judge Help Wales?

Cardiff, December 1953

Until 1963 Wales had never lost to the All Blacks at Cardiff. It is incredible to reflect today that their wins there in 1905, 1935 and 1953 once gave them a 3–1 lead in this series (they lost at Swansea in 1924). Even so, there was never more than one score between the sides in the matches won by Wales.

Probably the luckiest Welsh win of the three was in 1953 when they beat New Zealand for the last time. It was 8–5 to New Zealand as the game entered its last quarter. Welsh threequarter Gareth Griffiths had gone off the field with a badly dislocated shoulder in the first half, but pleaded with the Welsh Rugby Union's surgeon, Nathan Rocyn Jones, to allow him to return to the match. Griffiths was very persuasive and, soon after he returned, Wales redoubled their efforts and managed to kick a penalty goal that levelled the scores. Five minutes from time Griffiths was to figure in the move that led to the winning score of the match.

He and left wing Gwyn Rowlands put pressure on New Zealand's Allan Elsom, some 20 yards from the All Blacks line. As the ball went loose, Clem Thomas picked it up and, finding himself cornered close to the touch-line, cross kicked. The ball bounced into the path of the Welsh right wing, Ken Jones, who raced over for a try at the posts which Rowlands converted – 13–8 to Wales and that was that.

It was another Welsh winner against New Zealand, Viv Jenkins of the 1935 side, who later spun an intriguing tale around that winning move. He became a leading post-war rugby journalist, first with the *News of the World* and later for the *Sunday Times*. Jenkins attended the dinner after the 1953 match and was seated beside another former Welsh great, Ifor Jones of Llanelli, who regularly acted as Wales's touch judge during the 1950s. Jones had been running the line that afternoon.

Discussing the day's game, Ifor Jones divulged to Jenkins that at the instant Clem Thomas picked the ball up, he had yelled, 'Cross kick, Clem; Ken Jones is unmarked.' Did a touch judge really help Wales to beat the All Blacks?

Although referees were neutral of course, those were the days when each of the sides playing provided their own touch judge for international matches. Usually these were members of the participating Unions' committees or distinguished referees. More than 30 years were to pass before neutral touch judges arrived on the international match scene.

Ifor Jones and Clem Thomas, sadly both dead now, were great characters and wonderful story tellers. The truth of the tale has never been proved. But certainly the film of that winning move shows the Welsh touch judge right up with the play at the time of Thomas's cross kick. Ifor Jones was unquestionably in the ideal position to influence the kicker. Clem Thomas, moreover, was described as looking pale and worried during the match, weighed down no doubt by the distress of having been involved in a fatal road accident on his journey down to Cardiff on the eve of the game.

It is easy to believe that Clem was operating on auto-pilot for once in a distinguished rugby career that culminated in his captaincy of Wales in nine matches in 1958 and 1959, and that he was quite happy to follow the inspired instructions of 'his' touch judge. But many of Clem's friends on hearing this story years later insisted that the tale was more likely to be the product of Ifor Jones's fertile imagination.

Clem was a well-known rugby journalist up to the time of his death. His former press-box colleagues, all of whom retain the fondest memories of him, categorically dismiss the story: 'Can't be true', they say almost to a man. 'Clem would never have done as he was told.'

Where's Our Crossbar?

Twickenham, January 1958

That same England–Wales game at Twickenham in January 1958 is remembered in West Wales for a very different reason. During the match the Welsh full-back, Terry Davies, very nearly landed a winning penalty goal with a colossal kick from 50 yards into a swirling wind. His attempt missed, veering into the posts at the last minute and the match ended in a 3–3 draw. But the miss prompted a most peculiar incident during the weekend.

Later that evening in central London, a plan was hatched by a young Welsh supporter. Aided and abetted by the brother of his fiancée, who lived in nearby Ealing, the Welshman returned to Twickenham during the early hours of Sunday morning, climbed over the turnstiles and proceeded to saw down the cross-bar from the offending posts at the north end of the ground. In a 20-minute operation the bar was cut into three lengths before it was whisked away down the A40 back to West Wales later in the day.

On his way home the phantom woodworker from south Pembrokeshire stopped in a Cotswold café for some refreshment. By coincidence, Terry Davies had also pulled in to the same café while motoring back to his home in Bynea outside Llanelli. The prankster promptly told Terry the story and persuaded him to autograph the mementoes.

The then secretary of the Rugby Football Union (RFU) was Colonel Frank Prentice who broke the news of the incident to the press on the Monday morning. Taking the loss in a sporting manner he added that the RFU had made arrangements to replace the bar. It was at that stage that Terry Davies intervened. Davies, as it happened, was a timber merchant and offered to replace the crossbar.

'If it will save the lad any trouble,' he told the *Western Mail*, 'I would be glad to replace the bar. I am sure many people in Wales would like to know who the joker was. But I hope cross-bars are not going to keep vanishing after international matches and that I shall not be expected to continue replacing them. That could lead to bankruptcy.'

At length, the joker and his conspirators' consciences got the better of them. They had thought that their prank would have been quickly forgotten, but such an incident had never occurred at Twickenham before and when the respected Welsh critic and rugby writer, Bryn Thomas, advised them to write a letter of apology to the RFU, they decided to make a clean breast of the matter. A couple of days after the joke they decided to write to Colonel Prentice.

The perpetrators of this good-humoured prank were revealed as Fred Mathias, the Welsh champion jockey from Manorbier in Pembrokeshire, and his bride-to-be's brother, Brian Attewell of Ealing. Thus blame was shared by an Englishman and a Welshman and fortunately there the matter ended.

To this day, one of the autographed pieces of crossbar has pride of place in Mathias's local pub in Pembrokeshire.

Please Can We Have Our Ball Back?

Coventry, February 1958

The last match played by the Fourth Wallabies in England was against the Midland Counties at Highfield Road, the ground of Coventry City football club. The match play was not particularly distinguished, although the home side, comprising thirteen Warwickshire players, did achieve its first win over a touring team for 30 years.

The bare playing surface, which in wet conditions churned into a mud-bath, did not ease the running and handling for the backs of either side, though both fifteens did attempt to play open rugby. Coventry scrum-half George Cole put the Midlands ahead with a left-footed penalty goal after 20 minutes and Ron Harvey equalised early in the second half with a similar score for the Wallabies.

Fenwick Allison, an England full-back and the home side's captain, won the match ten minutes later when he was up in support of a threequarter move and took an inside pass from wing Peter Jackson to score wide out. Cole converted to conclude the scoring: an 8–3 win for the Midlands.

If the play was forgettable, one moment stood out. A hugely entertaining episode of farce made this match a memorable one for the 10,000 who saw it. George Cole and Fenwick Allison on the home side together with Jim

Lenehan and Terry Curley in the Australian XV were four of the most prodigious out-of-the-hand kickers of a rugby ball playing in the late 1950s. Twice during the early stages of the game match balls were kicked on to the top of the Highfield Road stands where they remained.

But when Allison had lodged a third ball on top of the roof, play ground to a complete standstill. Only three balls had been provided for the game and, this being a football ground, there were no spare or practice rugby balls lying around anywhere.

Allison himself, together with a couple of policemen, made earnest inquiries as the crowd became restless at the lack of action on the pitch. Eventually the long-suffering spectators were provided with the best entertainment of the afternoon. There was no alternative but for the groundstaff to march on to the pitch with an enormous ladder and clamber up to the roof. This brought light relief to the crowd, who burst into laughter and began clapping as a full-scale operation to recover the balls began.

While the intrepid groundsman spent five minutes recovering three rugby balls from the roof, a spectator tossed a souvenir miniature one on to the field, where it was enthusiastically received by the Australians who proceeded to further amuse the crowd with a mock game.

The Long Arm of the Law Tries to Intervene

Wanganui, August 1959

One of the hardest earned victories by the Lions in New Zealand in 1959 was against Wanganui. Bev Risman gave the tourists the lead with a penalty goal in the fifth minute but the determined hosts equalised when their wing, Boswell, landed a similar score. A tough, uncompromising forward battle developed in which no quarter was asked and certainly none was given.

Shortly before half-time Risman was given the opportunity to regain the lead for the Lions with a penalty awarded on the Wanganui ten-yards-line. As the English fly-half began making his preparations there was a commotion among the crowd on the far side of the pitch near the home side's 25. Unknown to the referee they were trying to draw his attention to the fact that the touch-judge's flag was up to indicate that an earlier line-out had been awarded.

As Risman steadied himself to take the kick the baying from the crowd reached a crescendo. A policeman on patrol along the kicker's side of the field moved in at this stage and tapped the referee on the shoulder to point out the cause of the disturbance. The referee had lost sight of his touch judge in the far distance against the jumbled background of faces.

What followed was more extraordinary. The official permitted Risman to take his penalty and a low-trajectory kick just scraped over the crossbar. As the Lions withdrew to their half to receive the kick-off, the referee moved across to the touch-line and spoke with the touch judge, whereupon he disallowed the penalty and whistled for a line-out.

The Lions and their small band of press followers were dumbfounded by these events and it was to the players' credit that they picked themselves up to grind out a narrow 9–6 win in the second half.

Mother's Day

Timaru, August 1961

Rugby can be an aggressive game at the best of times. With 30 young players all striving to establish themselves in the hurly-burly of a contact sport played at speed, is it any wonder that tempers are occasionally frayed? But when spectators get angry and become physically involved in the action on the field then the line has to be drawn.

During France's tour of New Zealand in 1961, the French team were embroiled in brawls in several games. Strong refereeing was often required to cool eager forwards as the temperature began to rise. One game in particular, against South Canterbury at Timaru, stood out for the rough play involved.

South Canterbury had never beaten a touring side but in front of 23,000 this was to be their day. Their mobile forwards completely disrupted the French, whose tour form hit rock bottom in this match and the home side, who ran out 17–14 winners despite finishing with only fourteen men, led from an early stage.

Trouble broke out at the line-outs during the second half. Barging and pushing escalated into fisticuffs and it was the French who bore the brunt of referee Pat Murphy's ire. By the end of the game the penalty count went 17–4 against the tourists who were lucky not to have had a player sent off.

But the most astonishing incident occurred near the end of the match after South Canterbury's second five-eighth,

Eddie Smith, was felled by a stiff arm tackle. Michel Crauste, the French captain, incensed the crowd further by picking the listless Smith up by the scruff of his neck and promptly dropping him back to the ground – whereupon a 56-year-old woman in the crowd rushed out from her seat, spoke to Crauste and clouted him on the back of his neck with her clenched fist.

Two policemen had to intervene before escorting her, amid loud and approving cheers, from the field. Afterwards, the mother from Oamaru explained that she felt the tactics of the French team 'were totally uncalled for. I was so mad I did not know what I was doing. I hit him hard, but I don't think it hurt. I think he got a bit of a shock though.' Attending the match with her husband, two children and nephew, she added in her defence: 'It was not good for young boys to see that sort of play.'

Monsieur Crauste's reaction to the irate woman is not on record.

One Hundred and Eleven Line-outs

Murrayfield, February 1963

The one ground in Britain where every rugby match was guaranteed to proceed during the Big Freeze of 1963 was Murrayfield. The Scottish Rugby Union in its wisdom had installed underground electric heating there a couple of years earlier ensuring that the playing surface for big matches was always excellent, no matter what weather conditions prevailed overhead.

Wales desperately wanted to win against Scotland in February 1963, having been beaten by England at Cardiff a month earlier while fielding an experimental fifteen that included six new caps. In particular, Captain Clive Rowlands, who was one of those new caps, was determined to avoid leading Wales to two successive defeats.

As a leader he had a single-minded attitude to winning. Praise or scorn were irrelevant to him if his side was successful. He also wanted to dispel once and for all the theory that Murrayfield was a Welsh bogey ground. Four times since 1953, strong Welsh fifteens had journeyed to Edinburgh expecting victory only to return narrowly defeated.

For bedtime reading on the eve of the match the Welsh captain chose to study the match programme for the game. Totting up the masses of the two packs he discovered that their published statistics measured up roughly even

(121st 2lb against Wales's 121st 9lb). Getting out of bed, he roused his forwards to check their weights and discovered that the two Abertillery back-row men, Alun Pask and Haydn Morgan, had had their figures considerably understated. Wales, Rowlands reckoned, would take the field with a pack that was in the region of two stones heavier than the Scots.

There and then he formulated his match plan: Wales would keep the ball among their forwards whose superior physical presence would almost certainly deliver the much-sought victory.

Rowlands, an extrovert personality whose energetic captaincy was always full of colourful gesticulations, totally ignored his backs in a match that yielded 111 line-outs – the record number for any international match. Time and again Rowlands hooked the ball into touch to push his side into Scottish territory. A Welsh supporter among their 10,000 travelling fans on Murrayfield's lofty banks was overheard saying, 'Rowlands has six signals for his backs: every one means he's going to hoof the ball back to touch.'

Wales took root in the Scottish 25 for most of the afternoon and won 6–0, Rowlands himself dropping a goal from a difficult angle in the second half. But the unattractive nature of the victory did prompt an outcry afterwards.

Hancock's Half Minute
Twickenham, March 1965

Who scored Twickenham's most famous international tries? Old timers still claim that the two scored by the Russian Prince Alex Obolensky against the 1936 All Blacks on England's way to a 13–0 win would take some beating. Peter Jackson's sensational last-minute try to seize victory against the Fourth Wallabies in 1958 is still talked of today, and then there was Richard Sharp's Championship winner when he sold three outrageous dummies in the 1963 Calcutta Cup encounter. Those with shorter memories might plump for the breathtaking French try started by Pierre Berbizier and Serge Blanco on their own dead-ball-line, and finished by Philippe Saint-André under the England goal in the 1991 Grand Slam showdown.

Yet arguably the most memorable out of the blue solo effort was the 95-yard run by left wing, Andy Hancock, for England against Scotland in 1965. Scotland were leading 3–0 through a David Chisholm dropped goal and heading for their first Twickenham win since 1938 as play entered the final minute. None of the press photographers at the match rated England's chances of pulling the match out of the fire. All of them were camped in England's 25, expecting another Scotland score to seal the game.

Scotland's right wing, David Whyte, launched an attack and cutting in found himself engulfed by English forwards about fifteen yards in front of England's posts. A maul developed enveloping Whyte and the ball was fed back on the England side to Mike Weston, their fly-half whose main function during the afternoon had been to hoof the ball into touch. Moving left to the blind-side, he threw a pass to Hancock who was standing in isolation near the left touch-line.

It was only the third pass of the match that the Northampton wing had received: he'd dropped the other two. This time he latched on to the pass and began running up the left wing. He swerved outside the Scottish back row, evaded an ineffective tackle by the Scotland full-back and raced 90 yards, hotly pursued by Iain Laughland, before lunging desperately over the line at the north end of the ground, just as the despairing Laughland completed his tackle. It was the longest solo run for a try ever seen in an international and saved England's bacon.

'I remember being helped up off the ground,' Hancock later recalled, 'but little else. On the way to the dressing-room one of the spectators offered me a dram, which I gratefully accepted.'

Unfortunately, with the cameramen stranded in Hancock's wake, no press photographs of one of rugby's most famous scores exist. The only record of the try is the grainy BBC film of the move.

The Drop That Never Was

Dublin, March 1968

Mike Titcomb of Bristol was a referee noted for his empathy with players during a career that took in eight major international matches between 1966 and 1972. There was an occasion in Dublin in 1968, however, when even he would be the first to admit that he had no empathy with the Irish crowd.

The occasion was the Ireland–Wales match that season when he erroneously awarded a dropped goal to each side. The first of these was in the twentieth minute of the first half when Ireland, leading 3–0, went further ahead through a drop goal from 35 yards by their fly-half, Mike Gibson. The ball was touched in flight by Welsh flanker John Taylor, which should have invalidated the score, but Mr Titcomb ruled that the kick was good. Naturally, the Irish crowd did not object. Wales then pulled back a penalty goal, making the scoreline 6–3 at the break, and then equalised early in the second half with international rugby's most famous dropped goal that never was.

Gareth Edwards drop-kicked high towards the Irish posts. Practically everyone in the ground saw the ball curl at least a foot outside the upright, but poor Mr Titcomb signalled the goal. Edwards, with a cheeky piece of gamesmanship, had raised his arm high as if indicating a fine goal and the referee was clearly taken in.

The Irish players, unaware that the goal had been given, assumed their positions for a 25 drop-out. They then realised to their dismay that the Welsh team had retreated to their own half, expecting a restart from halfway. Eventually it dawned on the crowd that the goal had been awarded and, as a result, a near riot resulted. Bottles and cans were hurled on to the pitch as a crescendo of hoots, whistles and boos emanated from the Lansdowne Road enclosures. Play was held up for several minutes as spectators broke through the touch-line cordons to remonstrate with the referee.

When play eventually resumed the Irish, clearly roused by the injustice, raised their game to a fever pitch and the Welsh were swept aside in the tight and loose. At length, in the ninth minute of stoppage time, Ireland's wing forward Mick Doyle crashed over for the winning try. The conversion failed but that did not matter as the whistle for no-side went immediately afterwards, leaving Ireland deserved victors by 9–6.

'I thought the ball had gone over,' Mr Titcomb innocently explained after receiving a police escort from the pitch to the safety of the dressing-room at the end of the match.

At least justice was finally seen to be done that day, which is more than can be said for another match involving Wales, in 1978. In the second Test of that year's tour down under, the Grand Slam champions went down 19–17 to a late dropped goal by Australia's fly-half, Paul McLean, that was hotly disputed by the Welsh players, who protested that the kick had flown six inches wide of the posts. The Australian referee would have none of it and ruled that the kick was good.

A Secret Affair

New Brighton, November 1969

The Sixth Springboks to Britain and Ireland were the last official South African international team to visit these shores for more than 20 years. Their matches were played in difficult circumstances as protesters staged anti-apartheid demonstrations inside as well as outside the venues where they were scheduled to appear.

Even before the opening match of the tour, against Oxford University, the tourists had a taste of what was to come. Anticipating demonstrators, Oxford police informed the University Rugby Club that it would be unable to guarantee safe arrangements for a match at Iffley Road. It was touch and go whether the match would proceed, but on the eve of the fixture it was announced that Twickenham would stage the game.

Two groups of protesters arrived at the ground on the afternoon of the match. There was a peaceful demonstration outside the ground but a more militant group infiltrated the spectators inside to disrupt the match by blowing whistles. The game was surrounded by confusion, though a strong police cordon successfully restricted demonstrators from breaking onto the field of play.

Similar scenes followed the tourists more or less throughout the tour. At Swansea there were unpleasant violent scenes before, during and after the Springboks' game against the local club. By the time the South Africans were due to make their first visit of the tour to Ireland in

late November, concerns were being expressed that the
prevailing political troubles there, coupled with the threat
of anti-apartheid disruption, would make the Ravenhill
Ground in Belfast, where the tourists were due to play, the
focus for violent groups. And so the scheduled tour match
against Ulster was cancelled.

The Saturday that had been set aside for that game,
however, was also the date when New Brighton, one of
Northern England's most homely clubs, were due to
entertain the North of Ireland Football Club, one of Ulster's
oldest and most distinguished clubs. The tour committee
secretly arranged for the clubs to forgo their annual fixture
and to field a combined fifteen that would face the
Springboks instead. None of the players knew about the
plans until the morning of the match. The game was played
before a small crowd and went off without a hitch. It
remains the only major tour match in the sport's history to
be played in such secrecy.

The Springboks won 22–6 and their skipper, Dawie de
Villiers, said afterwards that they had thoroughly enjoyed
'playing in a purely rugby atmosphere'. For once the tour
demonstrators were absent, only learning that the game had
been staged when they read the newspapers the next day.

The Springboks were to feature in an even more clandes-
tine affair nearly a dozen years later in North America. On
that occasion they were making a three-match visit to the
United States after a full-scale tour of New Zealand.

In an effort to escape anti-tour groups, their international with the Eagles was hastily arranged for a
secluded polo field in the country districts of New York. The
pitch was littered with horse manure, the makeshift posts
were rapidly erected before the match and just as quickly
dismantled after it – preparations that were similar to
those of a Sunday morning park match. It was recorded
that 35 spectators, 20 policemen, a television crew, one
pressman and no protesters attended.

Up Your Jumper
Sydney, May 1975

The late Daryl Haberecht was one of Australia's most gifted and innovative coaches. Apart from studying the Union game in great depth he was a keen observer of both League and American grid-iron tactics, and was not averse to pinching ideas from other codes that could be usefully tried in the Union game.

He achieved notoriety in May 1975 when, as the coach of the New South Wales Country XV, one of his well-rehearsed tricks led to a sensational last-minute win over arch-rivals Sydney. The score was 20–16 to the city slickers with time running out when the Country XV were awarded a penalty 40 yards from the Sydney goal-line.

John Hipwell, the Country XV's skipper, a veteran Test scrum-half and also Australia's captain at the time, was preparing to take a tap penalty when the Sydney side were confused by about a dozen of their opponents lining up shoulder to shoulder in a shallow crescent and with their backs to them. Hipwell was at the focus of the crescent and took the tap whereupon the ball was handed pass-the-parcel fashion along the line of players. The attackers further bewildered the Sydney players by making dummy movements as if handling the ball.

At Hipwell's signal every member of his team appeared to tuck arms under his jumper, turn and run in different directions towards the Sydney line. One of the players, Greg Cornelsen, actually did stuff the ball under his shirt

but after running for ten to fifteen yards realised that he
would have to hold it properly.

Even so, the trick had its desired effect, causing mass
confusion in the Sydney ranks as defenders wondered who
had possession of the ball. They eventually picked up
Cornelsen, the big Country Number Eight, galloping
towards them. Though challenged, the forward managed to
make 30 yards before passing to Geoff Shaw who sent lock
Brian Mansfield over near the posts. Referee Bob Fordham
allowed the try and Country's fly-half, Jim Hindmarsh,
landed the easy conversion to win the match 22–20.

Several sides tried to mimic the move in the weeks that
followed before Australian referees referred the matter to
the International Board, who ruled that the up-your-
jumper tactic was against the spirit of the game and was
therefore illegal.

Haberecht himself went from strength to strength.
Within a couple of weeks of his side's infamous trick he
masterminded their 14–13 win over Tony Neary's England
touring team, and three years later he became Australia's
coach. Taking the Wallabies to New Zealand in 1978, he
unveiled a number of new tricks on tour, one of which was a
variation on the up-your-jumper ruse. In the Test at
Christchurch, John Hipwell arranged his team in a crescent
at a tap penalty and feinted to pass. Simultaneously, his
fourteen colleagues began sprinting in different directions
to confuse the All Blacks. Among the coach's other tricks
was the 12-man scrum, while a more dangerous move
involved the fly-half running up and over the backs of the
forwards at a scrum. Sadly, Haberecht's national appoint-
ment was cut short owing to his ill-health.

Flour Bombs Interrupt Play
Auckland, September 1981

It was the oddest tour ever undertaken by the Springboks. Anti-apartheid demonstrations during their visit to New Zealand meant that the tourists were kept under strict security for the best part of six weeks. At times the Springboks were unable to leave their hotel rooms and there were occasions when late changes of plan necessitated their sleeping on sports-hall floors. At every match venue they had to run the gauntlet of protesters to fulfil their fixtures.

Two of the games were cancelled. At Hamilton, in the first week of the tour, more than 200 demonstrators ripped down a chain fence to break on to the pitch where they sprinkled tacks and staged a sit-in on halfway. The sides had changed and tossed for ends and a crowd of 25,000 was in place to see the Springboks take on Waikato. But the protesters defied the attempts of the police to disperse them and after an hour it was reluctantly decided by the organisers that the match should be cancelled. Thereafter, barbed wire and batons were the order of the day at all of the Springboks' matches. But even this was not enough to allay the fears of the rugby authorities at Timaru where, anticipating a demonstration that they would not be able to handle, the rugby authorities cancelled the South Canterbury game.

Nevertheless, against such a grim and stifling backdrop, the tourists managed to maintain their cool and played some skilful rugby. They were unbeaten in their provincial matches and went into the third and final Test at Auckland with the series delicately balanced at one win apiece. Their star player was Naas Botha, whose kicking throughout the tour was a revelation. The fair-haired fly-half finished with 129 points from eight tour appearances in New Zealand, an impressive average of just over sixteen a match.

The most bizarre game of this most bizarre tour was the final Test – the series decider in Auckland. During the match a Cessna aircraft constantly strafed the pitch with flour bombs, flares and leaflets. The plane passed so low at times that there were fears that it might crash and in one of its missions the All Black prop Gary Knight was temporarily stunned by a flour bomb. But both captains insisted on referee Clive Norling of Wales allowing the game to run its course and the highest moment of rugby drama of the entire tour came in the final moments of time added on for stoppages. Allan Hewson, the New Zealand full-back, kicked a long-range penalty to win the Test 25–22 and wrap up the series.

'There will probably never be another Test match like this,' wrote the New Zealand rugby historians Rod Chester and Nev McMillan. 'The tension generated by the closeness and importance of the game, combined with the efforts of protesters inside, outside and above the ground, made for an exhilarating and yet terrifying afternoon.'

The Most Famous Streaker of Them All

Twickenham, January 1982

The streaking phenomenon began among American college students in the 1970s, but the first streaker to bare all in front of thousands at a sporting event was Michael O'Brien at Twickenham during the 1974 England–Wales rugby match. He started the craze for stripping off at big sporting occasions and was famously captured on photographic film, a Christ-like figure being frog-marched along Twickenham's east touch-line by local bobby, PC Perry, who had thoughtfully removed his helmet to cover young O'Brien's embarrassment.

O'Brien, who is now a respectable stockbroker living in Australia, was swiftly removed to Twickenham police station where he was charged and released. According to legend, he managed to get back into the ground to see the last 20 minutes of England's first victory over the Welsh for eleven years.

The most famous streak and certainly the most publicised one came at the same ground during an England–Australia match nearly eight years after O'Brien's pioneering effort. Erika Roe, a 24–year-old who worked for an art dealer in Petersfield, thoughtfully waited until half-time during a tense match to make her eye-catching appearance in front of the packed south stand on a day early in the New Year. 'I didn't want to interrupt the game – I wanted to watch it,' she explained to an interviewer later.

The media had a field day. 'Titters at Twickers,' it was revealed in one tabloid, while the game's bible, the *Rothmans Rugby Yearbook*, referred to a highlight of the season being 'when a lady named Erika erupted on to the field like a galleon in full sail, but minus her spinnakers.'

But perhaps the best comment of all came from one of the England players who was temporarily distracted from the captain's pep-talk during Ms Roe's half-time interlude. Bill Beaumont was the England skipper at the time and his side were only 6–3 ahead with the wind to face after the break. The result was far from a foregone conclusion and Bill was earnestly trying to rally his troops for a big effort in the second half when he realised no one was listening to him. 'What's the problem?' he asked. 'Everyone's watching a girl over there who seems to have your bum on her chest, Bill,' came the reply.

Erika's display inspired England to great heights in the second half as they ran out 15–11 winners.

A Very Peculiar Sending Off

Laugharne, January 1988

Gerry 'Ginger' McLoughlin was a bulwark of the Ireland pack that won the Triple Crown and Championship in 1982. A man of tremendous strength, he provided the abiding memory of the famous win at Twickenham that year when, early in the second half, he led a raid for the corner from a maul in the English 22 and finished off scoring the only try of his Test career to set Ireland on course for a 16–15 victory.

He was a typical son of Munster, hailing from Limerick, and his shock of red hair made him stand out in even the most protracted scrum or maul. Never one to start trouble, he would be the first to admit that he was never an angel on the rugby pitch. Certainly he was well able to mix it with the best of them during a successful playing career that culminated in a Lions tour to New Zealand in 1983.

Long after his international career was over he took up a position as bar steward at the Gilfach Goch rugby club in Wales and frequently turned out for the first XV. He was a part of the side that enjoyed a run to the fourth round of the WRU Challenge Cup in 1988.

In the third-round match of that campaign at Laugharne, he was involved in a very peculiar incident. An argy-bargy involving some of the front-row forwards at a line-out attracted the attention of Roy Rees, the referee. Ginger, never one to argue with authority but perhaps revealing his guilty conscience, heard the referee's comments and trudged quietly off the pitch to his early shower and thought nothing more about the incident.

Some fifteen minutes or so later Mr Rees realised that Gilfach were a man short when a scrum went down minus a tight-head prop. It then dawned on everyone that Ginger had thought that he had been sent off and had left the field. Apparently, when he lectured the players for that bit of nonsense at the line-out Mr Rees had said sternly: 'Push off and let's get on with the game.' Ginger literally took 'push off' to be his marching orders.

Gilfach's fourteen men won through all the same, beating Laugharne 28–19.

Green Volvo Stops Play

Sunbury, March 1996

The current hum that surrounds the London Irish club dates from 1996 when, as a second division side, two strong personalities, Clive Woodward the coach and Gary Halpin the captain, stamped their mark on a team that began to play expansive rugby. Strong running backs and competitive forwards provided the momentum that drove the club to the top of the table and promotion to the top flight of English rugby.

The 1995–6 season was also memorable as it saw London Irish's best Cup run since their appearance in the 1980 final when they were beaten by Leicester. The Tigers were again their opponents at Sunbury in March 1996 when the clubs were drawn to meet in the semi-finals.

A capacity crowd was in attendance to set both a gate record and a Guinness consumption record for the club. London Irish boldly set out to play their wide game, making no concessions to the forward power of the renowned Leicester forwards. Although the Tigers were ahead 22–8 after only 27 minutes, the storming play of Rob Henderson and the effective goal kicking of Michael Corcoran brought the Irish back into the game and by the interval they only trailed by the slim margin of one point with the score at 21–22.

Then, five minutes into the second half, the concentration of the London Irish team was broken by an event that could only have happened at London Irish. So many had turned up at the ground to watch the match that parking arrangements had been chaotic right up to the time of the kick-off with cars being parked anywhere and everywhere. As the referee prepared to restart the game with a scrum after a break in play, the public announcement system rumbled into action to request that the owner of a green Volvo, registration number . . ., remove it immediately otherwise the police would do so.

As the scrum was about to go down, Gary Halpin, at tight-head prop, held the front rows up. The tannoy message had suddenly sunk in: that green Volvo belonged to none other than the London Irish skipper himself. Play had to be held up while he ambled across the pitch to the dressing-room, where he recovered his car keys and gave them to a friend so that the car could be moved.

Unfortunately, the poor Irish never recovered after that, and Leicester raced 46–21 ahead and into a Cup final against Bath.

Cross-code Challenge
Twickenham, May 1996

A meeting of the Rugby Football Union (RFU) on 19 September 1895 outlawed professionalism in any form and adopted strict new bylaws to govern the structure of the amateur rugby union game. These laws were framed as a reaction to a number of clubs in the north of England who had met two months earlier to vote for a breakaway and formation of what was then known as the Northern Union and which became the rugby league. The main plank of the newly formed organisation's constitution was that a six shilling (30 pence) broken time payment would be made to compensate players for loss of employment, something which the die-hards of the RFU could not and would not entertain.

The two games went strictly down their own paths for a century except during wartime. On the 14 November 1939, the RFU temporarily lifted the ban so that rugby league and rugby union players could join arms to play in service matches until official matches began again in peacetime. Interestingly, the Scottish Union saw no reason for removing the bar on league men.

There were two cross-code challenges during the war, the League XV winning the first match 18–11 at Headingley in January 1943. A year later, in April 1944, another special match arranged by Northern Command in which a Rugby League Selection played a Rugby Union Selection was staged at the league's stronghold, Odsal

Stadium in Bradford. The match, again played under the 15-a-side code, attracted more than 18,000 curious spectators and raised over £1,350 for charity. As expected, the strong Union XV went ahead early on and led 10–0 at the interval. The League outfit, however, staged a remarkable comeback in the second half and ran out deserved winners by 15–10.

But it was not until rugby union went open in September 1995 with the introduction of the seamless game that the drawbridge between the two codes came down permanently. To celebrate the end of the 100 years' war between league and union, a pair of interesting and unusual challenge matches involving Bath, the English rugby union champions, and Wigan, their rugby league counterparts, were enacted.

The first leg of the challenge, under rugby league rules, was at Maine Road, Manchester early in May 1996. Former Welsh rugby union international and distinguished league coach, Clive Griffiths, was drafted in to give the Bath boys a crash course in the subtleties of the 13-a-side game. A trial match against the South Wales League XIII was a useful taster for the Union boys who did well to score four tries despite conceding eight.

Then it was up to Manchester for the match against the side that had been the cream of the league game for several years. What Bath had done for modern English club rugby union, Wigan had done for rugby league.

Of course, Bath were smashed to smithereens in what amounted to a massive culture shock. It was 82–6 at the end, Wigan strolling in for 16 tries to one scored by Jon Callard. Wigan's lines of running, superior basic skills and imaginative use of space left a deep impression on the Bath players. 'Wigan are a fantastic side,' said Bath captain Phil de Glanville, reflecting on the pace, power and superior fitness of his opponents after the match. 'We turned up,' was the final word of the Bath director of rugby, John Hall.

When Wigan met Bath in the return match, this time under union rules at Twickenham, the kings of the north had already paraded their skills at the ground as special guests of the organising committee of the annual Middlesex Sevens. The Sevens tournament was the first time that a rugby league side had set foot on the hallowed turf of RFU headquarters, something that could not possibly have been envisaged even five years earlier. Wigan again displayed their sublime skills and entertained a hugely appreciative crowd, beating Harlequins and Leicester before winning the final against Wasps.

Honour at least was restored in the 15-a-side part of the cross-code challenge with Bath winning the Twickenham match by 44–19. Even so, Wigan certainly threw down the gauntlet to the English Union champions. It was felt that they would struggle in the scrums, line-outs and rucks, but bolstered by former exponents of the Union game such as Scott Quinnell, Martin Offiah (who had scored six tries at Maine Road) and Inga Tuigamala (who began the match as a flanker), and to a lesser extent, by some sympathetic refereeing from Brian Campsall, the northern champions managed three sparkling tries.

European Fiasco
Llanelli, April 2000

It was billed as the most important Welsh club match of all time. Llanelli versus Cardiff at Stradey Park in the quarter-final of the Heineken European Cup.

The match turned into a yawn. A dull game ensued with virtually no passages of back play for the sell-out crowd to savour. Llanelli went through to the semi-finals comfortably, but at a time when senior rugby needed the oxygen of good publicity for its increasingly important new competition, once again an opportunity for promoting the game was spoiled by inefficient administrators.

Mid-way through the first half the referee Didier Mené of France, who had experienced a difficult time quelling the tempers of two charged-up packs, sent loose forwards Owain Williams (Cardiff) and Ian Boobyer (Llanelli) to the sin-bin after a dust-up. Quite right, too, thought the sizeable audience watching the match on BBC television. After all, only an hour earlier in the other European quarter-final being played that day, Stade Français's New Zealand-born centre, Cliff Mytton, had been dealt similar justice playing against Munster by referee Steve Lander.

The two Welsh forwards had been off the field for five minutes when a fiasco began. There was a break in play during which Monsieur Mené's attention was caught by fourth official Ken Brackston and one of the Heineken tournament's organisers. The Frenchman was informed that there was no sin-bin in operation in the European competitions and that, while the yellow cards shown to Williams and Boobyer should stand, the players should be reinstated immediately. So, after only five minutes off the field, the two forwards re-joined the fray and the match continued its otherwise uneventful course to half-time.

It was during the interval that the farce reached Brian Rix proportions. What about the events over in Munster barely an hour earlier? Munster had piled on nine points during Mytton's absence. If, as now seemed likely, the sin-bin did not apply to the tournament, what would be Stade Français's reaction? Would they demand a replay?

Frantic telephone calls were made to Roger Pickering, head honcho of the European Rugby Committee that oversees the Heineken tournament. He at last cleared up the misunderstandings. In January, it transpired, the European Rugby Committee had taken on board the International Board's recommendations regarding use of the sin-bin. The quarter-finals of the Cup were the first Euro matches to be staged since those guidelines had been issued. Unfortunately, a lack of communication had meant that clubs, referees and tournament organisers were unsure of the yellow-card and sin-bin procedure.

Fortunately, the misunderstanding had no bearing on the outcome of the match. For good measure, Monsieur Mené sent Cardiff flanker Martyn Williams to the sin-bin for the full ten minutes after a second-half offence, but the whole affair did little to inspire public confidence in those who administer professional rugby.

Fifteen Minutes of Fame
Bucharest, April 2000

The Dorchester Gladiators enjoyed their fifteen minutes of rugby fame on an Easter tour of Romania in 2000. The occasional team of rugby enthusiasts were visiting Bucharest to distribute toys to an orphanage when, thanks to the intervention of a kindly embassy official, they were invited to play a rugby match against one of the Romanian clubs. The Dorchester party, comprising a lively but unfit group of forty-somethings, jumped at the opportunity of playing what they imagined would be a social match against the locals, with the chance to down a couple of pints of Romanian best afterwards.

Unfortunately, an error in translation led to the Romanians greatly overestimating the quality of their English opponents. As a result, the Dorchester boys arrived for their 11 a.m. kick-off only to find that the venue was the National Stadium, that an expectant crowd of thousands had turned up and that the match was to be broadcast live on Romanian television. Their opponents, moreover, were Romania's crack club side, Steaua Bucharest. The hosts fielded half-a-dozen full international players as well as the captain of the Romanian national side.

'We were a bit suspicious when the hosts offered us a training session the night before,' said lock forward Nigel Jones when the Gladiators returned to Britain. 'Not exactly our style,' he continued, 'we did our pre-match build-up in the bar.'

The Romanians, perhaps confusing the name Gladiators with Saracens or the Barbarians, believed their visitors were packed with England's top professional players, despite attempts from the Dorchester players to explain otherwise.

It was only on the pitch that the truth began to dawn on the Romanians. 'They warmed up like professionals while we stood around smoking cigarettes, knowing we were in for trouble,' one of the Gladiators revealed. Once the match started, Steaua quickly piled on the points before realising that they were involved in a mismatch. Consequently, the hosts eased up for the second half and the final score was 60–17.

The Gladiators' full-back, Dave Scaddon, told reporters: 'They were incredibly fit and all in their 20s. People kept telling us they thought we had done brilliantly under the circumstances.'

GOLF

by Andrew Ward

Holed in One . . . But Lost the Hole

Musselburgh, 1870

It was all-square in a foursome at Musselburgh, and almost dark, when Robert Clark played his tee-shot at the short eighteenth hole. The green wasn't visible from the tee, and no one saw where Clark's ball went. The golfers walked forward and started searching.

They looked everywhere. Clark and his partner were particularly concerned, given the balanced state of the match. Eventually, they admitted their ball was lost, conceded the hole and with it the match.

Yes, you've guessed. Clark's ball was in the hole. They never thought of looking there.

Clark, an Edinburgh printer, was the author of an early golfing anthology, and we can assume he was a reliable witness. Since his unsuccessful hole-in-one, I believe the rules have been changed so that the ball is dead and the hole finished the moment the ball goes in the hole. Hence, even if you concede the hole as lost, the position of the ball takes precedence. Worth checking though. You never know when it might happen next.

Golfers have stumbled on other ways to lose a hole with an 'ace'. One method is perhaps more obvious than Clark's. Reverend H C Moor gives an example in a letter to *The Times* on 2 February 1940: 'On the Castle Bromwich links, near Birmingham, there was, some 30 years ago, a green set in a hollow, blind from the tee. Two brothers playing together drove to the green and found that they had both holed in one. But it was not a halved hole, for one brother had to give the other a stroke.'

A third possible method of losing a hole with an 'ace' was discovered accidentally by two golfers at Walsall's fourth hole in May 1950. The 182-yard hole was not visible from the tee, concealed by bunkers. Dr E R S Grice and L Watson, playing in a club competition, could see they had put their tee-shots somewhere on the green. When they walked on to the green they discovered one ball in the hole, the other nearby. Unfortunately, on examining the balls, they found that both were brand new and of the same make and number. There were no distinguishing marks on either ball. It was impossible to say which ball was which. All they could do was assume the balls were lost, return to the tee and start again. So the player who holed in one – whoever he was – may, or may not, have won the hole eventually.

No hole is safe. Even if you hole in one.

Cross-country Golf
Maidstone to Littlestone-on-Sea, April 1898

'Undoubtedly the longest hole ever played at golf is one measuring a distance of no less than 26 miles in a bee-line and 35 in actual play, the tee being at Linton Park, near Maidstone, and the putting-green at Littlestone-on-Sea.'

So started an article in *The Strand Magazine* (July 1913).

It was written by T H Oyler of Littlestone Golf Club, who played the 26-mile hole, the longest at the time, with A G Oyler. The freak match was an outcome of a conversation on Appledore railway station which went something like this.

'How many strokes would it take to cover the distance from Maidstone to Littlestone-on-Sea?'

'One player?'

'No, two men playing alternately.'

'I should say two thousand would be a fair number.'

'Two thousand?' queried a sporting parson in the party. 'I'll wager five pounds that none of you could do it in two thousand.'

The rules were laid down within five minutes: the match should take place within three months; the ordinary rules of golf should be observed; and an umpire should be appointed to keep score. A Cambridge undergraduate,

H M Wyatt of St Catharine's College, agreed to umpire, not realising how tedious it would be.

On a beautiful spring day, they set off from Linton Park with two or three of each club – brassie, cleek, niblick and driving-iron – and half a gallon of old balls which were newly painted and carried in a bag. The first drive, their only tee-shot, played with a brassie, landed in a rhododendron bush, 'out of which we dropped with a penalty'.

Progress through the park was slow, but eventually they reached the River Beult (for 65 and another lost ball). They stuck to pastured land, where the principal hazards were hedges and ditches. They ticked off landmarks like Hertsfield Bridge (for 97), Hawkenbury Bridge (for 158) and Frittenden Road Bridge (for 201). After 213 strokes, at Headland, they stuck a stump in the ground to mark the ball, and retired to the village inn for lunch. It was 2.30.

After lunch, they played along the road rather than across fields, but anything other than a short putt brought problems as the ball tended to roll into a ditch either side of the road. They returned to the fields and woods, although 'one very rough arable field gave us much trouble,' wrote Oyler, 'and for a time a heavy niblick was the favourite club.'

Just before six o'clock, they stopped play for the day, close to Crampton House Farm (for 427), between Biddenden and High Halden. Near there they were met by their carriage and driven home after 'a fair day's work of fourteen miles'.

The next day they were back with their clubs, caddie and umpire. On they went. Over hedges, into ditches, out of ditches and into small woods. At Moat Farm they were treated as trespassers.

'What are you doing on my premises?' the owner demanded to know.

'We're playing golf.'

'I must request you to leave as quickly as possible.'

Fortunately a capital brassie shot into a rough wheat-field took them to another farm, and peace was restored, although another problem remained: 'Here our caddie gave us some trouble, as he had evidently an old quarrel to settle with some other lad of his own age, and we had to dismiss him and engage another.' Altogether they went through six or seven caddies. The caddies usually gave up when they were worried about getting lost on the way back home.

Then it was one problem after another. A strong cross-wind made play tiring. A high fence cost them five strokes before they put the ball through it. And several strokes were wasted in a hop-garden where the poles restricted the swing of a club. When they finally reached Ingledon Park (for 500) they celebrated with a rest. On restart, a network of dykes caused them to retrace steps on several occasions. Instead of reaching Appledore for lunch at 2.30, they arrived at 4.25 – for 714, with another ball lost, this one in the Military Canal.

After lunch they headed for Appledore railway station, taking tea at the Railway Hotel at 5.50. Their first attempt to clear the level-crossing gates hit the gate and rebounded on to the rails. They putted over the railway-crossing, then kept to the road for a distance, before losing a couple of balls in dykes and giving up for the night after 844 strokes.

Starting at eight o'clock the next morning, they per-severed along the strange course. After being fortified by a friend's sloe gin at Brenzett, brassie shots were 'far and sure'. 'We now crossed the main sewer which drains Romney Marsh,' wrote Oyler in his account. 'Twice our ball hit a sheep, and we were frequently in small ditches, but could generally play out. After passing the quaint little church of Old Romney, we found many rushes and reeds, and strokes were short.'

They had now played more than a thousand strokes but were almost at their destination. Losing a ball down a rabbit-hole – the seventeenth lost ball of their journey – was barely a setback. A good mashie shot landed them on the first green at Littlestone-on-Sea, a putt rested within four feet of the hole, and another ended the wager after 1,087 strokes.

They learned several lessons from their cross-country feat. One was that golfers often take fewer strokes than first imagined, as distances on real golf courses include a lot of fairly short putts. However, the emphasis on distance with each cross-country shot acts as a prolonged strain on arms, wrists and hands.

Dry conditions helped them enormously. Cornfields had been recently rolled, and provided plenty of good lies. Otherwise many of their brassie and cleek shots might have relied on the niblick.

A modern text-book on cross-country golf would refer to many other experiences. Rupert Phillips and Raymond Thomas had to jump over a hedge to escape a bull that chased them during their 20-mile meander from Radyr, near Cardiff, to Southerndown in 1920. They covered the course in 608 strokes, including the proper penalty for 20 lost balls. Another tricky moment came when they had to wade knee-deep through a ford.

In 1927, Doe Grahame set off from the first tee of Mobile Golf Club in an attempt to play 6,160,000 yards to Hollywood, California. It was one of golf's all-time ambitious journeys. In Pearl River, not far up the road, the sheriff caught him acting suspiciously with a flashlight and golf clubs late at night, so Grahame spent a night in jail. He drove through the countryside, used a brassie in the suburbs and putted along city sidewalks. He completed 850 miles to San Antonio, Texas, in 30,930 strokes, having lost 105 balls. He was so confident that he spent his day off on a local golf course, where he played 36 proper holes. This was what O B Keeler referred to as 'the Mad

Twenties', the era when golf swept over the United States 'like a prairie fire'.

The Guinness Book of Records notes an even more amazing effort than Grahame's trek – Floyd Rood's journey from Pacific surf to Atlantic coast in the mid-1960s. He covered the 3,398-mile course in 114,737 strokes. He lost 3,511 balls, and was away for a year and nineteen days.

Some cross-country matches are competitive, though the prize rarely resembles that of P G Wodehouse's short story 'The Long Hole', in which Jukes and Bingham play a sixteen-mile hole to decide who Amanda Trivett will marry (forgetting that the woman had a choice). In 1892, scores of 114 and 118 were recorded across nearly four and a half miles of Gloucestershire countryside. In July 1931, a foursome from Australia's Port Pirie Club played a seven-mile hole through bush country. After seven hours, Mallyon and Leahy's 196 was good enough to win by four strokes.

Later that same year, 1931, a masked man golfed 700 miles from Brisbane to Sydney in about 25,000 strokes. He lost 57 balls, and his worst experience came when he was taking a short-cut through a zoo about 48 miles out of Brisbane. His ball rebounded into the leopard's cage for a very difficult lie.

If our cross-country text-book needs chapters on 'Dealing with animals' and 'Choosing your snake-bite kit', it also requires an essential section on 'Playing through towns and cities'. In 1899, William Patton, a member of the Allegheny Golf Club, played nearly five miles through the centre of Pittsburgh. Patton achieved his aim of breaking 150 (by 31 strokes) but broke a few windows too. He won just enough money to settle the bill for damages.

A similar wager took place in London 40 years later. Toby Milbanke bet that Richard Sutton couldn't play from the other side of Tower Bridge to the steps of White's Club, St James's Street, in fewer than 2,000 shots. This is a ridiculously high number, but Milbanke was relying on Sutton being arrested. Sutton was stopped by the police four or five times, but his explanation – 'I'm doing it for a bet' – was accepted each time. Sutton putted the course in 142 strokes and won £5 and a set of golf clubs from his friend.

With a Handkerchief Over His Eyes

Sunningdale, February 1912

He stood on the first tee at Sunningdale and addressed the ball.

'Alright,' he said.

A purple-and-white handkerchief was tied firmly over his eyes.

'Alright,' came the reply.

He let fly at the ball with no preliminary waggles.

As he played the shot he was conscious that his body was stiff down one side. That cursed bicycle accident the other day. He knew he wasn't in tip-top condition. He knew he wasn't at his best. Especially with a handkerchief over his eyes.

His drive was long but slightly sliced.

His opponent then stood on the first tee. This was Mr A Tindal Atkinson, a good scratch player who knew the course.

Tindal Atkinson pulled his tee-shot. It wasn't as long as the man with the purple-and-white handkerchief.

The match was underway.

Blindfolded professional against the all-seeing amateur.

Alf Toogood against Mr A Tindal Atkinson.

Guy Livingstone started it all. One wet day, early that month, a *Daily Mail* golf-instruction article had annoyed him. More of that 'keep your eyes on the ball' advice,

Livingstone thought. No wonder all my pupils mesmerise themselves. They glue their eyes to the ball, play their shot, the ball moves, their eyes move, their head moves, and the stroke is ruined. It's wrong to keep your eye on the ball. You should keep your eye on the ground underneath the ball, and hold it there till you hear the ball click.

Livingstone believed there was better advice than keeping your eyes on the ball.

'Keep your head still.'

'Keep it in a vice.'

'Don't move it.'

Guy Livingstone had nothing better to do. He sat down at his desk at the Chelsea Golf School, where he was secretary, and wrote a letter to the editor of the *Daily Mail*.

Sir,

With reference to the first paragraph of your article 'The Golfer's Progress' I venture to make a somewhat startling assertion – viz, it is *not* necessary to keep your eye on the ball.

Given your stance is correct and that your swing is true, you will hit the ball perfectly truly whether you are blindfold or not.

The letter appeared at the bottom right corner of an inside page, but it was spotted by readers.

When people responded to Livingstone's comment, a challenge was issued. Alf Toogood, professional at the Chelsea Golf School and Livingstone's colleague, offered to play any amateur, and Toogood would play blindfolded. He was expecting an average club player to take the challenge. Instead it was Tindal Atkinson. Toogood knew that he would have to be at his best to beat Tindal Atkinson even if he weren't blindfolded.

Meanwhile the letters poured in.

J H Taylor doubted whether anything so heretical had
ever been said about golf as Livingstone's notion of not
keeping your eye on the ball.

Bernard Darwin didn't think it would catch on anyway.
Wrote Darwin: 'The prospect of a pause before every stroke,
during which the caddie, after the manner of a hangman,
slips a white cap over the victim's head, is positively
alarming to those who find golf on a crowded course quite
slow enough as it is.'

Harold Hilton gave Livingstone's comments some
credence. He agreed that a strong, forcing player ceased to
focus on the ball at some point. Hilton was certain that, on
long shots, he almost closed his eyes during the latter part
of the downward swing. On short-range shots, though, Mr
Hilton believed that you must look at the ball.

The *Daily Mail*'s correspondent went to watch Alf
Toogood at practice and had to admit that the blindfolded
professional looked good.

All over Britain, thousands of average golfers and
duffers were shutting their eyes in the hope that this was
the big breakthrough they wanted.

All would be revealed at Sunningdale.

He addressed the ball for his second shot.

'Alright.'

Guy Livingstone, acting as Toogood's second or bottle-
holder, tied on the handkerchief again.

'Alright,' Livingstone said. He stepped back smartly to
avoid the swing of the club.

At that moment a photographer knelt to take a daring
action picture of the strange golfer with a handkerchief
over his face. Toogood snatched at his approach shot
and topped and sliced it. The ball whistled past the
photographer's ear.

Old-timers in the gallery nodded sagely. Their mouths
formed the words, 'Keep your eye on the ball.'

Toogood took seven at the first, Tindal Atkinson five. The amateur was one up.

At the second Toogood reached the green in three excellent shots. The amateur was some distance away.

On the greens, where Toogood didn't swing his club so much, it was safe for Livingstone to hold the handkerchief in front of Toogood's eyes rather than waste time tying it. Unfortunately, on the second green, Livingstone had to do this four times. Another seven on the card. Toogood two down.

It was downhill from there. Toogood continued to out-drive the amateur and occasionally he played an excellent tee-shot. His pitching wasn't quite so good, and his putting was abysmal, not helped by Sunningdale's undulating greens. He persisted in slicing the ball, and, when putting, often sent it four or five yards to the right. But he played some good shots from the rough and on one occasion chipped beautifully out of a bunker.

He halved the third, ninth and tenth, but lost the rest. It was all over by the eleventh. In 85 minutes, the blindfolded professional had lost eight and seven.

The controversy continued. Shortly afterwards, a scratch golfer, receiving a stroke a hole and blindfolded with opaque motor 'goggles', went round in 92 and beat a six-handicap man three and two.

Golfer Plays in a Suit of Armour

Bushey Hall, April 1912

The sun shone brightly over the Bushey Hall course and Harry Dearth's resplendent suit of armour glistened and glittered as he clanked and creaked from hole to hole.

'Dear me,' remarked an infirm gentleman as he caught sight of the man in armour. 'I know it's dangerous to go round with golf balls hurtling in all directions, but it would never have occurred to me to take those precautions.'

Dearth's strange, imposing appearance had nothing to do with caution. It had more to do with risk. He was an actor hoping to win a bet that involved playing a nine-hole game of golf in a suit of armour. Dearth had worn the armour on stage when playing St George in a recent Sir Edward Elgar production called *The Crown of India*.

The game was played on 23 April – St George's Day. The correspondent for *The Stage* whimsically commented that Graham Margetson, Dearth's opponent, showed bad form in appearing in ordinary golfing gear. Mr Margetson 'should have completed the matter by disguising himself as Will Shakespeare, whose day it was also'.

'Mr Dearth represented St George,' stated *Golf Illustrated*. 'The opportunity to remark at this point that there was no dragon to be seen except the drag on his putts would cause a professional humorist to pause until the last echoes of the laughter had died away, but we propose to go straight on to make the critical observation that Mr Dearth looked every inch a polished golfer. In fact, he looked better polished than anybody we have ever seen on the links.'

Despite his 'polished' appearance, Harry Dearth was under several disadvantages, not to mention a certain discomfort. His hot and heavy outfit was hardly suited – oh, excuse me – to the distances he had to walk across the course in the heat of the day. At least he was spared having to wear a visor on this occasion. Even so, nine holes at Bushey Hall was not quite the same as the stage at the Coliseum, and Harry Dearth's suit of armour restricted his golf swing to about half its normal arc.

'Notwithstanding these disadvantages, however, Mr Dearth made a gallant fight of it,' summarised one report. 'There was never much to choose between the players and in the end Mr Margetson won the match, which was over nine holes, by two up and one to play. Mr Dearth secured the bye. The contest was on level terms.'

The reporter for *Golf Illustrated,* however, showed some resentment at the interest shown by the public in Harry Dearth's armoured play and Alf Toogood's recent blind-folded appearance. The reporter couldn't resist a facetious gibe at the future: 'It is understood that A H Toogood has now offered to play blindfolded against Mr Dearth in armour. The referee will crawl around on his hands and knees; while the caddies will be in chains, and will extract the clubs from the bags with their teeth. After that, semi-comic golf will be given up in despair.'

Tie After Tie After Tie

Glasgow and Gleneagles,
April, May and June 1924

The second annual Glasgow and District Professional Association competition took place on 30 April. It was a stroke competition, played over two rounds at the Pollok course, and a silver trophy donated by Whyte and Mackay was at stake. Early in the final round it developed into a straight competition between two players, and it remained so for several weeks.

The elder player was David Sutherland, the Balmore professional who was captain of the Glasgow and District Professional Association. The younger was John Campbell, a former colleague of Sutherland's at Balmore, now an unattached golfer who was teaching in a sports emporium in Glasgow. Campbell was the holder of the title.

Sutherland and Campbell each had a 75 for the first round of the tournament. They trailed McMinn by one stroke, but the third man soon fell away in the final round. Meanwhile Sutherland and Campbell's capacity for equality was uncanny. They both went out in 35, and all depended on the last nine holes of the tournament.

After his two at the thirteenth, Sutherland had a three-stroke lead, but Campbell immediately pulled back two of them at the next hole and drew level at the eighteenth. Two fine rounds of 70. Both had an overall total of 145, and a play-off was necessary. This was the scoring on the homeward nine:

Sutherland	354	254	435	–	35 (70)
Campbell	454	434	434	–	35 (70)

They went out again that evening. On a dull day, the light was not wonderful, so the play was not as good, but just as exciting. This time Campbell took a commanding lead – five strokes at the eighth – but Sutherland pulled them back by the fourteenth. Campbell gained two strokes at the fifteenth, but lost one at the sixteenth and another at the seventeenth. They went to the eighteenth all-square and halved it in fives. Two rounds of 77, and still no decision.

'It was certainly remarkable that after playing 54 holes there was not a single stroke between the players,' wrote the *Glasgow Herald.*

There was more to come.

The second play-off, at Pollok, began at 6 p.m. on Tuesday 13 May. The weather was delightful, the crowd large and the golf brilliant. Campbell was two strokes to the good after three holes, but the two players had identical scores for the next six holes.

Sutherland	545	443	444	–	37
Campbell	444	443	444	–	35

Campbell had lost his lead by the twelfth, but played the fourteenth magnificently for three. Sutherland was in a bunker at the same hole, but recovered well for a four. It kept him in the match, and the outcome was almost predictably equal.

Sutherland	344	344	434	–	33 (70)
Campbell	355	335	434	–	35 (70)

The third replay was again at Pollok – at 6 p.m. on Tuesday 27 May. The weather was poor, but nearly 700 people were curious enough to attend. The first nine holes were typically close, but Sutherland had a slight advantage at the turn.

Sutherland	454	453	535	–	38
Campbell	544	453	644	–	39

The 407-yard eleventh was played brilliantly. Both were on the green in two. Both holed fine putts for threes. They played inspired golf, but went to the last hole all-square, after Sutherland had pulled his second shot at the seventeenth on to the road. Campbell needed a long putt on the last green to keep the scores level. Naturally he sank it.

Sutherland	335	344	444	–	34 (72)
Campbell	334	354	434	–	33 (72)

It wasn't easy to arrange a date for the fourth replay. However, they agreed to play a round at Gleneagles on the eve of the *Glasgow Herald* tournament. About 200 spectators followed them round. After only five holes, Campbell had a three-stroke lead, but Sutherland recovered. Campbell three-putted at the eighth, reducing his lead to one, but his six-yard putt at the ninth widened the margin again.

Sutherland	545	545	534	–	40
Campbell	454	436	543	–	38

They went to the 170-yard eleventh with Campbell one stroke ahead. Sutherland's tee-shot hit the pin and he made a two. Campbell three-putted for a four. The lead had changed. Not for the first time.

The thirteenth hole at Gleneagles finally settled the

tournament. Campbell played two shots from the fairway, while Sutherland's approach drew up three inches from the hole. Sutherland became the new champion, but, in a fitting tribute to one of the most nearly equal contests ever, the two players did the last five holes in identical scores.

Sutherland	424	345	444	–	34 (74)
Campbell	544	545	444	–	39 (77)

After five equal rounds – 75, 70, 77, 70 and 72 – the competition was finally over.

You would think that ended the story, but the next day the *Glasgow Herald* tournament began. After two rounds of stroke play, the leading 32 players would go forward into match-play. Campbell started with a 77, Sutherland an 80, a three-stroke difference which compensated for the previous day, so perhaps it wasn't surprising that they both went round in 75 in the second round of the *Glasgow Herald* tournament.

Sutherland missed the cut with 155, but Campbell's 152 brought him . . . yes, you've guessed . . . a play-off. Seven players went out in pairs to play-off for the last six places, so obviously one player needed a marker. David Sutherland, the new Glasgow Champion, captain of the Glasgow and District Professionals Association, was an obvious person for the job. He partnered the odd man over the six-hole play-off. So there they were again, Campbell and Sutherland, taking part in a play-off in strange circumstances. Campbell's 26 for the six holes was equal to two other players, but good enough to make the cut as Ockenden had a 29.

Choice of Club Decided by Lottery

Atlanta, Georgia, February 1927

They called it 'the Monkey Tournament'. It was one of the strangest ever. Players didn't choose which club they would use for a shot. Instead they drew a slip of paper out of a hat, and, regardless of the stroke to be played, the slip of paper informed them of the club they had to use. Drivers were used on putting greens, and one woman drove off three times with a putter.

The tournament was organised by the Atlanta Women's Golf Association. It was a nine-hole event, with ten players on one team and eleven on the other. Besides the strange rule for deciding the club, there was one other violent deviation from the usual rules of golf. While a player was making a shot, her opponents were permitted to distract her with noise and action. Anything except touching an opponent and touching the ball was allowed.

The team captained by Mrs T T Williams took a lead at the first of the nine holes, with a four to Mrs Clarence Bradley's team's eight. But the scores shot up when the women realised the opportunities. Players took up their stances with an inappropriate club and then played their shots amid a glut of distractions. Opponents yelled, screamed, offered advice and criticism, blew police whistles and bashed tin cans together. An alternative distraction was to play practice-shots right next to the player doing the real thing.

Consequently, the Bradley team squared the match at the second hole with a twelve to the Williams fourteen, and then won the third hole by thirteen strokes. The Williams team couldn't really expect to win a hole in 21 shots, even if it were a 'Monkey Tournament'.

The next three holes were very close, but the Bradley team eventually picked up a two-hole lead at the vital seventh. The Williams team kept the match alive but lost by two up. The scores make unusual reading:

```
Williams team      4, 14, 21, 11, 9, 7, 9,  8, 7 – 90
Bradley team       8, 12,  8, 10, 9, 8, 6, 10, 5 – 76
```

How to Win With the Wrapping Still on the Ball

Wimbledon Park, November 1937

The Colas Products Golfing Society annual eighteen-hole tournament was held at the Wimbledon Park Golf Club. John Weaver of Worcester Golf and Country Club went very well for the first six holes.

The seventh was a short hole of 140 yards. The carry was over a pond with other hazards nearer the hole. John Weaver put his ball in a ditch three times. Having already taken eight for the hole, he had to drop yet another ball. He thought his chance for the tournament had probably gone, and his mind was elsewhere. He took a new ball out of his bag and dropped it over his shoulder. He turned round, and looked at the ball. The wrapping was still on.

Weaver played his approach shot with the paper covering still sealed on the ball. To his great surprise, he holed out.

He took the wrapping off the ball before the next hole, and his game was back to its best. He went round in 82, an excellent score for a twelve-handicap player. In fact, it was the best score of the day, but the officials didn't know what to do about the packaged ball. They presented John Weaver with the Cup, but it was conditional on a later decision. The secretary of the Wimbledon Park Club wrote to the Rules of Golf Committee of the Royal and Ancient Club of St Andrews and asked for a ruling.

The next day, Roland Allen investigated the possible outcomes in an article in the *Evening Standard*. A golf ball had to be *not wider* than 1.62in and *no heavier* than 1.62oz. Well, the width of an unwrapped ball was sure to be within the rules, but what about the weight? A leading manufacturer of the day claimed that every ball that left his company would be over 1.61oz and under 1.62oz. Otherwise it would be rejected by quality control. According to Allen, who spent time testing the various weights, the paper cover and seal of a wrapped ball almost certainly weighed more than 0.01oz, assuming it to be a first-class two-shilling ball.

Other students of a ball's weight asked delicate questions. What happens if a ball collects mud on the way round? Does the ball have to be the right weight before every shot?

The Rules of Golf Committee replied the following January. It was clear that if the ball was overweight when it was struck, the player was liable to disqualification, but if the ball was not overweight the player could not be disqualified.

The secretary of the Colas Products Golf Society consulted his committee. Together they decided that John Weaver should retain the Cup. It was argued that there was no evidence concerning the weight of the ball when it was struck, and it would be impossible to find out with any degree of certainty seven weeks after the event.

So John Weaver won a tournament after holing out at the seventh with a ball that was still in its paper cover.

A Plantation at Stake
Chicago, August 1938

Smitty Ferebee and Fred Tuerk jointly owned a 2,400-acre plantation in Princess Anne County near Norfolk, Virginia. They disagreed about how the land should be managed, but agreed that their dispute should be settled by a strange golf match. If Ferebee could play eight rounds of golf between dawn and dusk in one day, completing each round in no more than 95 strokes, he would win Tuerk's half of the plantation. If he failed, the plantation would revert to Tuerk.

J Smith Ferebee was confident about the task ahead. A 31-year-old Chicago investment broker, he played golf virtually every afternoon and usually averaged in the mid-80s. Also, he had played 90 holes in a day about a month previously, and the professional at his home course, Olympia Fields, said that he was in excellent shape.

Fred Tuerk was confident too. He didn't think Ferebee had a chance of completing eight rounds. It meant walking more than 29 miles around the same golf course. Far more than 29 miles, if Ferebee couldn't hit the ball straight.

Tuerk had obviously not kept up with all the stories of golfing marathons. Captain George Morris had played ten rounds in 889 at Walmer and Kingsdown Golf Club, but Bruce Sutherland's record 252 holes in a day seriously affected his health, and Stanley Gard had to retire with heart trouble after 220 holes of an attempt on Sutherland's record. Robert Coy had played 459 holes in 39 hours at

Potrero Golf Links before being taken to hospital with badly swollen ankles.

All Ferebee proposed was a mere 144 holes. Admittedly, there was the extra tension of staking his share of the plantation – valued at around $10,000 (£2,050) – plus side-bets of $2,500.

The weather favoured Tuerk.

'It looks like rain, Smitty,' we can imagine someone saying when Ferebee arrived at Olympia Fields and briefed his dozen caddies. At 5.05, as dawn broke, he prepared to tee off for his first round.

There were four courses at Olympia Fields, all heavily wooded, all perhaps longer than those tackled by previous marathon golfers. If Ferebee was going to complete eight rounds – two on each course – he would have to play 51,568 yards, an average of 6,446 yards per round. And, of course, he had to complete each round in a score of under 95.

He managed 90 for the first round. It was cause for concern. Then he put together three successive rounds of 82 strokes, and they didn't take him very long. It took only six hours to complete these first 72 holes. One round – the third – had been breezed in one hour sixteen minutes. He was halfway towards winning his bet without any real problem.

Then it started to rain.

Smitty Ferebee stopped playing for about fifteen minutes. The course was already drenched. He restarted, but the wind blew strong and it rained again before he had completed his fifth round, a terrific downpour that flooded the fairways. Ferebee stopped for more than an hour. He used the time to change his clothes and organise coffee for his caddies. Ferebee himself drank a glass of orange juice after 36 holes and a small beer after each nine holes thereafter. Following each round an attendant powdered his feet.

Back on the course, he completed the fifth round in 87 strokes. That still left him about seven hours of daylight for the last three rounds. After the next round – another 87 –

Fred Tuerk conceded that Ferebee looked like winning the plantation. Tuerk followed Ferebee round the last 36 holes, and sportingly applauded many shots. Some 600 persons were on the course towards the end of his final round. It was now around eight o'clock, and Ferebee looked pale and drawn, but he couldn't keep a grin from his face. At the sixteenth he took a six. Had he blown up after 142 holes? He had already taken 80 for the first sixteen of this final round, and had to do the last two in less than sixteen. But he finished well – four, five – and a round of 89 sealed the bet in his favour. His eight rounds were remarkably consistent – 90, 82, 82, 82, 87, 87, 88 and 89. He was only 119 over par for the day.

It took him fifteen hours seven minutes to earn half a plantation and $2,500, and he ate only three sandwiches and a chocolate-bar during that time. He took a shower and felt fine. That night he slept for more than eight hours. He got up, ate a hearty breakfast, did a day's work in his La Salle Street office and then played his usual round of golf in the afternoon.

The publicity from the event stimulated plenty of other 24-hour marathons – 171 holes from Bill Coleman, 196 holes from Carlton Brown, and 231 holes from Jim Caruso, just to mention three.

Smitty Ferebee was not one to be overtaken by events. His next marathon gave Tuerk a chance to win back the plantation and encouraged side-bets of $100,000 (£20,500). Ferebee said he could tackle 144 holes on four successive days, playing four rounds in each of eight different cities spread across the United States. On 25 September he began at Lakeside, Los Angeles, then after four rounds there, flew to the Encanta course in Phoenix, Arizona. A plane had been put at his disposal by Reuben Trane, a Wisconsin sportsman who took to the idea.

And so it continued . . . four rounds at the Blue Hills course at Kansas City in the morning of the second day . . .

four at Norwood Hills in St Louis, Missouri in the afternoon
... Tuckaway in Milwaukee in the morning ... his home
course of Olympia Field in Chicago in the afternoon ...
North Hills in Philadephia ... and finally Salisbury in New
York.

Drawn and haggard, lame and sore, he putted out on the
eighteenth green in his final round at 10.30 p.m. on the
fourth day, helped by flares and floodlights from a
borrowed fire-truck. Bandaged from ankle to knee, his feet
a mass of blisters, he hobbled from the final green into a
waiting car. He had played 576 holes with the same poor
ball.

One can sympathise with the sports editor of the *New
York Times* in August 1939 who, when asked for
information on the record number of holes and courses
played in one day, ducked the question: 'The marathon
golfers move at so fast a pace that the less hardy
statisticians have been left far behind, exhausted.'

Two Women and a Pilot
Jacksonville, Florida, March 1952

At ten o'clock in the morning, two women reached the 405-yard seventh hole at the Timuquana Country Club. They were good golfers. One of them, Bertha Johnson, had been city champion in 1938 and, now in her early fifties, was still good enough to compete in tournaments. She had been president of the Jacksonville Women's Golf Association for the two years after the war.

Bertha Johnson and Mary Dempsey, a 38-year-old mother, drove off from the seventh tee and started walking toward their balls. They were oblivious of any danger. It was just another golf round to be enjoyed.

The pilot was on a routine practice flight from the US Navy air-base that bordered the Timuquana Country Club. He was worried. The oil-pressure gauge of his Corsair fighter plane was registering a low reading and his engine power was below normal. He called for an emergency landing. The duty runway was cleared and prepared.

He made his approach to the runway, but all was not right. The engine of the single-seater plane was behaving erratically. The pilot didn't have enough control for a landing. He flew the plane on, turned right and hoped to reach the airfield again. Then the Corsair's engines died completely. The Corsair was now a glider. No power, no noise, and no chance of returning to the runway. The pilot looked at what was available below. Was there anywhere to land?

He saw a strip of grass on the golf course of Timuquana Country Club. It was the seventh fairway.

A man driving a van was making a delivery from his fruit-and-vegetable stall on Roosevelt Boulevard to the air station. He saw the plane come in low over the buildings with smoke pouring out.

'It's going to crash,' he said to his wife.

The plane pulled back into the air a little, but no higher than the tree-tops. The man and his wife watched it disappear behind the trees.

The two women played their second shots about 220 yards from the seventh tee. Then they strolled in a leisurely way down the centre of the fairway towards the green. Their caddie, 19-year-old Theodore Rutledge, walked about 35 yards behind them, along the eastern edge of the fairway. The caddie looked up. He saw the plane. It was coming in silently against the wind, strangely unobtrusive, its long nose and black engine smoke obscuring the pilot's forward vision.

The caddie yelled a warning to the women, who didn't hear, and then ducked and ran.

The plane landed on the seventh fairway and hit the women from behind with a propeller. One body was thrown 35 feet, the other 65 feet. The women were killed instantly.

The plane continued down the fairway for another 155 yards, veering towards a clump of pine trees in the rough, near the western edge. It crashed into the trees and the impact broke off the engine and nacelle. The pilot scrambled out of the wreckage and then watched it burst into flames. He was standing by the side of the plane when the golf-course grounds superintendent arrived.

'Are you hurt?' asked the grounds superintendent.

'No, thank God,' said the pilot. 'I got out before the fire started.'

The caddie rushed up and blurted out the news that two golfers had been killed.

The pilot went to pieces.

London to Oxford

The A40, June 1956

There was only one hole. It began at Marble Arch, London, and ended 55 miles away in Oxford. And the first hazard was particularly unusual. At the appointed starting time – 9 p.m. on 26 June – a large crowd of people blocked his fairway. They weren't waiting to see him tee off. They were waiting for Gina Lollobrigida. The voluptuous Italian actress was attending the premiere of *Trapeze,* a film in which she starred.

Humphrey Crum-Ewing waited patiently for fifteen minutes while the crowd disappeared into the Odeon Cinema. The 22-year-old Oxford University student could then begin his 55-mile golfing journey to the Canterbury Gate of Christ Church College. He stood to win over £135 if he could complete the journey inside 20 hours, which meant maintaining an average speed of 2¾ miles per hour. It was a tall order.

The Gina Lollobrigida interruption wasn't the first thing to go wrong. Crum-Ewing had originally intended to attempt the journey some three weeks earlier, but the Censors of Christ Church College had refused permission for him to be absent from college for a night. The Dean of the College, Dr John Lowe, felt that members of the college had received undue publicity that term. He might have been referring to an incident over the purchase of two pictures for the Christ Church Junior Common Room. One committee member had resigned over the way the pictures had been bought. Or he might have been referring to publicity given to another student, who, earlier that year, had attempted to beat the record time for an Oxford-to-London walk.

Crum-Ewing was reconciled to attempting the 'hole' in the privacy of his vacation. At Marble Arch he was accompanied by his caddie, 18-year-old Kamilla Jessel of Banbury, who planned to stay with him until he had reached the outskirts of London. Another Christ Church undergraduate, Viscount Furneaux, the Honourable John Dawnay, planned to keep pace with Crum-Ewing in a car during the earlier stages of the adventure.

By agreement with those placing the bets, who included the president of the University Dramatic Society, a University Divots' golfer and a golf blue, Humphrey Crum-Ewing was allowed 36 balls. In fact he carried only a dozen. He relied on his putter, sending the ball 20 or 30 yards along the A40 with each stroke. The major problem was the light, or, rather, lack of it. He tried tying pieces of cloth on the ball so he could see the ball on its journey, but the cloth came off. He ran after the ball to keep it in sight, but he lost one after another. He was tempted to hit them before they stopped to keep them in range but, of course, such a dribbling stroke was outside the rules.

When he reached Beaconsfield, at 5 a.m., he had covered about 25 miles of the 55-mile 'hole' in eight hours. He was slightly ahead of schedule but his hands were sore and in Beaconsfield he lost his last golf ball. He gave up and lost the bets. Because of his failure he was obliged to pay a penny to an Oxford bookmaker. No doubt there were further penalties – fatigue and plenty of teasing.

The Spectator Who Holed Himself

Bristol, May 1960

Sidney Gray went to Long Ashton golf course to watch a *Western Daily Press* league match between Long Ashton and Filton. He was a well-known local golfer, a past president and former captain of Filton Golf Club. He hoped Filton would win.

He disappeared near the ninth green.

The Filton golfers were back in the clubhouse when they realised he was missing.

Where was he?

The golfers had no idea. They began to search the course.

He had fallen down one of the biggest holes ever found on a golf course, a hole 120 feet deep, narrow at the top, wider at the bottom. He was lodged on a ledge down the hole. It was dark and depressing for the 62-year-old former civil servant, and he was in pain.

Eventually he was heard by the search party. His cries came from a thicket near the ninth green. When they investigated they found that the bushes concealed the entrance to a disused iron-ore mineshaft, fenced off with a warning notice posted at the top of its slope. Sidney Gray must have slipped and fallen into the shaft.

The golfers sent for help. Police and ambulance arrived.

They needed 120 feet of rope to make the rescue. A police sergeant was the first to be lowered down the shaft. He descended into the darkness, securely fastened to the rope that lowered him. He comforted Mr Gray, and examined his injuries – a head wound and abdominal injuries. Later, at Bristol Royal Infirmary, a fractured pelvis and fractured rib would be confirmed.

The policeman looked around the eerie mineshaft, and saw an earlier victim – a dead fox.

An ambulance driver was lowered down next. It took nearly two hours to complete the rescue. At 8.15 p.m., Mr Gray was secured on to a stretcher and lifted to safety. He was greeted at the entrance to the mineshaft by the concerned Filton captain.

'Did we win?' asked Sidney Gray.

A Hole Halved in One

Turnberry, August 1963

In 1991, two punters won hefty sums from small book-makers in northern England by seducing them into offering generous odds on a hole-in-one at three important British tournaments. They were quoted odds ranging from 7–1 to 33–1, yet Jay Townsend (Benson and Hedges International), Wraith Grant (Volvo PGA) and Brian Marchbank (British Open) duly sank tee-shots in the three tournaments in question. Obviously the bookmakers were unaware that European professionals were averaging a hole-in-one per tournament. Indeed, any bookmaker familiar with the detail of the 1989 US Open, when four players holed in one at the sixth hole in the second round, would shorten odds dramatically.

So what odds on a hole being halved in one?

It has happened plenty of times, though it doesn't always involve two players holing in one. There is a tale of James Braid, for instance, holing his tee-shot at Walton Heath's sixth hole only to halve the hole because his opponent received a stroke and did it in two.

The first time two golfers holed in one at the same hole was probably at Forest Hills Golf Club, New Jersey, in 1919, when Mr G Stewart and Mr F Spellmeyer did it at the eighteenth hole. An early reference book states that one of the players offered a bet of $10,000 (£2,055) to a dollar against it being repeated in his lifetime. It sounds a bit risky . . . unless he meant at the same hole.

The first time in Britain was in May 1925, when Gwendoline Clutterbuck (St Augustine Ladies) and Mrs H M Robinson (Herne Bay Ladies) halved the 110-yard fifteenth hole, one of seven short holes on the St Augustine course at Ramsgate. Two quick mashie shots and history was made.

Later in 1925, two players at Claremont Golf Club, Swinton, Messrs Evans and Matthews, halved the fourteenth hole in one stroke. The hole was nearly 140 yards, and the players sensibly called up witnesses before going near the hole. Two years later, Colonel F G Crompton and E Macey both holed in one at a much longer hole, one of 175 yards at Royal Eastbourne Golf Club.

In July 1936, there was a case in New Zealand. Two golfers halved a hole-in-one at the Shirley Links in Christchurch. Both balls landed in almost the same spot, slightly to the left of the flag, and then rolled gently into the hole. A true case of 'playing the like'.

Wales too. In 1948, two golfers holed in one at the sixteenth hole at Ashburnham. The beauty of this match was that it was all-square, and the golfer playing second had no choice but to go for the hole.

My personal favourite concerns a match at Turnberry on Sunday 4 August 1963, when a weekend four-ball reached the eleventh hole. Two men, George Gordon and Hugh Wilson, were playing against their wives, Margaret Gordon and Jean Wilson.

From the ladies' tee, Margaret Gordon sank her tee-shot from 137 yards.

The men must have been impressed.

From the men's tee, eight yards further back, Hugh Wilson put his tee-shot on the green. Not good enough.

Presumably Jean Wilson had no need to play.

Then came George Gordon. Yes, you've guessed. He emulated his wife by clipping a nine-iron shot into the air and watching the ball disappear into the hole.

Hole halved.

The men were fortunate that it wasn't one of the seven holes that they were conceding a stroke to the women. It must have been a demoralising blow. The men won the match by one hole.

De Vicenzo's Birthday Card
Augusta, Georgia, April 1968

The day of the final round of the US Masters was also Roberto de Vicenzo's forty-fifth birthday. He had achieved a lot during those 45 years, progressing from Buenos Aires caddie to British Open Champion, a title he had won the previous summer. He had also won a lot of friends.

In the major US tournaments, de Vicenzo's best finishing positions were eighth (US Open) and tenth (US Masters), but this particular Sunday he had a chance to win. After three rounds he was two strokes behind Gary Player, the formidable leader, and a stroke behind three other players. The list ran as follows:

Gary Player	72	67	71	–	210
Frank Beard	75	65	71	–	211
Bruce Devlin	69	73	69	–	211
Bob Goalby	70	70	71	–	211
Roberto de Vicenzo	69	73	70	–	212
Tommy Aaron	69	72	72	–	213

For the final round, de Vicenzo (fifth) partnered Aaron (sixth). It was a pairing that produced memorable golf and a sensational climax, albeit for the wrong reasons.

De Vicenzo began his final round by holing a nine-iron for an eagle two at the 400-yard first hole. He birdied the second and third to take a two-stroke lead, and reached the turn in 31. The crowd sang 'Happy Birthday' and de

Vicenzo celebrated. In the past he had had troubles with his putting. Not this year. Not on this occasion.

What made this a stunning day's play was that de Vicenzo wasn't alone in playing brilliantly. On any ordinary day the tournament might have been won by Yancey's 65 (for 279), Devlin's 69 (for 280), or Nicklaus's 67 (for 281). Frank Beard's 70 (for 281), Gary Player's 72 (for 282) and Tommy Aaron's 69 (for 282) could hardly be considered evidence of 'cracking up under pressure'. In the end, however, the contest was between de Vicenzo and Bob Goalby, a relatively little-considered 37-year-old American. Goalby was matching de Vicenzo's performance. When he putted in from off the fourteenth green and eagled the fifteenth with a fifteen-foot putt, Goalby went twelve under par, having gained five strokes on par in only eight holes.

De Vicenzo was playing the seventeenth while Goalby played the fifteenth. The seventeenth was to prove the crucial hole of the tournament, for bizarre reasons.

Watched by a huge television audience, the Argentinian reached the green in two shots, then holed a putt to go twelve under with Goalby. Most observers saw it as a birdie three, but Tommy Aaron marked de Vicenzo's card with a 'four' for the hole.

De Vicenzo's incredible golf was spoiled slightly by a bogey five on the final hole to give him a round of 65, but Goalby took three putts on his next hole – the seventeenth. With Goalby to play the 420-yard eighteenth, the two men were level.

Goalby's tee-shot on the par-four eighteenth struck trees on the right but bounced back into play. His second finished 60 feet from the hole, and a long putt left him with another stressful putt of four or five feet for par. He made it, and finished on 277, level with de Vicenzo.

The drama had begun. De Vicenzo, emotional at the end of the round, excited at such a birthday present, had one more task to perform. He had to sign his card. He looked it over three or four times. That 'five' at the last hole was what he saw, the bogey he thought had cost him an outright victory in the US Masters. He didn't notice too much else. He signed the card, handed it in and left the roped-off area around the last green. People wanted to talk to him. He had plenty to talk about, in his familiar charming manner.

The mistake on the card was noticed by officials. The rules were very clear. If a golfer signed for a score higher than that achieved, the score must stand. If a golfer signed for a lower score, the outcome must be disqualification. De Vicenzo's card showed a score too high – four rather than three – for the seventeenth hole. It had to be included in his total as a four, even if millions of television viewers had witnessed the birdie three. His 65 became a 66. He lost the Masters by one stroke, a stroke he had never played.

Bob Goalby	70	70	71	66	–	277
Roberto de Vicenzo	69	73	70	66	–	278
Bert Yancey	71	71	72	65	–	279
Bruce Devlin	69	73	69	69	–	280

When the mistake was discovered, everyone behaved with dignity. The officials checked whether there was any leeway. Had de Vicenzo really left the roped-off area? Yes, he had. The rule had to apply. The scorecard was part of the game, and the scorecard was de Vicenzo's responsibility.

De Vicenzo blamed only himself. 'What a stupid I am,' he said, endearingly, in his heavy English accent. He conceded that Goalby's final round had put him under pressure, and forced him to make two mistakes – a hooked drive at the last hole and signing for the wrong scorecard.

It was hard for Goalby, who would probably rather have played off and lost than won on such a technicality. He received little of the credit he deserved. Goalby had, after all, legitimately tied with de Vicenzo and was playing golf superb enough to win the play-off. He won eleven PGA events in his career, and no one could begrudge him the 1968 US Masters.

There were, of course, lessons to be learned. While playing partners were generally shown to be more expert markers than non-players, it was apparent that de Vicenzo might not have made his mistake if he had been taken somewhere quiet to check his card. The system was changed the next year, and officials went through the card hole-by-hole.

Golf on the Moon

Fra Mauro Driving Range, February 1971

'Houston, you might recognise what I have in my hand is the handle for the contingency sample return,' Captain Alan Shepard reported to base while standing on the surface of the moon. 'It just so happens to have a genuine six-iron on the bottom of it. In my left hand I have a little white pellet that's familiar to millions of Americans. I'll drop it down. Unfortunately, the suit is so stiff I can't do this with two hands but I'm going to try a little sand-trap shot here.'

Captain Shepard, commander of the Apollo 14 spacecraft and the fifth man on the moon, duly set up his lunar golfing experiment. He had prior permission to take the golf club on board, but some of his colleagues were surprised. The club had been devised by Jack Harden, a golf professional at River Oaks Country Club near Houston. The head was that of a normal six-iron, but the shaft was in three aluminium sections, which fitted together with Teflon joints and inserted into the 30-inch handle used by astronauts for moonwalk tasks requiring a shovel and an axe. The overall weight was 16½ ounces.

Millions of television viewers were captivated by the idea of hitting a golf shot on the moon. It was one giant shot for golfkind. If Shepard, a fifteen-handicap golfer, could hit a normal six-iron shot about 140 yards, how far could he hit one on the moon, where the gravity was one-sixth that of earth?

About 800 yards?

It wasn't going to be easy with the restrictions of his stiff space-suit and his one-handed swing.

Indeed, when Shepard waggled his space-suit, kept his head down and brought back his strange club, he was restricted immensely by his suit material, and his back-pack shortened the swing. He found it difficult to hit the ball.

'You got more dirt than ball that time,' commented Commander Edgar Mitchell, Shepard's companion on the moon. The third man in the party, Major Stuart Roosa, stayed in orbit while the other two collected soil samples.

Undeterred, Shepard threw down his second golf ball – he had brought three – and swung his six-iron again. The ball sailed away. It went a long way. He later estimated a couple of hundred yards, although it wasn't possible to measure it. His third attempt was even better, and Shepard estimated about 400 yards. But there wasn't a green in sight. Not even green rocks.

After Apollo 14 returned to earth, the Royal and Ancient Golf Club of St Andrews acknowledged Captain Shepard's feat by sending him a telegram: 'Warmest congratulations to all of you on your great achievement and safe return. Please refer to Rules of Golf section on etiquette, paragraph six, quote – before leaving a bunker a player should carefully fill up all holes made by him therein, unquote.'

Captain Shepard was later honoured by awards from the Metropolitan Golf Writers' Association and *Golf Magazine*. In 1974 he presented his custom-made six-iron club to the United States Golf Association Museum at Far Hills, New Jersey, where it can be seen today.

Rounds of 123 and 114
Tallahassee, Florida, April 1974

The 1974 Tallahassee Open coincided with the Tournament of Champions so none of the very big names in golf was competing, but it was a good opportunity for others to establish themselves on the circuit. Allen Miller won the tournament, playing great approach shots at the seventeenth and eighteenth when it looked as if his lead had slipped away, and the top four places looked like this:

Allen Miller	65	69	67	73	–	274
Eddie Pearce	68	68	70	69	–	275
Dan Sikes	67	69	67	72	–	275
Joe Inman	73	68	63	71	–	275

To students of strangeness, however, the bottom four places were more interesting. These four players made the cut but made no money.

John Quick	75	70	76	73	–	294
John Ruby	72	72	77	74	–	295
Steve Cain	73	72	75	76	–	296
Mike Reasor	73	71	123	114	–	381

You have to admit, something looks odd about Mike Reasor's scores. After two rounds he wasn't too far out of contention, only three strokes behind Joe Inman, who eventually finished joint second (though admittedly with the help of a superb third round).

So what had happened to Reasor?

The answer was that he had been horse-riding. While out on a horse, he had run into a tree, bruising his right knee and tearing muscles in his left shoulder and side. His left arm was out of action for the final two rounds.

Most golfers would withdraw with such injuries, but Reasor faced an interesting problem. In order to gain exemption from one week of the nerve-racking qualifying process, he had to play through *all 72 holes* of the Tallahassee Open. The automatic entry to the next tournament was for those who had *completed* the current tournament, regardless of score.

So Reasor played one-handed.

Spectators near the first tee laughed when they saw him, especially when his first attempt took the ball barely past the ladies' tee. Wearing check trousers, a white shirt and white shoes, he looked as good as usual, but his swing was not one for novices to study. His left arm hung limply at his side, his left hand rested on his left thigh, and he swung the club with his right arm, rather like someone chopping through long grass looking for a ball. He played his two Sunday rounds with only a five-iron and a putter. On the greens, he used his left hand to steady his putter. His scores of 123 and 114 showed a distinct improvement. On the first round, he was proud not to have strayed into double figures more than once – a ten at the seventh.

He earned his exemption from the next tournament, the Byron Nelson Classic, and looked forward to three days of rest beforehand.

A Head for Heights

Paris, October 1976,
October 1977

Golf and mountaineering are related.

Yes, you might think, remembering that ball on the clubhouse roof. Yes, you may agree, recalling how Bernhard Langer scaled a tree to play a shot in the 1981 Benson and Hedges International. Indeed, some people argue that golfers and mountaineers have similar temperaments – persevering, intrepid, disciplined and forever seeking a course that beats the weather.

The relationship, though, is simpler than all that.

One of the most extreme examples of combining golf and mountaineering features two United States Army sergeants who, in 1956, played a course of 4,132 yards. Most golf courses of that length would be par 59 or 60. This one was par 1,275. Their course was not 4,132 yards long but 4,132 yards high. It was the 12,395-foot Mount Fuji, a sacred mountain of Japan.

Mount Fuji presents a rocky course, but the daring sergeants, carrying one club, chipped and shovelled their way to the top, taking only ten hours 50 minutes. It was impossible to tee a ball on the mountain, and not always easy to reach the ball after hitting it. They went through 27 balls, and then lost the last one holing out into a two-mile wide crater at the top of the mountein. With a hole that size, at least the putting was easy.

Then they came down in one.

If you have a head for heights, you may be able to make money by betting that you can drive a golf ball a prodigious distance. In 1925, for instance, Waldo Chamberlain of Washington University drove 650 yards off Pinnacle Peak, a 6,562-foot mountain in the Mount Rainier National Park, Washington. Nine years later, Gust Kupka whacked a ball from the top of the Washington Monument. *Warning: Those who suffer from vertigo may wish to skip to the next paragraph.* Kupka climbed out of a window at the end of the elevator-shaft and edged himself up a ladder. He stepped on to the top of scaffolding that was surrounding the top of the Monument while it was being cleaned. He was 555 feet above the ground and fighting a 60-mile-an-hour wind, but he managed a swing at the ball.

In October 1976, on the morning of the first round of the Lancôme Tournament, French police stopped traffic in the Champ de Mars while Arnold Palmer drove a succession of golf balls from the second stage of the Eiffel Tower, that huge upside-down tee-peg in the centre of Paris. It was wet and windy that morning, and conditions were not good for ground-floor golf, let alone driving from a height of 377 feet. Palmer's best shot went only 276 yards. The wind ravaged the Lancôme Tournament itself, and on the final day a young Severiano Ballesteros out-Palmered Palmer by bravely making five birdies in the last nine holes and winning the tournament.

A year later, immediately before the 1977 Lancôme, Palmer tried again from the second stage of the Eiffel Tower. 'Two monuments are going to find each other again after a year's separation,' the press handout said, 'the monument of golf, Mr Palmer, and the monument of Paris, the Eiffel Tower. Together they are going perhaps to establish a new world record.'

Pressmen ate croissants and drank coffee, photographers swung from the tower above Palmer's head and clicked shutters, and die-hards talked about how the conditions were much better than the previous year. The sun shone, the air was still, and Arnold Palmer took out his number-one wood and considered his swing. The platform was cramped for space, handrails in front and a steel stanchion behind, and Palmer needed to position himself perfectly.

His first shot went 323 yards and landed in the pond halfway between the Tower and the Ecole Militaire. The second was a great bad shot. It was hooked towards the Invalides, but bounced off the roof of a passing bus. The distance was measured at 402 yards. Trust Palmer to find a daring shot.

The promotional stunt ended with a third shot of 363 yards. Palmer moved on to the Lancôme Tournament, where he scored a first-round 75 and was not really in contention.

The Top Stars Walk Off

Melbourne, Australia, November 1987

When the experienced Russell Swanson eight-putted on the third green in the final round of the Australian Open, it was obvious that the organisers had a problem on their hands. Playing the third hole was like playing a hole on a Crazy Golf course.

Before that final round, Greg Norman had led the National Panasonic Australian Open field by seven strokes. His third victory in the tournament seemed guaranteed. Only something extraordinary could stop him winning on the fourth day of the tournament. That something was the pin placement on the third green.

The third hole at the Royal Melbourne course was a par four of 333 yards. The Royal Melbourne greens were usually fast and contained many subtle humps and hollows, and in the mid-1970s Lee Trevino vowed never to return to such difficult greens. This day, though, there was the added hazard of a north wind that varied between 35 and 50 miles per hour. More crucially, the pin had been placed in an up-slope position where it was vulnerable to the winds. Later investigation showed that an assistant greenkeeper had set the pin two yards from the intended position.

The first three rounds had produced some superb golf. Terry Price had shot a 67 for the first-round lead, but Greg Norman's 70 kept him favourite. Norman followed this up with two successive rounds of 66, both magnificent, and his three-round score of 202 gave him a commanding lead.

Then came the final round. It took Norman over an hour to play the first two holes. The problem was the queue forming on the third tee. At one point there were over 20 players waiting on the tee.

Spectators on the third green saw three hours of comedy rather than skill. Players discovered that putts would not stop rolling within four yards of the hole. To get down in four putts was a good achievement – many took five or six – and the players lingered on the green while they studied the baffling problem. Caddies attempted to mark balls only to find them still moving, perhaps rolling back down a slope after going up it. Larry Nelson's caddie touched the ball, and Nelson took a two-stroke penalty.

Brett Ogle was more fortunate than most. His putt went a foot and a half past the hole, but as his caddie went to mark the ball the wind blew it back into the hole. Mike Colandro putted next and could be forgiven for thinking luck was against him. He hit four successive putts – all from around fifteen to 20 feet – and saw them all follow the same course. The ball ran round the edge of the cup for almost a complete circle and set off back towards his feet. Colandro sank his fifth attempt. He had been level par at the start of the final round. By the fifth hole he was eight over.

Ronan Rafferty and Sandy Lyle both refused to complete the third hole. The golfers on the third tee – the five waiting groups included leader Norman – walked off in support rather than risk humiliation on that green. The players were angry, the spectators were furious, and sponsors were confused.

The organisers considered the options available.

The 1985 Australian Open had been converted to a 54-hole tournament after a day had been lost to rain, but that decision had been criticised. Another option was a 71-hole tournament, eliminating the hazardous third hole, but this idea was soon rejected. That left only one option. They would have to switch the final round to the Monday and make sure the pin was correctly positioned on the third hole. But even that solution had problems, as many players had flights booked to New Zealand or Europe for their next tournament. A move to boycott the final round provoked a heated debate among the players. In the end they agreed to continue, although a few golfers pulled out to fulfil other commitments.

On the Monday Greg Norman clinched the title with a record ten-stroke victory. His 273 broke the Royal Melbourne course record by five strokes.

Saving a Child's Life
Phoenix, Arizona, March 1988

A man in Amish dress jumped into an outdoor swimming-pool.

Mary Bea Porter saw him in mid-air, fully clothed, about to hit the water. It distracted her from her next shot, a tricky one from the rough at the thirteenth hole at Moon Valley Country Club. She was on the LPGA tour, playing a qualifying round for the Standard Register Turquoise Classic, and her life was at an all-time low. It had been one thing after another – her husband's bankruptcy, divorce, debts, and her home and car gone – and now here was this strange scene.

Then she saw the child, lying face down in the pool. It was a boy of perhaps three years. She saw the Amish man pull the child out of the pool and hold him by the ankles, shaking him up and down.

Mary Bea Porter flipped off her shoes and ran towards the house, which bordered the rough on the thirteenth fairway. She faced a six-foot high fence. Wrought iron. Vertical bars. Nothing to climb on to.

'Do you know CPR?' someone asked.

Cardiopulmonary resuscitation.

Her caddie, Wayne, lifted her up. She put her right foot on top of the fence, jumped over, landed on two feet, stumbled forward and scraped her knee and her hand. The Amish man handed her the apparently dead child.

An Amish woman was on the patio, holding a telephone.

'What do I do?' she asked. She had not used a telephone before. The Amish family were visiting from Pennsylvania.

'Dial nine-one-one,' said Wayne, the caddie, who was trapped on the other side of the fence. He could have got over next-door's fence but their Dobermann looked hungry for legs.

The child in Mary Bea Porter's hands was grey and had a flat stomach and chest. She had a five-year-old boy of her own, and knew she had to do something, even with no training.

She tried to clear the baby's mouth, in case he had choked. Then she hit him hard on the heart. She desperately sought a technique. She put her hand in his mouth, moved his tongue to the side, held his nose and blew into his mouth. She tried again. His heart began to beat. It was like starting a lawn-mower engine.

The baby choked and moved his eyes.

'Bring a blanket, or a towel,' shouted Wayne from the other side of the fence.

The emergency services were on the telephone.

'What do I do now?' the golfer asked them.

'Keep the boy on his side.'

She yelled this advice at the boy's father. It wasn't how women usually treated Amish men.

The ambulance crew needed the address of the house. Mary Bea Porter had to search for a bill or a letter before she knew.

The child was being sick, expelling a very thick mucus. The rescue vehicles arrived. The boy screamed. The rescue team hugged everyone. The Amish were in shock.

Two women from a nearby house walked across to the scene. Mary Bea Porter had the child in her arms, her golf glove soaking wet, her clothes showing clearly that she was a golfer.

'Was it your ball that hit the little boy on the head?' one woman asked her.

'The child drowned,' someone said. 'She saved his life.'

Mary Bea Porter returned to the golf course. Her threesome had waited a few minutes before letting the next threesome play through. Then they had continued as a twosome.

Wayne handed Mary Bea a club. It could have been a Coke bottle for all she was concentrating. She hit a reasonable shot but it fluttered in the wind and landed in a bunker. She laughed. Well, there were more important things in life than golf shots . . . things like life itself.

Her round of 76 was three strokes short of qualifying. It was typical of her golf. She had won one tournament during her first spell on the tour, in the mid-1970s, and had finished thirty-seventh in the women's money-list in 1975, but times had been hard since her return. In 1987 she had won only $955 (£600) in prize money in 21 tournaments. This year it was only marginally better – $420 (£250) in three.

Newspapers and television stations queued up for her story, and the LPGA, receiving a petition signed by 50 golfers, granted her an unprecedented special exemption into the Turquoise Classic. But Mary Bea Porter was emotionally and physically drained by the events. Her first-round 83 was almost embarrassing, and she failed to make the cut.

Meanwhile, three-year-old Jonathan Smucker was taken to John C Lincoln Hospital and Health Centre, where he was found to be in good condition. He was transferred to St Joseph's Hospital and Medical Center for observation.

Professional Takes Nineteen on a Hole

Sydney, Australia, February 1989

Amateurs are often reassured when professionals take nineteen for a hole, whereas professionals have a right to be smug when they hear tales of amateurs losing count after 50. Robert Emond's experience at the 1989 Australian Tournament Players Championship should therefore be put in the context of stories from the world of amateur golf.

A letter in *Golf Illustrated* (9 July 1909) described how an amateur had taken 97 for a hole at Windermere: 'It was a downhill hole, about 230 yards – quite possible to reach the green if you hit your tee-shot. I didn't, nor did my partner, and his second found a whin brush to the left of the green. I played my second and waited. He had one smash, then another, and by the time I had walked up to the green had reached double figures. I told him to pick out, but he declared his intention of playing his ball out, and went on striking like a flail, and calling out each stroke as it was played till at 95 he found the green, having in the meantime cleared the whin brush quite away. And with that stroke he laid me a stymie, but I had 94 for the hole, so didn't worry over it. He holed out in 97, quite the biggest score I ever heard of, and I saw the whole of it.'

A second example occurred in 1912 in a qualifying round of a ladies' competition at the Shawnee Club in Pennsylvania. The number of entrants was exactly the same as the anticipated number of qualifiers for the later match competition, but there were special prizes for the best qualifying round, so that round had to be played. At one hole, a competitor hit her tee-shot into a fast-flowing stream just short of the green. Knowing she only had to complete the round to ensure qualification, she resolved to play out. Her ball was floating in the middle of the wide stream, and the only way to it was by boat. Her husband rowed the boat adjacent to the ball, while his wife slashed shot after shot with her niblick, showering him to saturation. She stuck to her task, and played shot after shot after shot, until she finally connected and put the ball ashore – a mile and a quarter downstream from the hole. Unfortunately, she had hit her ball into a dense thicket and it took her some time to find it. Then she thrashed a few more shots until she was safely in a clearing and could find a more direct way to the green. She holed out in 166, and the Shawnee Club presented her with a special cup – for qualifying.

Travers and Crowell later suggested that this story may have grown in the retelling, but they agree that something of the kind did happen, and point out that the winner of the tournament was Mrs Caleb Fox, a pioneer woman golfer.

Another story that varies in the telling is that of Tommy Armour's 23 at the 1927 Shawnee Open. The following day's newspapers give his seventeenth-hole score as eleven rather than 23, but folklore suggests that Armour hit shot after shot out of bounds and the only thing in dispute was whether he was down in 21 or 23. Whatever the correct details, it is a strange story because Armour had won the US Open a few days before, beating young Harry Cooper in an eighteen-hole play-off. His eleven (or 21 or 23) came in the third round, and his scores were listed as 80, 71, 82 and 79. The most detailed account I could find of Armour's third-round débâcle at the seventeenth goes as follows: 'Whatever hopes Armour may have had of finishing somewhere went a glimmering when he hooked three drives out of bounds at the seventeenth. The hole cost an eleven.'

At the 1938 US Open, Ray Ainsley was 'credited' with nineteen strokes at the 397-yard sixteenth hole in the second round. It is still a record for the US Open. That year's tournament was at Cherry Hills, Denver, and Ainsley began with a round of 78 that left him equal twenty-fifth. Then, on the second day, he hit a good drive at the sixteenth but his five-iron shot hit the edge of the green and bounced back into a five-foot wide brook which contained a couple of inches of water. The ball drifted with the current back towards the tee. Ainsley chased it and started swinging. 'Ainsley stood in the stream, chopping away and then backing up to chop again,' wrote Tom Flaherty in *The US Open*. 'The scorekeeper stood over him like a referee, counting "seven, eight, nine". Finally the scorekeeper doubled up in laughter and he fell to the ground. Ainsley's playing partner, Bud McKinney, took up the count.' On a few occasions the ball teased Ainsley by jumping the bank before dropping down again. Eventually, he popped it out on to dry land, and spectators debated whether it was for 19, 22, or even 23. It made little difference to Ainsley, whose round of 96 (even with a 19) wasn't good enough to make the cut.

Ah, you might say, those anecdotes are from long ago. What about more recently? Has a professional golfer taken nineteen for a hole in the last few years?

The answer is yes.

In the 1989 Australian Tournament Players Championship, Robert Emond had an 81 for his first round. His second round began at the tenth hole and he progressed well on the first nine. He was out in 36, which included birdies at the fifteenth, sixteenth and seventeenth. All was well until the first hole, which he was playing tenth. That first hole at Riverside Oaks was a 573-yard par five, and Emond, a 20-year-old rookie from Geelong in Victoria, began by hooking his drive into the water (one). He took a penalty drop (two) and hit a new ball along the fairway (three). His next shot put the ball on a bank at the front of the green, but it rolled down into more water (four). He removed his right shoe and sock and made two attempts to hit the ball out of the water (five and six) before picking up for a one-stroke penalty (seven). He dropped in the rough and hit it back into the water (eight), conceding another one-stroke penalty (nine). Flustered by now, he dropped another ball but it hit his shoe for a two-stroke penalty (ten and eleven). He dropped again and hit the ball into water again (twelve) for another on stroke penalty (thirteen). Then he hit the ball to the fringe of the green and marked it (fourteen). Unfortunately, as the ball was technically off the green, another two-stroke penalty was in order (fifteen and sixteen). Finally, Emond three-putted (seventeen, eighteen and nineteen).

In the circumstances, the rest of Robert Emond's round – he had a 90 on his card – was creditable but he failed to make the cut by 23 strokes. His nineteen at the first dwarfed Adam Nance's eleven at the 152-yard fourteenth the previous day. Nance had hit four balls into a lake on the left-hand side of the green before landing one two yards from the pin and two-putting.

The tournament was won by Greg Norman, who came with a typical late charge – 70, 70, 69 and 67 – to pip Roger Mackay by two strokes. At the twelfth, in the final round, Norman's ambitious tee-shot came to rest over 300 yards away, right by the pin. He holed his putt for a stunning eagle.

Three American Presidents, Three Wounded Spectators

Palm Springs, February 1995

When two former presidents, George Bush Snr and Gerald Ford, joined the then incumbent Bill Clinton in a foursome at the Bob Hope Chrysler Classic it promised to be exciting for spectators. Ford assessed the situation correctly on the first tee when he suggested that the general public should take up positions *behind* the golfers. Indeed, plenty of ducking and dodging was in store for spectators.

Bill Clinton, at 48, still had time on his side to improve his game. A few months previously he had holidayed on Martha's Vineyard with the expressed ambition of completing a round in less than 80. He managed an 82 on the first day of his stay but it was downhill thereafter.

George Bush, now 70 years old, had been an eleven-handicap player in his prime but his goal now was 'just to get the ball in the air'. Gerald Ford, 81, was another who was probably past his best. The fourth member of the group was professional Scott Hoch, whose golf had one thing in common with Clinton, Bush and Ford – he had never won a major.

The foursome was joined by Bob Hope himself. The 91-year-old comedian travelled the course in a golf-cart and played at all the holes. He didn't keep a proper score and sometimes started a hole on the fairway.

The first tee was a portent of what was to come.

A nervous Gerald Ford hooked his drive into the crowd.

'Fore,' he yelled, almost before his swing had come to rest.

An equally nervous Bill Clinton sliced his first tee-shot into a bunker.

George Bush hit a reasonable first shot but his second shot resulted in the day's first casualty. Bush's drive rebounded from a tree and hit an elderly lady, Norma Earley, in the face. The impact broke her glasses and cut her across the bridge of the nose.

George Bush hurried across to the woman and offered sympathy while the tournament officials provided first aid. Norma Earley was taken away to hospital in a golf-cart. Her cut required ten stitches.

Bush made a birdie at the sixth hole, but at the fourteenth his ball struck another spectator. John Rynd was sensible enough to have turned his back on play. According to differing reports, the ball hit Rynd on either the back of the leg or the buttock.

'How's the wound?' Bush asked him.

'No blood, no problem,' the man replied.

Bush autographed the ball for him.

Gerald Ford then hit a spectator, Geraldine Grommesh, at the seventeenth hole. The ball drew blood from the spectator's left index finger but no stitches were needed.

Clinton erred in other directions, barely topping his ball with one tee-shot and landing another in a yard next to the fairway. Clinton had to check with tournament officials before picking up the ball and dropping it on the fairway.

If Hoch was worried about always being in front of the other golfers, it didn't ruin his game. His round of 70 was by far the best of the group (although it was a par 68 course). The personal battle between Bush and Clinton was more interesting. Bush (92) was delighted to beat Clinton, who pleaded that his 93 was his worst score for three or four years. Gerald Ford went round in 100. However, one observer pointed out that these scores did not include 'mulligans' (free shots).

The journalists loved it. They were able to ask questions like 'what sort of lies did we have from the President today?'

Bill Clinton can at least claim to have played with great golfers. In 1996 he went round with Greg Norman in Australia. It was on a visit to Norman's Florida home, however, that Clinton tore the quadriceps tendon on his right knee when he slipped on the guest-house steps. Presidents always have strange golf careers.

MOTOR-RACING

by Geoff Tibballs

Working Up a Head of Steam
Paris to Rouen Trial, July 1894

Motoring was still very much in its infancy when Pierre Giffard, editor and owner of the Parisian newspaper *Le Petit Journal*, hit upon the idea of staging the world's first motor event. It was not a race as such but an 80-mile trial along the bumpy roads between Paris and Rouen, the winner to be the vehicle which, in the opinion of the judges (all of whom were on the staff of *Le Petit Journal*) most closely adhered to their ideal of '*d'être sans danger, aisément maniable pour les voyagers, et de ne pas coûter trop cher sur la route*', in other words safe, easy to handle and cheap to run. Hoping for a large turn-out to ensure maximum publicity for his newspaper, M. Giffard was no doubt heartened to receive entries from 102 drivers putting their names forward to compete for the handsome first prize of 5,000 francs. The entry list contained a vast array of vehicles, hardly any two alike, and featuring no fewer than 20 different methods of propulsion. These ranged from the more conventional steam-powered designs or the new-fangled petrol-powered cars to contraptions driven by compressed air, clockwork, gravity, a system of pendulums, 'a combination of animate and mechanical motor' and even the rocket-like Baricycle, a device which was propelled solely by the weight of its passengers!

The organisers laid down strict regulations governing which vehicles would actually be allowed to compete. First there was an inspection test which eliminated all but 25 of the original 102, principally the more bizarre entries. The event itself was scheduled for 7 June but with a number of vehicles still not ready by the start of that month, it was postponed until 22 July. This allowed more opportunity to arrange a 32-mile qualifying trial, which every competitor had to pass. The time limit set was three hours, thus necessitating an average speed of just over 10mph, but this was deemed too harsh and so the time was extended to four hours, thereby reducing the required speed to a more attainable 8mph. Seventeen vehicles took part in the first qualifying run on 19 July, but only 13 passed. A second run on the 20th saw all six starters pass and two more qualified the following day, to leave a starting line-up of 21 (all powered by either petrol or steam engines) for the 80-mile journey to Rouen.

The festivities began at 8 a.m. in the Paris suburb of Neuilly and the route ran via Nanterre, St Germain, Mantes (where drivers would stop for lunch) and Vernon to Rouen. Along the way entire villages turned out to cheer and to shower the vehicles with flowers and fruit. Families set up picnic tables at the side of the road so that they could gawp at the great monsters as they trundled by. For some, it would be the first time they had ever seen a motor car. On board each car, in addition to the driver and passenger, was an official observer to determine whether the criteria for the first prize were met. The vehicles were flagged off at 30-second intervals, but it soon became apparent that the most powerful vehicle by far was a giant De Dion articulated steam tractor driven by wealthy playboy and renowned duellist Count Jules de Dion. The leaders covered the 30 miles to Mantes by 11 a.m., de Dion showing the way to Georges Lemaître in a Peugeot and Emile Levassor in a Panhard. The attempts at official timekeeping at Mantes were singularly chaotic, but after a leisurely lunch, the drivers began the second leg of their journey at 1.30 p.m.

It came as no surprise that Count de Dion maintained his lead all the way to Rouen. He had the odd hair-raising moment along the way, once having to be hauled free by spectators after his vehicle became stuck on the road's loose stone surface, and on another occasion taking a wrong turning and ending up in a potato field. He finished in 6hr 48min at a commendable average speed of 11.66mph, three and a half minutes ahead of Lemaître. However, the Count did not win the coveted first prize, the judges ruling that because it needed two people to handle it – a driver to steer and a stoker to tend the engine – the de Dion tractor did not comply with the event's aims. Therefore he was demoted to second although he was praised for his 'interesting steam tractor which . . . develops a speed absolutely beyond comparison, especially when going uphill'. Instead the prize was awarded jointly to Lemaître and Levassor for their petrol cars. Indeed the day was a triumph for the brash new petrol machines. For while all thirteen petrol-powered cars completed the course, four of the eight steam-powered vehicles broke down. For reliability, it was clear that the future of motoring lay with petrol.

Charron in Reverse

Tour de France, July 1899

Buoyed by the success of its enterprising racing calendar, the Automobile Club de France began preparations for the longest motor-race in the world to date – a 1,423-mile circuit of France to be spread over nine days. The schedule was as follows:

Day 1 – Paris to Nancy (180 miles)
Day 2 – Nancy to Aix-les-Bains (274 miles)
Day 3 – Rest day
Day 4 – Aix-les-Bains to Vichy (238 miles)
Day 5 – Rest day
Day 6 – Vichy to Périgueux (186 miles)
Day 7 – Périgueux to Nantes (210 miles)
Day 8 – Nantes to Cabourg (216 miles)
Day 9 – Cabourg to Paris (119 miles)

Sponsorship by *Le Matin* had attracted 48 starters – nineteen cars, 25 motorcycles, and four lighter vehicles or voiturettes. The favourites were the French trio of Fernand Charron, René de Knyff and Léonce Girardot, whose Panhards had finished first, second and third in the Paris to Bordeaux race two months earlier. The start took place on a Sunday morning at the foot of a long hill just outside the Parisian suburban town of Champigny. One absentee was the Panhard driven by Comte Berthier de Savigny who, on his way to the start, tried to avoid a pedestrian in the centre of Paris, but went up on the pavement and knocked down a lamp-post. While the Comte was unharmed, the car was wrecked. Charron was first away at 8 a.m., followed by Girardot 30 seconds later, the remainder of the field following at similar intervals. Last away was the Vallée car driven by Flash, a pseudonym for Dr E Lewhess. It was expected to create an impression and it certainly did, although not quite in the way its driver had envisaged. For it was unable even to climb the first hill. It eventually reached the summit after ten long minutes but only because the mechanic got out and pushed. As if this ignominious start was not enough to have the good doctor reaching for his pills, a tyre then burst. With no spare on board, Lewhess had to catch a cab back to Paris to fetch a new one. Not surprisingly, he decided to retire shortly afterwards.

There were numerous hazards en route. Several drivers ended up in ditches trying to avoid spectators or wagons, while dogs were a constant menace, packs of them chasing the drivers through every village. The route was also littered with level crossings which damaged the wheels and suspensions, leading to further retirements. An added obstacle was that, on approaching Nancy at the end of the first day, the drivers discovered that a steep hill was not fit for vehicles, requiring them to seek an alternative way into the town. De Knyff led the field after that first stage, but Charron had forged ahead by Aix-les-Bains. The much-fancied Girardot suffered a setback when he broke a wheel but, resourceful as ever, he managed to borrow a replacement from a farmer's cart. It is not known whether he ever actually returned the wheel to the farmer. And Camille Jenatzy ended up in a ditch after smashing a wheel. He was able to continue after repairing the damage but had lost precious time.

At the outset of day four, de Knyff lost 30 minutes repairing the springs on his car and more time ebbed away when he stopped to help one of the motorcyclists, Williams, who had come off his machine. Nobly, de Knyff drove the injured rider to St Etienne, where Williams suddenly came to his senses and refused to let de Knyff help him further in case the delay cost him the race. Remarkably, de Knyff was able to make up the ground and finished the day five minutes ahead of Charron. Less fortunate was a M Degrais, whose motorised tricycle skidded out of control after a chicken had got caught between the front wheel and the mudguard . . .

Following the second rest day, there were 30 competitors still going at the start of day six. A minor – but time-consuming – accident to Charron put de Knyff 35 minutes ahead at Périgueux, by which time the field had been thinned to 23. De Knyff was still ahead at Nantes, and his victory was sealed on the next stage to Cabourg when Charron's forward transmission gear broke near Le Mans. Unable to go forward, Charron refused to admit defeat, turned the car round and drove the 25 miles to Alençon in reverse! Alas, the prospect of reversing all the way to Paris proved too daunting and he was forced to retire.

De Knyff was never troubled after that and went on to win the first prize of £240 by five hours from Girardot, with Comte Gaston de Chasseloup-Laubat third in another Panhard. De Knyff's average speed was 30.2mph, and there were 20 finishers – ten cars, eight motorcycles and two voiturettes.

The Firing Squad

US Grand Prize, November 1908

Although the home of motor-racing was Europe, the sport had started to take off in the United States. However, the hopes of attracting the leading European drivers had been dealt a severe blow by the 1906 Vanderbilt Cup race at Long Island, New York – an event marred by poor crowd control. Many drivers had felt intimidated by spectators who had broken through the wire-netting barriers and swamped the circuit. So the authorities decided to take no chances for the Grand Prize of the Automobile Club of America, to be run on Thanksgiving Day, 1908, at Savannah, Georgia, and arranged for the track to be patrolled by armed soldiers and policemen. These officers didn't quite operate a 'shoot to kill' policy, but they were decidedly trigger-happy.

The 25-mile Savannah circuit wound its way along roads lined with palm trees, and the race distance of 402 miles was relatively short for that time. There were 20 entrants, including a strong European contingent with three Fiats and three Italas from Italy, three Benz cars from Germany and two Renaults from France. The Fiat team consisted of Felice Nazzaro, Louis Wagner and Ralph de Palma, a young Italian-born American driving in his first big race. His riding mechanic was Pietro Bordino, who went on to become the leading Italian driver of the early 1920s. In addition there were six American drivers – Ralph Mulford, Joe Seymour, Bob Burman, Willie Haupt, Len Zengle and

Hugh Harding – each at the wheel of an American car. The Fiats and Renaults appeared to have a major advantage when it came to tyre stops thanks to the introduction of detachable rims. When a car sustained a puncture, the old tyre usually had to be slashed off with a knife, then a new inner tube and outer casing had to be fitted using levers before finally being inflated. It was a laborious process that resulted in lengthy pit stops. But Fiat and Renault were now using detachable rims which could be unbolted and bolted back on complete, thereby reducing the time taken by around ten minutes.

Following an extensive ten days of practice, the race was due to start at 9 a.m. but was postponed 45 minutes because of fog. As was the norm in those days, the cars were started at intervals (massed starts not being widely introduced until 1922) with the result calculated on time rather than finishing position on the track. When the cars got away, it was de Palma who took the lead, followed by Wagner, René Hanriot in a Benz and with the fancied Nazzaro back in sixth. De Palma retained his lead until the third lap when tyre trouble dropped him back to last place. This allowed Hanriot to take over at the head of the field, pursued by Hungarian driver Ferenc Szisz in a Renault, Wagner, Victor Hémery (Benz) and Nazzaro. All the while the militia men, rifles poised, were keeping a close watch on the spectators. Then suddenly for some inexplicable reason, one of the locals tried to drive a horse and buggy across the track at the height of the race. The soldiers fired on the driver in an instant. He got the message.

Hanriot maintained his advantage until lap eight, by which time Hémery had moved up to second. As Hanriot fell away, Hémery began to dispute the lead with Nazzaro and Wagner. On lap eleven Erle, who was in fourth place, was knocked unconscious when a tyre burst and his Benz careered along the course for a further quarter of a mile before overturning. Luckily he received only minor injuries and his mechanic escaped unhurt. Then came more drama when the police captain shot at Hanriot for what was described as an infringement of the regulations. Somehow the black flag seems a more civilised method of dealing with transgressions. Remarkably, Hanriot bore no ill feelings and later presented his gloves and goggles to the officer.

Starting the final lap, Nazzaro had a lead of nearly two minutes over Hémery who, in turn, was just two seconds ahead of Wagner. Hanriot, still running despite his scare, was twelve minutes back in fourth. But fifteen miles from the finish Nazzaro lost a tyre and was relegated to third. Hémery crossed the line first but it was Wagner who, by virtue of a storming last lap, was declared the winner on corrected time – by 57 seconds after more than six hours of racing. Wagner and Hémery made it a French one-two with the Italian Nazzaro back in third.

Despite the over-zealous policing, the event was declared a resounding success. The drivers much preferred Savannah to Long Island and were delighted when the 1910 Grand Prize was switched from New York to Georgia. For that occasion, a new course was laid out using convict labour, the prisoners being rewarded with a special enclosure on race day. 'It will be grand,' enthused Hémery. 'Not even Europe has ever furnished a more perfectly patrolled course.' Then again, he hadn't been shot at in 1908.

Champagne Jules
Indianapolis 500, May 1913

The 2½ mile oval circuit at Indianapolis was laid down in 1909 at a cost of $250,000. The original surface was natural rock which had been steamrollered flat, but this proved too dangerous and so the circuit was paved with three million bricks, earning it the nickname of 'The Brickyard'. This surface remained until 1935 when, with the exception of the start/finish straight, the track was asphalted. The last of the brick paving disappeared in 1961 when the entire circuit, apart from a symbolic brick strip at the finish line, was asphalted. Until 1971, the 200-lap, 500-mile spectacular was raced on Memorial Day, the day each year on which the United States remembers its war dead, but that year it was moved to the last Sunday in May. The first '500' took place in 1911 and the following year Ralph Mulford completed the race down the field at a leisurely 56mph solely to qualify for starting money, even stopping for lunch on the way! In 1913 it was drink rather than food that would make the headlines.

The first two years of the '500' had been essentially an American preserve, but in 1913 there was a significant European challenge. Five foreign drivers ('swarthy-skinned aliens' as the American press called them) took part and the line-up included eight foreign cars – two Peugeots, two Mercedes and three Isotta-Fraschinis and a Sunbeam. As the American cars were much smaller than their European counterparts, none of the monster machines was entered. Of the European contingent only Frenchman Jules Goux had any experience of a banked circuit like Indianapolis, having raced in the spring of that year at Brooklands where he had lapped at a highly impressive 109.22mph. For Indianapolis Goux was at the wheel of the same 7.4-litre Peugeot in which Georges Boillot had won the eventful 1912 French Grand Prix. It was to prove a good omen.

America's Robert Evans led for the first few laps in a Mason but the race soon settled down into a battle between the Peugeots of Goux and Paul Zuccarelli, American Bob Burman in a 7.2-litre Keeton, and Albert Guyot in the strongly fancied Sunbeam. Alas, Guyot did not enjoy one of his more auspicious drives. R F Crossman accompanied him as riding mechanic and some observers thought the Sunbeam might have fared better had the situations been reversed. For despite having to change just one tyre throughout the 500 miles, Guyot could only finish a disappointing fourth, never really threatening the leaders. Up front, Goux made numerous tyre stops and during each one he guzzled a quantity of the Frenchman's favourite tipple, champagne. In the course of the race, he downed no fewer than six bottles! Far from having an adverse effect on his driving, the alcohol intake spurred him on to greater heights and when Burman dropped out in the second 100 miles, then Zuccarelli retired with carburettor trouble while lying second, Goux was left unchallenged in the lead. He went on to become the first European to win at Indianapolis (pocketing the prize money of £8,750), finishing well ahead of Spencer Wishart's 4.9-litre Mercer, which crossed the line on fire, and Charlie Merz's Stutz.

Goux's triumph saw him acclaimed as a national hero on his return to Paris. Over the ensuing years there was much debate as to whether or not the champagne story was apocryphal, but Goux himself subsequently confirmed that it was definitely champagne and not water that he had consumed during those pit stops. He added that it was the finest vintage, procured before the race with great difficulty by a Mr Kaufman of New York, Peugeot's representative in the United States.

Across the Line Backwards
Targa Florio, November 1919

The brainchild of Count Vincenzo Florio, the Targa Florio was first run in Sicily in 1906. When the suggestion of staging a race on the mountainous island had initially been put to the count, his response was that there were no roads. Undeterred by this minor obstacle, the organisers found a tortuous 90-mile loop which proved more than a match for man and machine. Following a twelve-year absence, the race was revived in 1919 over the 67-mile Madonie circuit. This may have been of a lesser distance than the original but the mountain twists ensured that there was no shortage of hazards. Among the 25 starters were a number of interesting names. Enzo Ferrari was making his racing debut at the wheel of a CMN; graduating from hill climbs, Antonio Ascari, the new hope of Italy, was driving a Fiat; André Boillot, younger brother of Georges who had been killed in the First World War, was in a 2.5-litre Peugeot; and René Thomas was driving an Indianapolis Ballot car which had been entered so late that Thomas had been obliged to drive it all the way from Paris to Naples. At one point on the journey through Italy Thomas had to wait while scaffolding was erected to replace a stretch of road that had been washed away by torrential rain. Most of the starters were Italian, including the Alfa Romeos of Giuseppe Campari and Nino Franchini and the pair of 1914 Grand Prix Fiats driven by Ascari and Count Giulio Masetti.

Thomas may have been forgiven for thinking that he had seen off the worst of the weather in Italy but on the eve of the race a raging storm deposited a two-inch covering of snow on the mountain section. The following morning at 7 a.m. Enzo Ferrari was first away, followed by Ascari, in a devilish combination of snow and high winds, swiftly followed by rain, hail, sleet and sun, although not always in that order. To cope with the conditions, the drivers wore gauze masks but discarded their goggles because of the snow. The principal casualty on the first lap was Ascari, whose Fiat skidded on the treacherous road, plunged down a 30-foot ravine and was not found until halfway through the race! André Boillot was proving a worthy successor to his illustrious brother and an opening lap of 1hr 54min 36sec gave him a lead of nearly four minutes over Thomas, with Domenico Gambino third in a Diatto and Count Masetti's Fiat in fourth. But starting the second lap Boillot's Peugeot skidded, struck a bank, leapt three feet in the air, dropped on two wheels and was only prevented from plunging 200 feet over a precipice by a handily placed pile of stones. A lesser driver might have been unnerved by this experience but Boillot pushed on regardless, maintaining a healthy lead over Thomas despite having a car that boasted just half of his rival's cubic capacity.

When Thomas came in for fuel at the start of the final lap, having driven flat out, he discovered to his horror that he was still seven minutes behind. Boillot's carefree approach to this treacherous circuit had seen him leave the road on no fewer than six occasions but between accidents he was by far the quickest driver in the race. He didn't even bother to stop for fuel when beginning the last lap. Instead his equally manic mechanic grabbed a can from the pits and refuelled on the move. Thomas pressed on boldly but couldn't hope to compete with such daredevil tactics and in the end he pushed too hard and crashed, leaving Boillot with a lead of around half an hour.

Others might have been content to coast home but the Frenchman continued to drive like a madman right to the finish. It very nearly proved his undoing. For as news reached the crowd in the stands of Boillot's impending arrival, knots of spectators began to trickle excitedly on to the circuit. Boillot came roaring round the final corner and suddenly saw hordes of people in front of him. He jammed on the brakes and swerved to avoid the clusters of well-wishers but merely succeeded in spinning into the grandstand . . . just ten yards from the finish. Perhaps feeling guilty at their part in the proceedings (although three of their number were injured in the collision), the spectators started to push Boillot's car back on to the track until a journalist helpfully pointed out that Boillot would be disqualified unless he and his mechanic did the pushing. Although in the latter stages of exhaustion, the pair succeeded in dragging the battered Peugeot back on to the road, from where Boillot rolled across the finish line backwards. But that wasn't the end of it. Ernest Ballot reminded them that reversing over the finish line was also illegal so they were lifted back into the car, drove down the road, turned round and this time crossed the line facing the right way. A yard or so over the line, Boillot collapsed over the wheel, muttering gloriously, *'C'est pour la France!'*

His average speed of 34.2mph had spreadeagled the field. Antonio Moriondo's Itala finished second, half an hour adrift, and Gamboni was a further twelve minutes back in third. Enzo Ferrari completed the race (no mean achievement in itself) but was well down the field. On the day nobody could cope with the new Boillot.

A Pit Stop For Lunch

European Grand Prix, June 1925

The first Grand Prix to be staged in Belgium was held at the 8.76-mile Spa circuit in 1925. A race had been scheduled for 1914 but by then a different sort of battle was being fought on Belgian soil. The 1925 event was run under the title of the European Grand Prix but a low turn-out and a monotonous race was scarcely the best advert for European motor-racing. In fact the day was memorable for just one reason – the most amazing display of arrogance by the Alfa Romeo team. If you can imagine Michael Schumacher prolonging a pit stop to tuck into a picnic, you'll get the picture.

Twelve cars were supposed to take part but when the Sunbeams and Guyots scratched, that left four Delages against three Alfas. The Delage drivers were René Thomas, Robert Benoist, Albert Divo and Paul Torchy, while the Alfa team comprised Antonio Ascari, Giuseppe Campari and Count Gastone Brilli-Peri. There should have been everything to play for since, although the World Championship did not begin in earnest until 1950, a short-lived experiment did take place for manufacturers from 1925, and this was one of the races which counted, in company with the Indianapolis 500 and the French and Italian Grands Prix. The other innovation for the year was the abolition of riding mechanics in Grand Prix events. Most racing cars now became single-seaters.

Ascari led the way round the first lap from Campari, Benoist, Brilli-Peri, Divo, Torchy and Thomas but on the next circuit Benoist dropped out with a split fuel tank. Then on lap four Torchy stopped for new plugs and retired soon after. The Delage misery deepened three laps later when Thomas's caught fire. He burnt his left hand trying to beat out the flames and retired. So after little more than 50 of the 500 miles, there were already only four cars left running.

At half-distance Ascari was still showing the way to Campari, Divo and Brilli-Peri. It was hardly riveting entertainment for the Belgian crowd but it was to get much, much worse. For soon Brilli-Peri retired with a broken spring and Divo exited the race after making two long stops – one for tyres, the other for plugs. Now it was just the two Alfas. Round and round they went, separated by over a quarter of an hour. The crowd, partly disappointed at the lack of French involvement but even more disgruntled by the tedious procession, began to jeer and boo the Alfa drivers. Irked by this show of disapproval, Alfa team manager Vittorio Jano decided to rub in the Italian superiority by arranging for a sumptuous lunch to be laid out in the pits. Then, to a crescendo of boos and hisses, he called in his two drivers and they sat down to a leisurely meal while the mechanics polished the cars. The spectators could hardly believe their eyes.

Their stomachs satisfied, Ascari and Campari resumed the 'race', remaining in that order to the finish at which point Ascari was 22 minutes ahead of his team-mate. He had led from start to finish at an average speed of 74.46mph.

The joy of Ascari and Alfa was to be short-lived. He was killed in his next major event, the French Grand Prix, following which the Alfa cars withdrew from the race as a mark of respect. Alfa still won that inaugural World Constructors' Championship (beating Duesenberg and

Bugatti), but the season had been tarnished by the death of their star driver. It was all a far cry from that picnic in the pits at Spa.

Le Mans Victory Sealed by Chewing Gum

Le Mans 24-Hour Race, June 1933

More than a few eyebrows were raised when Alfa Romeo announced its pairings for the 1933 Le Mans Endurance Race. Raymond Sommer and Tazio Nuvolari in the same team? Neither was exactly fond of playing a supporting role. What were Alfa thinking of?

The Frenchman had won the previous year's race in partnership with Luigi Chinetti, but had insisted on driving 20 of the 24 hours himself as he had infinitely more confidence in his own ability than that of his co-driver. Chinetti was probably not in a position to argue too much with this high-handed approach, but Nuvolari was a different matter altogether. He would not act as anyone's chauffeur. The potential clash of egos was frightening.

True to form, Sommer loftily declared that he would be doing most of the driving in 1933 since Nuvolari was not as familiar with Le Mans as he was, and anyway the Italian was a known car-wrecker. If Nuvolari was allowed to remain at the wheel for more than a few hours, he would be sure to blow the Alfa's engine. No, the only hope of success was for Sommer to take the lion's share. For once, Nuvolari exercised considerable restraint, pointing out politely but firmly that he was a leading Grand Prix driver who knew his way round every circuit in the world and would not be troubled by a simple configuration such as Le Mans.

Sommer backed down and, albeit reluctantly, agreed that they should divide the driving equally.

In the end this unlikely arrangement worked, but for all the merging of two great talents, it was a simple piece of chewing gum that won the day.

Sommer and Nuvolari's short-wheelbase Mille Miglia type Alfa was one of 29 starters. Others included a noisy 6.8-litre V8 Duesenberg, entered by Prince Nicholas of Romania. The American car was popular with European royalty, but was too cumbersome for Le Mans where its high fuel consumption led to its downfall, it being disqualified after just 22 laps for refuelling sooner than was permitted.

Sommer took first turn in the favourites' car and got away to a good start, leading at the end of the first lap from the fellow Alfas of Louis Chiron and Franco Cortese, Chinetti and Varent, and the English duo of Brian Lewis and Tim Rose-Richards. By 24 laps Sommer had established a healthy advantage, at which point he was persuaded to hand over to Nuvolari. Contrary to fears, Nuvolari did not break the car and when he handed it back to Sommer that night, they had a lead of more than two laps over Chinetti and Varent. Everything seemed to be going smoothly until half-distance, when Sommer came in to the pits because the front wing had broken loose and the petrol tank had developed a leak through the constant vibration. Hasty repairs were carried out, the hole in the tank was plugged with chewing gum, and fifteen minutes later Nuvolari rejoined the race, now over a lap behind the Chinetti/Varent car. Such a deficit was nothing to a man of Nuvolari's stature and over the next few hours he set about catching and eventually overhauling the lead car. By ten o'clock on the Sunday morning – when little more than half of the field were still running – Nuvolari and Sommer led by a lap. This position was strengthened by the departure of Cortese, who rolled his car out of the race at the Esses.

Until now the chewing gum had done its job admirably, but suddenly the makeshift fuel tank repair gave way and Sommer was forced to make another unscheduled pit stop. With no satisfactory means of sealing the leak, it was evident that more stops might be necessary and so, being the faster driver, Nuvolari took the wheel in the hope that he could minimise the effect of the frequent fuel stops. How Sommer reacted to this order is not documented.

With less than an hour to go Nuvolari was barely two minutes ahead of Chinetti, but then another wretched fuel stop allowed Chinetti to take the lead. It seemed that Nuvolari's valiant efforts would be in vain. With just one lap remaining Nuvolari moved up into a challenging position and swept past Chinetti. But the latter was not about to surrender and surprised Nuvolari by regaining the lead. Then at Arnage, Chinetti, under intense pressure, missed a gear change, allowing Nuvolari through once more and he held on to win by 400 yards, the lead having changed hands three times in the final eight miles of a classic 24-hour race.

Encouragingly for the British contingent, of the thirteen finishers, they filled the next five places. Lewis and Rose-Richards were third, 287 miles ahead of a 1.1-litre Riley driven by Peacock and van der Becke. Aston Martins finished fifth and seventh, sandwiching a new 750cc MG.

But the day belonged to Nuvolari, who had broken the lap record no fewer than nine times. It is doubtful whether Sommer ever questioned the little Italian's driving skills again.

Nuvolari Versus the Germans

German Grand Prix, July 1935

By the summer of 1935 German nationalism was reaching its height. The self-styled master race could not countenance defeat in any shape or form – in the political arena, on the battlefield, or on the football pitch or running track. This sense of superiority applied equally to the motor-racing circuit, where the sleek silver Mercedes and Auto-Unions were sweeping all before them. Germany not only had the fastest cars, but also the finest drivers – men like Rudolf Caracciola, Manfred von Brauchitsch and Bernd Rosemeyer, the new sensation who, like so many of his predecessors, had risen from the ranks of motorcycling. In their spotless white overalls, the Germans appeared clinical and efficient, and their public came to view them as unbeatable.

The march to power had begun in 1934 when, after Alfa Romeo victories in Monaco and France, Mercedes and Auto-Union had carved up the rest of the season between them, notching wins in Germany, Switzerland, Italy, Spain and Czechoslovakia. They carried on the good work in 1935. Luigi Fagioli won the Monaco Grand Prix for Mercedes; Achille Varzi (Auto-Union) triumphed in Tunis; and Caracciola's Mercedes won in Tripoli, France and Belgium. Nothing was expected to stand in the way of the silver machines on home soil, and a regiment of dedicated Nazis marched 350 miles to the Nürburgring in anticipation of another German clean sweep. The line-up was headed by five Mercedes (Caracciola, Fagioli, von Brauchitsch, Hermann Lang and Hans Geier) and four Auto-Unions (Rosemeyer, Achille Varzi, Hans Stuck and Paul Pietsch). The best the Italians could muster by way of competition were three Alfa Romeo P3s, driven by Tazio Nuvolari, Louis Chiron and Antonio Brivio. But even on a circuit with 176 corners, the Alfas' 265bhp would surely be no match for the Auto-Unions' 350bhp and the Mercedes' 400bhp.

Despite the drivers' preference for starting positions on the grid to be decided by practice times, the organisers insisted on a ballot, which put the crowd favourite, Caracciola, back on the fourth row. Any spectator apprehension was quashed immediately when Caracciola, shooting off almost before the flag had fallen, stormed straight into the lead. Fagioli lay second but before the end of the first of the 22 laps had surrendered that position to the slender figure of Nuvolari who, in his familiar uniform of sky blue trousers and yellow sweater, had steered the Alfa around the outside of the pack in a daring manoeuvre. At the end of that opening lap, Caracciola sped past the pits at 170mph, followed twelve seconds later by Nuvolari who clocked 150mph, and Fagioli close up in third. On the second lap it was Rosemeyer's turn to force his way through the field, relegating Nuvolari to fifth behind Caracciola, Rosemeyer, Fagioli and von Brauchitsch. Soon Chiron passed Nuvolari and moved up to fourth when Rosemeyer had to stop for a wheel change. But by lap five both Chiron and Brivio had retired, with transmission trouble and a broken differential respectively, leaving Nuvolari alone against the might of the Germans.

The situation certainly seemed to appeal to the little Italian, who took the fight to the Germans in inspirational fashion. By oversteering round each corner in a four-wheel drift (a technique which he pioneered), Nuvolari was able to gain precious seconds and work his way back up through the field. By lap ten only Caracciola remained ahead, but even he could not hold off the irresistible Nuvolari who, to the horror of the German crowd, swept past him into the lead. Then came the high drama of the race. At the end of the eleventh lap – half-distance – the leading five cars came into the pits to refuel and change wheels. Von Brauchitsch got away in 47 seconds but in the Alfa pit a pumping device broke and, amid much panic, the refuelling operation had to be completed by hand with a funnel. Excitable at the best of times, Nuvolari went spare and, in his frustration, downed an entire bottle of mineral water, pausing only to swear at his hapless mechanics. The stop took a calamitous 2min 14sec and when he eventually rejoined the race, Nuvolari had fallen back to sixth. It was nothing short of a disaster.

The efforts of von Brauchitsch's pit crew had hoisted him into the lead from Caracciola, Rosemeyer and Fagioli, but Nuvolari quickly began to make up some of the lost ground and in the course of one lap – the thirteenth – he passed Stuck, Fagioli, Caracciola and Rosemeyer to rise to second place, just 69 seconds in arrears. Von Brauchitsch responded by setting a new lap record of 10min 30sec and by fourteen laps had increased his advantage to 1min 26sec. He then appeared to ease off in the belief that victory was a foregone conclusion, and this enabled Nuvolari to make renewed inroads into the lead, cutting it back lap by lap – to 63 seconds, then 47, 43 and, starting the final circuit, 35. Such a lead should still have been sufficient for the German to take the chequered flag in first place, but as he passed the pits he could be seen pointing frantically at his left-side rear tyre. The same tyre had begun to show alarming signs of wear at the start of the previous lap, but Mercedes team boss Alfred Neubauer had overridden his mechanics' pleas to bring von Brauchitsch in for a tyre change. 'Brauchitsch will make it,' he snapped, 'and so will the tyre. It's only a question of a few minutes.' The tyre didn't make it. Coming out of a corner less than six miles from the finish, the Mercedes' tyre collapsed. Von Brauchitsch skilfully managed to retain control but could do nothing more than grind home slowly on the rim. Nuvolari swept past imperiously to win what the world's press described as 'a historic triumph of man over machine'. Stuck was nearly two minutes behind in second with Caracciola, who later complained of having felt unwell during the race, third, Rosemeyer fourth and von Brauchitsch fifth.

The 250,000-strong crowd were stunned by this blow to German supremacy. The loudspeakers, which had been prepared to announce another German victory, remained ominously silent. The organisers eventually conducted a search for the Italian flag, which was then half-heartedly raised but without the accompaniment of the Italian national anthem, for the simple reason that nobody had bothered to bring the record. Except Nuvolari, that is. He always carried a record of the anthem in his suitcase for good luck, so he sent his mechanic to fetch it and the spectators were finally able to listen to the least popular tune in Germany that afternoon. It must have been a bitter pill to swallow, but for Nuvolari it was probably his finest hour. One of motor-racing's strangest races was also one of its greatest.

An Encounter With a Stag
Donington Grand Prix, October 1938

In an era when motor-racing had a disturbingly high mortality rate, most drivers regarded serious injury – or worse – as an occupational hazard. But few treated it in quite as cavalier a fashion as Tazio Nuvolari. From the moment he first arrived on the scene on two wheels back in the 1920s, the Italian ace had made it clear that in the event of a pre-race accident, only a formal death certificate was likely to prevent him competing. Doctors despaired of him. A crash in the 1925 Italian Grand Prix at Monza put him in hospital, where he was swathed in bandages like an Egyptian mummy. Yet seven days later he took part in a motorcycle race, having persuaded medics to bandage him in such a manner that he could be placed on his machine in a riding posture.

Having moved up to four wheels on a regular basis, he broke a leg at Alessandria in 1934 when his Maserati skidded into a tree on the wet road. After four weeks in hospital as the world's most impatient patient, Nuvolari defied the advice of the doctors and entered to drive a Maserati in the Avus Grand Prix in Germany. He had the pedals of the car specially adapted so that all three could be operated with one foot (the other still being in plaster), and before the race he was presented by a local gymnastic club with a chunk of the tree which he had hit in Alessandria. The inscription read: 'To Tazio Nuvolari, intrepid ace of the wheel as a record of the providential obstacle which though

preventing a sure victory saved a precious existence.' The
sight of him hobbling out on crutches for practice sessions
and having to be helped in to and out of the cockpit must
have done wonders for his opponents' confidence but,
despite being plagued by cramp, he managed to finish a
gallant fifth. The fourth-placed Earl Howe said of
Nuvolari's drive: 'Let any who say it was foolhardy at least
be honest and admit it was one of the finest exhibitions of
pluck and grit ever seen. By such men are victories won!'

Two years later, while Nuvolari was practising for the
Tripoli Grand Prix, a wheel of his Alfa Romeo caught a
marker stone at over 125mph. The tyre burst, the car
turned over and ended up in the sand which bordered the
circuit. For his part, Nuvolari was flung into the air like a
doll and landed in a heap of parched grass. Helpers who
rushed to the scene found the smoking car but no sign of its
driver until, ten minutes later, the stricken Nuvolari was
located deep in the grass, lying unconscious with damaged
ribs and severe bruising. In hospital he was put into plaster
and ordered to rest for several days. 'But of course,' came
the reply. 'After the race I shall do so!' The next day,
although scarcely able to move in his plaster corset, he
drove a replacement Alfa into seventh place. It was the
stuff of which legends are made.

The Donington Grand Prix had first attracted the mighty
German teams in 1937 and had proved such a success
(Bernd Rosemeyer winning in an Auto-Union) that they
returned in force to the tree-lined Leicestershire circuit for
the 1938 race. It was scheduled to be the last major event of
the season, listed for 2 October, but when the German
teams arrived a week earlier to start practice, they found
themselves slap in the middle of the Munich crisis. In case
war was about to break out, the Germans hurried home and
the race was cancelled, but once Chamberlain had returned
with his promise of 'peace for our time', the contest was
rearranged for 22 October and the Germans returned.

Three days before the race the 45-year-old Nuvolari took his Auto-Union out for a practice session. That he was now at the wheel of a German car was the result of a considerable fall-out with his Italian employers. He was approximately halfway round the circuit when a huge stag emerged from some woods and ran straight across the track, ploughing into Nuvolari's car. Nuvolari stopped 200 yards further on and limped back to attend to the animal which was lying in a pool of blood. Back at the pits ambulance men were worried by Nuvolari's non-appearance and so they drove off to search for him. They found him stroking the dead stag. 'You cannot take anyone to the hospital,' he said gravely, 'not even this unfortunate one. He died on the spot.' In fact Nuvolari was in need of hospital treatment, having fractured a rib in the collision, but he no longer wanted to be bothered with doctors and nurses. He was not prepared to risk being told he could not drive in the race. Instead he asked for the stag to be taken away and prepared himself for the race. After persuading the organisers to agree to his request to have the stag's head stuffed and mounted, he got out his lucky corset, which he had improvised for himself using tight bandages, and set out to thrill the British public in the same way that he had captivated spectators all over mainland Europe.

In the absence of Rudolf Caracciola, who had burnt his foot during the Italian Grand Prix and in any case was said not to like Donington as a circuit, Hermann Lang took pole in a Mercedes from Nuvolari, Manfred von Brauchitsch in a second Mercedes and the great British hope, Richard Seaman, in a third. Near the back of the grid was an ERA driven by band-leader Billy Cotton. A crowd of 60,000 turned up to watch the Duke of Kent start the 80-lap race with a Union Jack. From the off, Nuvolari shot into the lead from his Auto-Union team-mate Hermann Müller and the Mercedes trio of von Brauchitsch, Seaman and Lang, and stayed at the head of affairs until lap 20 when he went into

the pits for a change of plugs. Emerging in fourth spot
behind Müller, Seaman and Lang, Nuvolari was about to
lap Hanson's Alta when the tail-ender dropped a sump full
of oil on the descent to the hairpin. Nuvolari picked his way
through the hazard but Seaman was not as fortunate and
spun off the road, promoting Nuvolari to third. He was still
third after the mid-race refuelling stops but Lang had now
taken over pole position from Müller. Driving with typical
verve and flair and, according to contemporary reports, a
huge grin on his face, Nuvolari proceeded to reel in the
front two. He passed Müller and on lap 67 overtook Lang
for a lead he was never to relinquish. Showing no ill effects
from his severely restricted movement, he pulled away to
win by 32 seconds from Lang, Seaman, Müller and von
Brauchitsch.

Nuvolari received a rapturous welcome from all except
some of the serious punters in the bookmakers' enclosure.
They had torn up their tickets when he had looked to be
out of the race following his practice accident and now
they were furious with themselves. Two days after
crossing the finish line the 'Maestro', as he was known,
was presented with the Grand Prix trophy along with the
mounted stag's head, which he intended to take with him
to other tracks as a lucky mascot. It would be another
sixteen years before a German Grand Prix car would
again race on English soil, but in the meantime Nuvolari's
epic drive under unbelievably difficult circumstances
would provide a lasting memory through the dark days of
the Second World War.

Hell in Buenos Aires

Argentine Grand Prix, January 1955

With echoes of the energy-sapping 1926 European Grand Prix, this race was run in unbearably hot conditions. At the start of the three-hour ordeal, the temperature in the shade at Buenos Aires stood at 100 degrees Fahrenheit while ground temperatures exceeded a staggering 125 degrees. Only the strong or the acclimatised could hope to survive and in the event only two drivers – Juan Manuel Fangio and Roberto Mieres – were able to last the distance. Not surprisingly, both were Argentinians. Everyone else either gave up altogether or had to stop at some point for a rest, enabling a fresher driver to take over, so that in the course of the 96-lap race there were sixteen driver substitutions among the 21 starters and more than 50 pit stops.

Froilan Gonzales put his Ferrari on pole, and back on the third row was up-and-coming British driver Stirling Moss, new to Mercedes-Benz for 1955, having been with Maserati. There was a typically mad rush into the first bend and when things sorted themselves out at the end of the opening lap Fangio's Mercedes had a slender advantage over Alberto Ascari (Lancia), Moss, Gonzales and Nino Farina (Ferrari). On the second lap a multiple crash involving Jean Behra and Karl Kling reduced the number of participants to sixteen, and on the following lap Ascari moved to the front, only to be overtaken soon after by Gonzales. The battle between Ascari and Gonzales raged until lap 22, when Ascari spun on a patch of oil and crashed into the fence.

As early as quarter-distance, drivers were coming into the pits in a state of extreme fatigue. After Ascari's retirement, Gonzales stopped for a rest, his car being taken over by Farina who himself had been relieved a matter of a few laps earlier by the Ferrari spare driver, Umberto Maglioli. When Farina soon found the going too tough, he was replaced for a time by Maurice Trintignant who, in a distinction shared with Behra, would go on to drive three different cars in the race. Meanwhile Moss retired on lap 30, too exhausted to continue, and abandoned his Mercedes at the side of the track. Four laps later Fangio, the new leader, stopped for refreshment and the welcome opportunity to pour cold water over himself. The delay allowed Harry Schell's Maserati to seize the initiative but soon the American, too, was affected by the heat and was substituted by Behra. Mieres had a stint in front until he was kept in the pits for ten minutes with fuel pump problems.

It was so hot in the stands that halfway through the race all of the soft drinks supplies had run out, forcing parched spectators to buy wine bottles filled with tap water which were brought in by an emergency fleet of lorries from the surrounding area. An indication of the debilitating nature of the heat was that one Ferrari actually had five different drivers, the car standing idle in the pits for an entire lap because none of the drivers was fit enough to take the wheel. Finally it was Gonzales who, after a prolonged rest and an injection to alleviate back pain, climbed into the cockpit, earning the nickname of 'Cabezon' (the stubborn one) from his home crowd.

Gonzales resumed the struggle a considerable distance behind Fangio but began closing at the rate of five seconds per lap. Fangio was now on the brink of collapse himself and on more than one occasion contemplated giving up. He later recalled: 'Once or twice I felt as if my Mercedes-Benz had caught fire. I turned right round to look, but there was nothing to be seen. It must have been the wind carrying the hot air from below the car, and up round the cockpit to burn my shoulder and neck.' A few laps from the finish Mercedes team boss Alfred Neubauer signalled to Fangio to come into the pits to hand over the car to Moss, who was now suitably refreshed by a shower, but Fangio pretended not to understand and pressed on. He kept going by imagining that he was lost in the snow. His predicament was helped by an accident to Gonzales who pressed so hard that he spun off, bending the Ferrari's front suspension. He was more than happy to hand the car back to Farina, who drove on to the finish. With one supreme last effort, Fangio came home almost two minutes ahead of the Gonzales/Farina/ Trintignant/Gonzales/Farina Ferrari with the Farina/ Maglioli/Trintignant/Maglioli Ferrari in third. When it came to the prize-giving, Fangio was so tired he could hardly stand. It had been that sort of a race.

Helping Hands

Italian Grand Prix, September 1956

The 1956 Formula One World Drivers' Championship all boiled down to the last race of the season, at Monza. The destiny of the title lay between two men with hitherto contrasting careers – Juan Manuel Fangio, the brilliant Argentinian who had been world champion in each of the past two seasons, and Peter Collins, the young British driver who was just beginning to make his mark in Formula One. Fangio had won that year in Argentina, Britain and Germany, while Collins had triumphed in Belgium and France. Under the complicated points scoring system of the time, which took into account a driver's best five finishes, Fangio had 30 points from his best five. In order to add to his total, he had to finish first or second at the Italian Grand Prix. Going into that race, Collins had 22 points from four finishes. So if he were to win at Monza, set fastest lap (which earned an extra point) and Fangio were to finish outside the first two, Collins would snatch the title by 31 points to 30. There was everything to play for.

To complicate matters, Fangio and Collins were team-mates at Lancia-Ferrari. In the absence of Mercedes, who had withdrawn from Formula One in the wake of the 1955 Le Mans tragedy, Lancia-Ferrari had swept virtually all before them in 1956 and Monza looked like being no exception. Fangio took pole position from team-mates Eugenio Castellotti and Luigi Musso, but Collins could do no better than row three. Before the race Fangio had expressed concern about tyre wear, believing that it was the only thing that stood between his team and victory. He suggested to Castellotti and Musso that they carve up the race between them. Fangio offered to set the pace and then towards the finish, to allow the other two through to fight out victory. Fangio was perfectly content with third place so long as Collins wasn't in with a chance of winning. Fangio hoped that the idea of tucking in behind him and thereby conserving their tyres for much of the race would appeal to the two Italians but they wanted no part of it, preferring to go their own way.

As the flag fell, Fangio moved smoothly into the lead but was passed almost immediately by Musso and Castellotti, who seemed to be treating the race as one of five laps rather than 50. Their pace was suicidal and after just five laps, exactly as Fangio had predicted, both dived into the pits with their tyres in shreds, leaving the front four as Fangio, Stirling Moss in a Maserati 250F, Collins, and Harry Schell in a Vanwall. Further down the field, Jo Bonnier, in his first championship race, had taken over Luigi Villoresi's Maserati after four laps but had to retire himself just three laps later with valve trouble. And on lap six the Marquis de Portago's Lancia-Ferrari slid dramatically down the banking after losing a tyre and quit the race with a bent suspension.

Back at the sharp end, Castellotti lost another tyre on lap nine and retired after spinning wildly into the barrier, and two laps later Collins had to stop for a new tyre when lying in fourth. Then on lap nineteen, sensation. Fangio pulled into the pits with a broken steering arm. The damage could be repaired but the delay would wreck any chance Fangio had of winning the race. The pit signall⌐ for Musso, who had moved up to third, to come in hand over his car to Fangio so that the champⁱ quest could be resumed, but Musso ign⌐ instruction and drove on. Eventually, after fo⌐

been lost, Castellotti drove away in Fangio's repaired car, there being no point in Fangio returning to the fray so far adrift. As each lap passed the Argentinian could see his title hopes disappearing a little further. A world champion without a car.

Moss was now in the lead and pulling away from Schell. By half-distance the Englishman's advantage was thirteen seconds. On lap 28 Schell stopped to refuel, promoting Musso to second, but two laps later Musso came in for a tyre check. Everyone expected that Fangio would take over, but Musso insisted on continuing. To Fangio's credit, he bore no malice.

Collins managed to get past Schell (who then retired on lap 32 with transmission trouble) and was still in third place on lap 35 when he came in for a tyre check. With Fangio seemingly out of the running, Collins had a very real chance of taking the title but when asked by Fangio's manager if he would consider handing his car over to the world champion, Collins did not hesitate. He jumped out of the cockpit, allowing Fangio to inherit third place. Fangio threw his arms around Collins in sheer exuberance and gratitude and sped off, hell-bent on making the most of his good fortune. Moss was still half a lap ahead of Musso until on lap 45 he ran out of fuel on the back straight. As the car slowed to around 120mph, Moss spotted Luigi Piotti's privately entered Maserati coming up behind in seventh place and gestured to the Italian to give him a shove. The compliant Piotti tucked in behind Moss and proceeded to nudge the works Maserati round the curve to the pits, where Moss was able to refuel!

Moss rejoined in second place behind Musso but with only a ten-second margin over Fangio. Three laps from the finish, however, the steering arm on Musso's car broke as he was exiting the banking and he coasted to a halt in front of the pits. Despite a tyre that was almost bald, Moss held ff Fangio's challenge to win by 5.7 seconds.

Moss took the race, Fangio the title, both having received a helping hand in different ways. Afterwards, track officials tried to disqualify Moss because he had been given a push, but Moss protested that Piotti was his team-mate and was therefore permitted to give him a push. In fact, Piotti was a privateer, but the officials swallowed the argument and allowed Moss's victory to stand. As for Collins, was his decision to throw away the chance of the championship an illustration of supreme sportsmanship or sheer stupidity? Collins tried to explain it away by saying that Fangio deserved the title and hinted that he (Collins) would never have been able to cope with the adulation anyway. Whether that would have been the case, we were never to know. For two years later, Collins was killed at the German Grand Prix before ever realising the chance to be world champion.

The Final Push

United States Grand Prix, December 1959

The final race of the 1959 Formula One season was the United States Grand Prix at Sebring, Florida – the first time that race had counted towards the World Drivers' Championship. Going into it, three drivers still had a chance of winning the title – Jack Brabham (in the revolutionary, rear-engined Cooper-Climax), Stirling Moss (Cooper-Climax) and Tony Brooks (Ferrari). With the best five finishes from the nine races counting, Brabham was six points ahead of Moss and eight ahead of Brooks, but the permutations were such that Moss could snatch the championship with a win and a fastest lap (provided Brabham didn't finish second) and Brooks could tie with the Australian if he won and Brabham failed to score.

During qualifying Brabham was unhappy with his car and decided to swap with his team-mate, 22-year-old New Zealander Bruce McLaren. But this car also needed some fine tuning and Brabham and the mechanics were up until one o'clock on the morning of the race. Grid position was all-important, but here the colourful American Harry Schell threw a spanner into the works by recording what appeared to be an unfeasibly fast time in his very moderate Cooper. Rumours circulated that he had taken a short cut along the back stretch of the bland airfield circuit, but Schell pleaded his innocence. His time of 3min 5.2sec (the third fastest, just ahead of Brooks) seemed too good to be true and Ferrari, who naturally wanted Brooks on the three-car front row, immediately protested. After much argument, Schell insisted on taking his place on the front row alongside Moss and Brabham, thereby relegating Brooks to the second rank. Ferrari were not happy.

The race was to be run over 42 laps (218 miles), and as the flag fell Brabham roared into the lead, only to be quickly passed by Moss. On the first lap Taffy von Trips accidentally rammed his Ferrari team-mate Brooks going into a corner and both went off. This was not the start Ferrari wanted and, after coming into the pits for a precautionary check, Brooks rejoined in a lowly fifteenth. Of course, if Brooks had been allowed to start on the front row he would, in all probability, have been well clear of von Trips, who started from row three. But for the time being, speculation could wait for another day.

By the fifth lap Moss had increased his lead to ten seconds but the next time round he coasted to a halt with a broken transmission. It would not be the first or the last time that Moss would stand accused of wrecking a car by setting off too quickly, but more important than the whys or the wherefores was the fact that he was now out of the championship equation. Brabham and McLaren proceeded to pull well clear with the race – and the title – seemingly sewn up. By the end of lap 24 there were only seven cars still running. Brooks did his utmost to make up the lost ground, but the deficit was too great and he was left languishing over a minute behind the leading pair in fifth. Although the race appeared to be in his pocket, Brabham was taking no chances and let McLaren slipstream him so that if anything should happen to the leading car, the New Zealander could take over at the front and still beat Brooks to the finish.

Starting the final lap, less than five seconds separated the front three of Brabham, McLaren and Maurice Trintignant, also in a Cooper. Then about a mile from the finish and with victory almost in sight, Brabham's car suddenly began to run on two cylinders. The engine went dead. He was out of fuel. McLaren slowed in sympathy, but Brabham frantically waved him on, fearing that Brooks might somehow snatch an unlikely win. McLaren got the message. Trintignant sped past moments afterwards as Brabham's car crawled around the track, eventually grinding to a complete halt some 500 yards from the finish. He took off his helmet and goggles, climbed out of the car and started to push. 'Why must home straights always be uphill?' he later lamented.

With McLaren and Trintignant already finished, the crowd wondered anxiously what had happened to Brabham. All eyes looked down the track. Then in the distance they spotted a hunched figure in blue overalls pushing his car up the straight. Brooks flashed by to take third and Brabham inched slowly but surely towards the line, encouraged in his efforts by the man waving the chequered flag. Police on motorcycles kept back the excited spectators, who were all too eager to give the weary Australian a helping hand which would probably have resulted in his disqualification. As Brabham himself remarked: 'It must have been the first time the new world champion was escorted to the line by a motorcycle escort.' After five minutes of pushing, he made it across the line and slumped to the ground in exhaustion . . . safe in the knowledge that he had won the World Championship by four points. It was a most unusual end to a season.

Punch-up at the Palace

Shell Formula Three Championship, Round Eleven, October 1970

By 1970 James Hunt had only been racing for three years, but in that time he had already earned a reputation as someone whom trouble seemed to follow around. His proposed debut, at Snetterton in 1967, came to nought after he was refused permission to race because his Mini had no windows. Two years later he had worked his way up to Formula Ford but was prevented from taking part in a European Championship race at Vallelunga in Italy because he did not have the necessary medical certificate. His reaction was to sabotage the start of the race by deliberately parking his car at right angles across the front of the grid! As controversy continued to dog his every move, a fellow competitor's mother remarked that Hunt always carried £5 on him in those days so that he had enough money for a protest. He was never one to shrink away from confrontation.

But by 1970 he had entered the ranks of Formula Three and was making people sit up and take notice for the right reasons. Competing in the Shell Formula Three Championship, he had scored points in five of the ten rounds, including a second at Oulton Park and a third at Cadwell Park. In between he had also posted his second major Formula Three win, in a non-championship race at Zolder in Belgium. So his star was definitely in the ascendant when he came to the compact Crystal Palace circuit in South London for round eleven, the penultimate race in the series.

Driving a Lotus 59, Hunt finished second in his heat, thereby qualifying for the final. With BBC *Grandstand* cameras covering the event, there was huge anticipation that the drivers would put on a memorable show for the armchair audience. Hunt made sure the TV viewers got more than they bargained for.

Australian David Walker, lying second in the championship, took the race by the scruff of the neck and so the main interest centred on the six-car battle for second place, which included Hunt's Lotus and a March 703 driven by Dave Morgan. Approaching the last corner on the penultimate lap, the two cars were virtually abreast but Hunt appeared to have the better line. However Morgan refused to yield, with the result that the pair collided, the Lotus ending up in the middle of the track and the March embedded in the pit wall, both minus one wheel. Hunt exploded, leapt from his car, rushed over to Morgan and lunged at him, aiming a punch which, perhaps fortunately for both parties, missed by a country mile. Morgan recalled: 'The silly arse leapt out of his car and ran across the track, all these racing cars coming past him. I was amazed he wasn't run over. I was trying to undo my helmet and as he turned to punch me I lost my balance and fell so he missed. Then other people got hold of him and dragged him off.'

Autosport wrote that 'a justifiably enraged Hunt felled Morgan in the heat of the moment' but *Motor Sport* adopted a less partisan line, reporting: 'A stewards' enquiry was convened but by then Hunt had regrettably resorted to fisticuffs to settle his differences. This is very much against the spirit of camaraderie which exists in motor racing and was greatly deplored.'

Hunt was widely pilloried over his latest transgression by people who saw him as a hot-headed upstart who was bringing the sport into disrepute. Hunt protested his innocence and at the subsequent RAC tribunal, which both drivers were summoned to attend, he produced BBC footage of the incident. This clearly showed that his car had not hit Morgan's first. Furthermore three other drivers testified that, in their opinion, Morgan had overtaken in a dangerous manner. Consequently the outcome of the tribunal was that Hunt was exonerated and Morgan was banned for a year.

For Hunt at least, the punch-up at the Palace had a happy ending. But it would by no means be his last brush with authority.

Hunt's Flag Day

British Grand Prix, July 1976

Feelings were running high in the build-up to the 1976 British Grand Prix courtesy of a simmering feud between Ferrari and McLaren which was about to boil over. The bad blood had started at the Spanish Grand Prix earlier in the season, when James Hunt's apparently victorious McLaren had been disqualified two hours after the race for exceeding the maximum allowable car width by 18mm. The Ferrari number one, Niki Lauda, was awarded the race but two months later, on appeal, Hunt was reinstated as the winner. This controversial decision met with a frosty reception from Ferrari, not least because it cut Lauda's lead over Hunt in the World Drivers' Championship to 27 points – 52 to 25. The British Grand Prix at Brands Hatch was the next race on the calendar.

The year 1976 saw the long, hot summer when the British public basked in unexpectedly high temperatures and found a new sporting hero in 28-year-old Hunt, the dashing blond bombshell with the film-star looks and the aristocratic accent. Hunt had acquitted himself creditably with the Hesketh team over the previous three seasons but this was the year which really catapulted him into the big time. Lauda was his friend and great rival, so it was fitting that the pair lined up alongside each other on the front row at Brands as the season reached its halfway point. The second rank was made up of Mario Andretti's Lotus and Clay Regazzoni's Ferrari. Having qualified on pole, Lauda chose to start from the left side of the track, thereby avoiding the steep camber of the opening right-hander, Paddock Hill Bend.

Lauda got away well but Hunt missed a beat, enabling Regazzoni to fly past from the second row and attack his team-mate at Paddock. It was a bold but misguided assault, one which saw the two Ferraris touch wheels. Regazzoni spun, Hunt veered left to avoid him but hit the sliding Ferrari. The McLaren rode over the Ferrari's wheels and was launched into the air, crashing down to earth in an upright position but with the right front steering arm broken. In the midst of the mayhem Jacques Laffite crashed his Ligier into the bank. Hunt motored on slowly up the hill to Druids with one front wheel at a crazy angle and drifted down the other side towards Bottom Straight. He thought he was out of the race until he saw red flags indicating that proceedings had been stopped, so he turned off the track on to a little back road that led to the pits. As a crowd gathered around, Hunt climbed out and asked the mechanics to push the McLaren to the pit.

Half an hour later it was announced that the race would restart as if the first lap had not occurred, but that no car would be allowed to take part in the rerun if it had failed to complete the first lap. Additionally, no spare cars would be permitted to start. When the crowd heard that Hunt and, to a lesser extent, Regazzoni and Laffite, would be excluded, there was uproar. The McLaren spare car was wheeled on to the grid and as Hunt climbed into it, the bulk of the 77,000 crowd started to boo and whistle at the stewards. The slow handclap started up and some frustrated spectators threw beer cans on to the track. Hunt later remarked: 'It soon became clear that the organisers were going to allow me to start because if they didn't, they would have a riot on their hands!' In a miraculous change of heart, the stewards did indeed suddenly rule that Hunt could start after all because his car had been mobile when the race had been stopped. And the issue of the spare car no longer applied since in the intervening period between the original crash and the restart, the McLaren mechanics had managed to repair the front suspension of Hunt's race car. So he got into that while Regazzoni and Laffite used their training cars.

In the restarted race Hunt sat behind Lauda for 45 of the 76 laps until he took the Austrian at Druids. With the Ferrari slowed by gear trouble, Hunt pulled away to win by a minute but even as he stood on the victory podium, moves were afoot to snatch away his moment of glory. Ferrari, Tyrrell and Copersucar all objected to Hunt's win on the grounds that his car hadn't technically been running when the original race was halted. Tyrrell and Copersucar subsequently withdrew their objections but Ferrari held firm.

Ferrari's appeal against the result was heard two months later. The McLaren hierarchy knew they were on to a loser when Lauda, having climbed out of his deathbed following his dreadful crash at the Nürburgring, was wheeled in by Ferrari swathed in bandages. Ferrari claimed that Hunt had abandoned his car, that the mechanics had pushed it with the race still in progress and that the McLaren would have been incapable of completing that first lap anyway. McLaren countered that Hunt had only stopped on seeing the red flag. Even though video evidence was produced to show that Hunt was still driving at the time, the FIA ruled that he hadn't actually been taking part in the race when it was stopped, and disqualified him. Lauda had won the sympathy vote, the general feeling being that Hunt's disqualification was to appease Ferrari following his reinstatement in Spain. It was a severe blow to Hunt's title aspirations. But the season was by no means over yet.

A Falling-out Among Friends

San Marino Grand Prix, April 1982

The 1982 San Marino Grand Prix was shrouded in controversy even before the start. Most of the British FOCA teams boycotted the event in protest at the disqualification of Nelson Piquet's Brabham and Keke Rosberg's Williams from the top two places in the Brazilian Grand Prix for brake water-cooling irregularities. As a result only fourteen cars stood on the grid at Imola – Ferrari, Renault, Alfa Romeo, Tyrrell (who were only competing because they were sponsored by an Italian washing-machine company), ATS, Osella and Toleman. Despite the fanatical support of the home crowd, the Ferraris of Gilles Villeneuve and Didier Pironi were unable to compete with the Renaults driven by René Arnoux and Alain Prost. Arnoux took pole with Prost half a second slower. Villeneuve and Pironi were third and fourth on the grid, separated by 1.4 seconds, Pironi having survived a hairy high-speed accident during qualifying which saw him fly backwards into a barrier. There is no rule that says that team-mates have to get on – indeed most drivers regard their team-mate as their fiercest rival – but the Ferrari pair got on better than most. Both were highly talented drivers. Pironi was determined and resourceful while Villeneuve was fearless and flamboyant, a throwback to the likes of Nuvolari. Villeneuve was by nature a trusting guy, and he trusted Pironi. On the evening before the race the two men had dinner together with their wives. All was sweetness and light.

Come the off and Arnoux was first away, pursued by
Prost, but the latter was passed by the two Ferraris before
the end of the opening lap, and when Prost retired with
piston failure on lap seven, the leading three were the only
serious contenders. The trio were separated by less than a
second when, on lap 44 out of 60, Arnoux was forced to
retire, his car belching out smoke. This left the Ferraris to
win as they pleased, the only threat, apart from some
unforeseen mechanical problem, being fuel consumption,
since Imola was the thirstiest circuit in Formula One.
Villeneuve now assumed the mantle of leader. Eager to
conserve fuel, he eased off for a few laps and did not worry
when Pironi passed him. The French-Canadian soon
regained first place. To the crowd, the pair were simply
putting on a show to liven up what might otherwise have
turned into a dreary procession.

However, the Ferrari pit, which was without team
leader Mauro Forghieri (absent on family business),
became concerned that this constant jousting was drinking
up the fuel, of which there was only just enough to see them
through to the finish even at normal levels of consumption.
So they ordered Villeneuve to slow, and he immediately
responded by easing off to the tune of two seconds per lap.
Ferrari team orders were that the man ahead when the red
cars became first and second (in this case Villeneuve)
should be the man ahead at the finish. Villeneuve clearly
understood that and, backing off as ordered, was not
unduly perturbed when Pironi put on a sudden spurt to
overtake him again seven laps from the finish. This time
the lead was not so easy to retake. On lap 58, Villeneuve
drew alongside his team-mate under braking at the right-
hander known as Tosa, only to be unceremoniously cut off.
But on the following lap, Pironi did let him past. As far as
Villeneuve was concerned, that was that. Pironi's antics
had been nothing more than showmanship and now the
pair would cruise around for a stress-free one-two. Then as

they headed down towards Tosa for the last time at a conservative 180mph, Pironi suddenly shot past on the approach to the corner, catching Villeneuve totally unawares. The two cars nearly touched. Since that was the last overtaking point on the track, there was no opportunity for Villeneuve to retaliate, and it was Pironi who crossed the line the winner of the 1982 San Marino Grand Prix.

Pironi stood on the victory rostrum waving happily to the crowd but next to him Villeneuve had a face like thunder. He didn't want to be there at all and had to be persuaded by his wife to appear before the Imola fans. As soon as the ceremony was over, Villeneuve stormed away from the circuit without saying a word to Pironi. In Villeneuve's opinion, Pironi had stolen the race in an act of treachery. Pironi pleaded his innocence and expressed the hope that he hadn't upset his team-mate, but Villeneuve did not appear interested in platitudes. He told reporters: 'The first two or three times he came inside and passed, I thought, well, he wants to play a little bit, and I never defended myself. But him, he was just racing, and I was too stupid to realise it. I thought he was an honest guy . . .'

They never did make up. Villeneuve was killed while practising for the next Grand Prix at Zolder in Belgium. Some say his mind was still on Imola.

The Battle of Suzuka
Japanese Grand Prix, October 1990

To say that there was no love lost between Ayrton Senna and Alain Prost is like saying that Britain and Germany didn't get along terribly well between 1939 and 1945. Although they were McLaren team-mates for a while, they were poles apart. Senna was the wild, hot-headed Brazilian, capable of moments of genius and moments of madness. Prost was the analytical – sometimes aloof – Frenchman, nicknamed 'the Professor'. Both were great drivers, but both thought they were king of the road.

The presence of two such strong personalities in the same team may have looked good on paper but in practice it was little short of a nightmare. It was similar to having an orchestra with two conductors, and neither was happy to play second fiddle. The tension between the pair first surfaced at the 1988 Portuguese Grand Prix when Senna ruthlessly chopped Prost at 190mph as the Frenchman tried to pass. Senna took the title that year, but in 1989 Prost was ahead on points as the season entered its penultimate round in Japan. Prost needed only to finish in front of Senna to become champion for the third time. Ominously, he issued an advance warning that he was not prepared to tolerate any of the Brazilian's rough-house tactics on this occasion. He would fight fire with fire. Prost led from the start but Senna, in a typically determined drive, gradually pegged back the advantage. With ten laps remaining the cars were running nose to tail, Senna desperately searching for a hint of an opening. Six laps from the finish he thought he had found one – up the inside at the chicane. He left the braking as late as he dared and dived for the gap. Prost simply turned in on him and took both cars out of the race. Prost was champion. Each blamed the other for the collision.

For the 1990 season Prost had joined Ferrari. Again the Japanese Grand Prix at Suzuka was the penultimate round but this time the positions were reversed. With only five wins to Senna's six, Prost had to score at least one more point than Senna to keep the title battle alive going into the final race at Adelaide. More significantly, as it transpired, if neither car finished at Suzuka, Senna would be champion. Senna put the McLaren on pole with Prost alongside him, just three-tenths of a second behind. It had all the makings of a charge into the first corner. Whoever got there first would have an outstanding chance of staying there. Senna knew that, and was furious at being ordered to start from the right-hand side of the track, which was much dustier than the left. Having gained pole, he thought he had earned the right to decide where he would prefer to start from. He protested, but FISA president Jean-Marie Balestre refused to reconsider. Senna simmered and sulked. In his eyes, Prost, although only second fastest, had been given the side of the track with the superior grip. Senna made a mental note of his race plan: 'If Prost gets the best start, then I'm warning him, he'd better not turn in on me because he isn't going to make it.' It was to prove a chillingly accurate prophecy.

Race day was warm and sunny, a deceptively tranquil backdrop to the drama that was about to unfold. On the front row of the grid, the two combatants sat in their cars a matter of yards apart, waiting anxiously for the green light. When it finally came, Prost, as Senna had feared, got the better start from the cleaner side of the track. Prost, with a slight advantage, inched towards the racing line which he would need to negotiate Turn One, the Ferrari's superior power giving him a lead of almost a car's length approaching the corner. Instead of coming across and blocking Senna completely, Prost edged back a fraction towards the outside. Senna sensed a gap, albeit a minimal one, and made for it. Prost eased off slightly to take the turn but Senna kept his foot hard down and smashed into the Ferrari, taking both cars out of the race. Mission accomplished. Senna was champion.

Prost was outraged. 'I am not prepared to fight against irresponsible people who are not afraid to die,' he stormed. Senna maintained the pretence of innocence . . . at least for another year. But in the meantime the shortest championship decider in history had gone his way. Sure, it was controversial, but in Senna's book the ends always justified the means.

Schumacher Wins in the Pits
British Grand Prix, July 1998

A rain-soaked British Grand Prix at Silverstone ended in mayhem with nobody seeming to know whether Michael Schumacher or Mika Hakkinen had won. It all centred on the interpretation, delivery and timing of a ten-second penalty to Schumacher but when the fuss had died down, it emerged that the German had earned the distinction of becoming the first driver ever to win a Grand Prix in the pit lane.

After a lightning start to the season when they looked destined to sweep all before them, the wheels had come off the McLaren wagon over the previous two Grands Prix. Comprehensive defeats in Canada and France – coupled with two Schumacher successes – had put a different complexion on the championship race. After eight rounds, Schumacher was within six points of Hakkinen with Coulthard – perhaps beginning to regret his largesse in Australia – languishing fourteen points behind the German in third. Suddenly there was a real race on. Ferrari could sniff McLaren blood and their drivers, especially the outspoken Eddie Irvine, were making plenty of capital out of the Woking team's sudden vulnerability. But now McLaren were back on home soil. The British Grand Prix would be the perfect venue to answer their critics.

Hakkinen did his bit, qualifying on pole, but Coulthard was only fourth fastest – behind Schumacher and Jacques Villeneuve. Irvine and Heinz-Harald Frentzen made up row three. Hakkinen was cautiously optimistic but the weather forecast for Sunday's race was heavy rain, and Schumacher was the acknowledged rain-master.

Hakkinen and Schumacher both made good starts but Villeneuve was away slowly and found himself behind Coulthard and the Sauber of Jean Alesi, who gained four places from his grid position. Irvine also made a poor start and things looked grim for Ferrari when Coulthard eased past Schumacher at Abbey Curve. After a dozen laps light rain began to fall and when it became increasingly persistent, the cars started a mad scramble for the pits. Some didn't make it in time. To the dismay of the crowd, Damon Hill spun off on lap fourteen and was followed two laps later by Frentzen. Only Hakkinen of the leading bunch moved on to wet tyres, the rest opting for intermediates. Coulthard made steady inroads into his team-mate's advantage until the rain suddenly started to get heavier around lap 26. Soon Johnny Herbert and Mika Salo (Arrows) went off and Esteban Tuero's Minardi was involved in a shunt with Ricardo Rosset's Tyrrell. Coulthard, in particular, was struggling in the wet conditions and spun three times in quick succession, finally exiting the race on lap 38. He later expressed his anger at being put on intermediates while Hakkinen had the benefit of wets.

The rain had now reached monsoon level, resulting in further casualties including Rubens Barrichello (Stewart), Olivier Panis (Prost) and Pedro Diniz (Arrows). Even Hakkinen went off on to the grass at Bridge Corner but managed to keep going. Conditions were so treacherous that the yellow flags were brought out, but while lapping the Benetton of Alexander Wurz, Schumacher failed to spot the flags and passed the Austrian. Moments later the safety car appeared. In an instant Hakkinen saw his 38-second lead over Schumacher reduced to nothing. To make matters worse, the McLaren had not emerged unscathed from its excursion on to the grass, although Hakkinen was unsure as to the extent of the damage. Six laps later the rain had eased sufficiently for the safety car to withdraw. Almost immediately Hakkinen went off at Becketts and Schumacher swept through into the lead.

But behind the scenes there was high drama. Schumacher had been awarded a ten-second penalty for passing Wurz under the yellow flags, but the Silverstone stewards took 31 minutes to notify Ferrari of the decision when the rules state that it should be delivered within 25 minutes of the offending incident. Moreover, the piece of paper handed to Ferrari sporting director Jean Todt was, at best, ambiguous and, at worst, illegible. Ferrari were unsure whether it was a stop-go penalty, which would necessitate Schumacher coming into the pits for ten seconds before rejoining the race, or if the ten seconds was simply to be added to his final time. In the absence of any clarification from the stewards, Ferrari let Schumacher continue on his way and then brought him in for the penalty at the end of the final lap, by which time he had a 20-second lead over Hakkinen. So at the end of the 60th and last lap, Schumacher came into the Ferrari pit, which was beyond the finish line, and served his ten-second penalty, this being added to his overall time. He thus won the British Grand Prix while stationary.

Not that any of the soaked crowd had any idea who had won at that point, for it was some time before it filtered through that Schumacher had officially been declared the winner. McLaren protested, arguing that as the yellow flag incident had occurred twelve laps before the finish the transgressor was supposed to sit out the ten seconds in the pit in a stop-go penalty rather than have them added to his time. However, the protest was rejected since the delay was deemed to be the fault of the stewards rather than Ferrari.

So Schumacher kept the race. Hakkinen's championship lead was down to two points. Game on.

The Shed, the Bed and the Boot

Donington Park Wacky Races, August 1999

In the summer of 1997 the *Sun* newspaper came up with the idea of staging an alternative British Grand Prix for bizarre customised vehicles. But what started out as a spoof has developed into a proper race, held annually at Donington Park's August Bank Holiday meeting.

The 1999 event was so popular that it had to be divided into two classes – road-going and non-road-going. The second category attracted no fewer than ten entries, including a motorised garden shed, a four-poster bed, a roller boot, a sofa, a giant orange, and a toilet and bath combination.

The shed was the brainchild of Derbyshire farmer George Shields, who originally built it in 1997 as a practical joke for a friend's wedding. 'I couldn't find the pony and trap he wanted,' said Shields, 'so I decided to make some transport of my own. My friend thought his stag party had finished the night before. Little did he know he was going to show up at the church in a garden shed!' The Shields machine, which held the distinction of being the only garden building ever to have completed the journey from John O'Groats to Land's End under its own steam, consisted of a quad bike engine underneath and a six-by-four garden shed on top, complete with five hanging baskets. It had a top speed of 55mph and did 50 miles to the gallon. 'Where to put the exhaust pipe was a bit of a problem,' he admitted, 'but I got it to go out of the door. The whole conversion is really comfortable, with a big cushion on the seat. It's very noisy and smelly to drive, but that's OK because there is a television and radio inside. And it doesn't like corners much – especially at 55mph.'

Race organiser Edd China had three entries – the sofa, the toilet and bath, and the four-poster bed. The bed, welded to a 1,600cc Volkswagen Beetle engine, was inspired by the 1960s TV series *The Monkees*. 'Their show would start with them pushing a bed around town,' said China. 'I just thought I wanted to live my life like that. It cost £5,000 and took two months to build, but it's a car that impresses the women.'

The toilet and bath combination was driven by 65-year-old Donington Park track marshal Frank Richardson. 'It is terrible to drive,' he confessed, 'although once you get it up to 40mph it tends to straighten itself out.' Richardson had a nasty moment during practice when clothes from the laundry basket on the front became entangled with one of the wheels.

At the wheel of the giant rollerskate, a promotional vehicle for Derby Rollerworld, was the firm's general manager Terry Wilcox. Other entrants included Mick Pike in a dodgem car, Geoff Quaife in the Outspan Orange, and Mike Hand driving a stuffed horse and covered wagon, in which the indicators were in the horse's eyes. Among those sadly missing for the 1999 event was a motorised skip.

It may not have been the full Grand Prix distance but a few laps of Donington Park still produced plenty of excitement. In the end victory went to the dodgem car from the Outspan Orange, which just pipped the bed. The shed broke down. The non-road-going class resulted in a win for a customised fire engine, beating an armchair and a gondola on wheels.

No Tyres For Irvine

European Grand Prix, September 1999

The 1999 World Championship season had been turned on its head following Michael Schumacher's broken leg at the British Grand Prix. The Silverstone race left Schumacher's Ferrari team-mate Eddie Irvine eight points behind championship leader Mika Hakkinen, but victories in the next two races – in Austria and Germany – had propelled the Ulsterman into pole position. Hakkinen fought back with a win in Hungary and a second in Belgium but missed out at Monza where Irvine, too, could only finish sixth. Going into the European Grand Prix at the Nürburgring, with just two more races to follow, the two chief protagonists were level on points. Irvine was relishing his new-found, albeit temporary, status as Ferrari number one while Hakkinen, judging from the way he broke down in tears at Monza after spinning off while comfortably in the lead, was definitely starting to feel the pressure. With Schumacher's legions of German fans rooting for Irvine, the Nürburgring appeared the ideal place to increase that pressure, yet in the heat of battle it was Ferrari that buckled.

The European Grand Prix was a race that had everything – tension, farce, joy, despair, drama, anger, and at one stage seemingly a new leader every lap. There was enough excitement for half a dozen Grands Prix.

As is so often the case in Formula One, the overriding

factor was the weather. The morning rain had stopped before the end of the Saturday lunch-time qualifying session but the track remained wet and the best times were set in the closing minutes, with Heinz-Harald Frentzen's Jordan snatching pole from David Coulthard and Hakkinen. Irvine could manage no better than ninth. He would be starting from a long way back.

The track was dry for start time but the overcast sky suggested that it was unlikely to remain so for the full 66 laps. An aborted start, after Minardi driver Marc Gene had signalled a problem on the grid, was an indication of the drama that was to follow almost from the moment the lights went out. As the field flowed into the first corner, Damon Hill's Jordan lost power and Alexander Wurz had to swerve to avoid it. In doing so, he clipped Pedro Diniz's Sauber which flipped over on to the grass. The safety car was called out while Diniz was extricated, happily with nothing more serious than a few bruises. When the safety car departed, Frentzen led from Hakkinen, Coulthard, Ralf Schumacher and Giancarlo Fisichella. By lap 17 Irvine had worked his way up to fifth. At that point it started to rain.

Three laps later Hakkinen, in second, pitted for wet tyres. This proved a grave misjudgement, as the shower soon passed and he found himself losing up to ten seconds per lap. But his move seemed to spread panic. On lap 21 the Ferrari pit were getting ready to bring Irvine in for new tyres when Mika Salo (Schumacher's replacement in the Ferrari team) came in unexpectedly, needing a new nose-cone and tyres. He was away again after a 30-second stop, but the unscheduled visit had caused his tyres to become mixed up with those of his team-mate. To complicate matters further, Irvine and Ferrari technical director Ross Brawn, seeing the rain easing off, hastily switched their choice of tyres from wet to dry, forcing the mechanics to shelve one set of tyres and find another four. Irvine wanted to stay out for an extra lap to give the mechanics time to prepare, but he didn't have sufficient fuel and so he had to come in just 23 seconds after Salo had left. As the Ferrari crew scrambled for Irvine's fresh set of tyres, they could find only three. The right rear tyre was still in the garage. This Keystone Cop performance cost Irvine a pit stop of 28.2 seconds – 20 seconds over the norm – and dropped him out of the points-scoring positions. It was an unmitigated disaster.

Irvine's only consolation was that Hakkinen had fallen back to tenth on the unsuitable wets, but on lap 24 the Finn tried again, this time calling in for dry tyres.

Eight laps later, the first and second-placed drivers, Frentzen and Coulthard, pitted together. Frentzen got away first but the Jordan ground to a halt with an electrical problem at the very next corner, handing Coulthard the lead. By lap 38 it had started to rain heavily again. Coulthard, on dry tyres, was slipping and sliding his way around the track but was hanging on to his ten-second lead over Ralf Schumacher until he pressed too hard and slithered into the gravel and out of the race.

This presented the younger Schumacher with a 20-second advantage over Fisichella, but Schumacher was on a two-stop strategy and when he pitted on lap 44, the Benetton driver became the new leader. But four laps later Fisichella, like Coulthard before him, failed to cope with the wet track and spun out of the race. Presented with the lead once more, Schumacher was prevented from taking advantage when, on the following lap, he suffered a right rear puncture and limped to the pits. With Schumacher down to fifth, Johnny Herbert, who had started a lowly fourteenth on the grid, suddenly found that it was his turn to lead.

Greatly assisted by a switch to wets on lap 35, Herbert kept his head while all around were losing theirs. Having previously finished just four races that season, the popular Englishman held on for his third Grand Prix win and, more importantly, the Stewart team's maiden victory. And with team-mate Rubens Barrichello finishing third behind Jarno Trulli's Prost, it was a highly emotional day for Jackie Stewart and his colleagues. There was joy, too, for Minardi. Luca Badoer seemed set to pick up the Italian team's first points for four years, only for his car to die on lap 54 when he was lying fourth. All was not lost, however, as team-mate Gene came through to finish sixth and earn Minardi a priceless point. But it was another hard luck story for former world champion Jacques Villeneuve, still seeking BAR's first point. He was poised for fifth place when his clutch failed.

Villeneuve's loss proved Hakkinen's gain. Having appeared to give up, Hakkinen found a new lease of life towards the end and, four laps from the finish, harassed Irvine into a costly mistake. Once past Irvine, Hakkinen profited from Villeneuve's late exit to finish fifth and pick up two vital points. Irvine ended up seventh to round off a hugely disappointing day for Ferrari.

Irvine was understandably angry at the prolonged pit stop. 'It is a problem when you have one team of mechanics serving two cars,' he said. 'We should have two teams doing it. We screwed it up.' Ferrari president Luca di Montezemolo was even more scathing. 'Ferrari's fans are rightfully very upset and we cannot tolerate it. We made a complete mess of it and it must never happen again.'

CRICKET

by Andrew Ward

One-legged Against One-armed
Manchester, July 1863

In the early days of the sport, in the era of 'picnic cricket', there were frequently games played between men with one leg and those with one arm. The participants were usually wounded servicemen, and the purpose was to raise money in their cause. Often the games were played to a backcloth of sideshows and events for all the family. Apparently the one-legged cricketers were usually the winners.

As early as 1796 there were games between handicapped Greenwich Pensioners. At Montpelier Gardens, Walworth, that year, there was a real rumpus. The match started at nine o'clock, and the one-legged team made 93 runs. The one-armed men were batting when the crowd broke down the gates to get into the packed ground. There were casualties in the crush, but, three hours later, the game was restarted. The one-armed team were soon all out for 42, and the one-legged men reached 60 for six in their second innings before the light faded. A rematch, the following Wednesday, saw the one-legged team win by 103 runs.

At Old Trafford, in July 1863, the two teams showed their relative merits. The one-legged players fared well while batting but were slow in the field and between the wickets, while the one-armed players were lively in the field, but less assured while batting and taking catches. One reporter, covering a game of the same era, at Peckham Rye in 1862, described the fielding of the one-legged players as 'something painfully wonderful and ludicrously horrible'. All the players in that game were young, so they had developed compensatory muscles.

In the exciting two-day, two-innings match at Old Trafford, all the players were pensioners. The one-legged team won the toss and elected to bat. The crowd's favourite was undoubtedly Letford, who had lost both legs yet batted at number ten and scored ten in the first innings, and then an unbeaten ten in the second innings when he was promoted in the order. Letford fielded bravely at long-stop, and the *Manchester Daily Examiner and Times* could not resist the obvious painful description of his value to the one-legged team: 'No-legs, as he is usually called, has often pulled a match through when, without him, the eleven would hardly have a leg to stand on.'

Two excellent innings by Langsden, who 'showed a remarkable mastery of the bat by a succession of first-rate off-drives', kept the contest interesting. Langsden surprised the spectators with the strength of his hitting, despite having only one arm. He scored over half the one-armed side's runs, but it was not enough. The one-legged team won by 21 runs.

That same year, at the Oval, a team of one-legged Greenwich Pensioners beat a team of one-armed Greenwich Pensioners by nineteen runs. And, in the last year of the century, another team of one-armed players lost a one-innings match at Brighton.

There have, of course, been many examples of individuals playing with one leg or one arm, or of injured cricketers doing the best they could with one good leg or arm. Perhaps the highest achievement was that of Lionel Tennyson, the Hampshire and England captain, who, having been injured on the hand when fielding in the Leeds Test match against Australia in 1921, batted one-handed and scored 63 and 36.

THE ONE-LEGGED TEAM

Hammond b Smith	0	b Langsden	3
Swann b Langsden	9	run out	12
Scott b Smith	17	b Smith	20
Crabtree b Langsden	41	b Langsden	27
Page b Smith	27	b Smith	35
Hampsher b Smith	30	c and b Smith	8
Jeffries b Langsden	2	b Smith	7
Woolley b Smith	0	b Smith	1
Smith b Langsden	0	c Graves b Langsden	1
Letford b Langsden	10	not out	10
Lisle not out	1	c Rosier	0
Extras	1		9
	138		**133**

THE ONE-ARMED TEAM

Rosier c Jeffries b Page	0	b Page	13
Cook b Crabtree	7	b Crabtree	12
Sate b Crabtree	17	b Page	3
Langsden st Hampsher	56	not out	77
Smith c and b Hampsher	12	c Hampsher b Page	6
Graves st Hampsher	8	b Crabtree	8
Brown not out	6	c Hampsher b Page	7
Watson b Hampsher	0	c Hampsher b Crabtree	0
Groombridge b Hampsher	0	c Crabtree b Page	1
Bicknell st Hampsher	0	run out	4
Smith run out	5	hit wicket	0
Extras	7		1
	118		**132**

Cricket on Ice

Cambridge, December 1878

The fields of the Fens were full of water, and the water froze. People took to skating and races were organised across the smooth fields.

But there was one other sport which generated interest during the cold winter of 1878–9, a sport which automatically comes to mind when looking out of frosty windows on to a field of perfect ice in the midst of a harsh winter. Yes, it was, of course, cricket.

The Cambridge University term had ended, so Charles Pigg challenged a team from the town to a game on an ideal icy field at Grantchester Meadows, scene of Chaucer's 'Reeve's Tale' and close to the residence (in different eras) of Rupert Brooke and Jeffrey Archer. The Town–Gown game was played over three days on a wicket which didn't show the slightest sign of wearing badly. No fast bowling was allowed. The umpires were severe on anything other than lobs.

The Town batted first and the scoring was heavy. The renowned Robert Carpenter opened the innings and helped himself to the first 50 of the match. Charles Pigg, the Gown captain, gave his team two overs each in order to assess what they could do. He eventually settled on Lilley and Boucher as his mainstream lob attack. Boucher, writing to *The Times* 50 years later, recalled a sweet moment when he lobbed up a full toss to Dan Hayward when the crack batsman was going strong. Hayward, forming strong images of how the ball would look in the next county, swung heartily and overbalanced on the ice. The ball bowled him, and the twelve-man Town team were all out for 328. I should think the Gown captain would have opted for a light roller if he had had a choice.

The Gown batted and were 61 for one at close of play on the second day. Fielders chased and slid across the ice in exhilarating fashion as they tried to keep down the Gown score. Three of the first five batsmen raced to fifties, and the two Piggs put together a solid fifth-wicket stand. Time ran out when the Gown team needed another 55 runs for victory with seven wickets standing. The game was an honourable draw.

That was only one of a number of games on ice that winter. Cricket on ice has occasionally been revived since, such as the game between Broadwater Park and Charterhouse in 1895 (see *The Carthusian* for March, 1895), but conditions abroad are often more favourable than in Britain. Cricket in a frozen fiord, or on a Swiss lake, would really be something, but a word of caution. It needs specially qualified umpires to test the thickness of the ice.

CAMBRIDGE TOWN		CAMBRIDGE GOWN	
R Carpenter c Scott b Boucher	89	von E Scott run out	88
W Thurston run out	37	Lilley b Newman	6
F Pryor c Scott b Boucher	13	W Deedes b Newman	56
J Warrington b Lilley	1	A D Wawn c and b Carpenter	7
G Hoppett b Lilley	3	H Pigg not out	69
J Fordham b Wawn	42	C Pigg not out	34
H Mason c Wawn by Lilley	9	Extras	14
W Newman run out	65		274–4
A Fromant lbw b Lilley	19		
W Richardson b Lilley	0		
D Hayward b Boucher	41		
J Cain not out	9		
	318		

A Team of '50 or More Farmers'

Yatton, Near Bristol, October 1887

It is a rare game that has as many as 23 ducks in one
innings, but here we have an example. The game was billed
as Yatton against '50 or more farmers' and there is little
indication of how many farmers turned up to play the
regular cricketers. The scorecard shows that 41 batted, and
the Yatton bowling figures must have been impressive. The
wickets were shared between eight bowlers, Radcliffe
taking eleven, Chamberlayne and Gage five each, Blew and
Shiner four apiece, Atherton three, Winter two and Clapp
one. Five batsmen were run out, and there was an amazing
dearth of catches, unless the scorecard fails to record the
full details of the innings.

It is unlikely that all the 40-plus farmers fielded during
the Yatton innings. That would have been some field for a
radio commentator to describe. Yatton, a team including
some renowned local cricketers, batted to make 75 for six
(including two men retired) so we can assume the game was
a draw.

The scorecard is reproduced from *Cricket* (27 October
1887), which also includes a brief background to the game:
'Mr Tankerville Chamberlayne, of Cranbury Park,
Manchester, and of yachting renown, who has for many
years done so much by purse and presence to uphold and
support cricket, both in Hampshire and Somerset, was
again to the fore on Friday October 14, at his pretty seat at
Yatton, near Bristol, catering for his many hundred guests

with unbounded liberality. This was the third successive year of the festivities. The day was very cold, but this did not deter the many hundreds of both gentlemen and ladies attending and witnessing the novel sight, and partaking of the good things provided. Nearly 300 sat down to luncheon, the self-esteemed host presiding, supported by the well-known amateur cricketer Mr O G Radcliffe, Rev. O Puckridge, Frank Wills, J H Fowler . . . About 500 partook of tea and indulged in the dancing until a late hour.'

This is just one example of a game of unbalanced teams, some of which were responsible for what now appear as astonishing bowling figures. Perhaps the most sensational was Johnny Briggs's fifteen for four (match figures of 27 for 23) against 22 of the Cape Mounted Riflemen at Williams Town, South Africa, in 1888–9. As late as 1923 MCC beat fifteen of Northern Orange Free State by an innings and 35 runs.

The many early matches where numbers were unbalanced include an All England XI's victory by an innings against 33 of Norfolk on Swaffham Racecourse in 1797 and Lord Winterton's XI against 37 Labourers at Shillinglee Park in 1843, the Lord's team winning by five wickets. Three years later, Lord Winterton's XI took on 56 Labourers and this game was drawn.

THE FARMERS

B Marshall b Chamberlayne	20
B Burgess run out	1
C Hawkins b Radcliffe	0
J Pavey run out	0
J Hill b Radcliffe	0
S B Griffin run out	2
J Edgell c Clapp b Radcliffe	2
A Williams c and b Radcliffe	4
T Price c and b Radcliffe	0
A Osmond b Chamberlayne	0
T Champion b Radcliffe	0
W Cavill b Chamberlayne	0
H Wall b Gage	0
W Marsh b Radcliffe	0
R Wilcox b Gage	0
M H Thatcher b Winter	0
W Gill b Clapp	0
J Wallis b Winter	0
W Hennessy b Gage	0
R Harding b Blew	0
F W Wills run out	1
C Burgess b Clapp	0
J Gage b Clapp	10
G Hardwick b Blew	3
W Luff b Blew	0
G Badman b Blew	0
S M Harding run out	2
A Batt b Radcliffe	4
T Pearce b Shiner	12
C Griffin b Radcliffe	0
H Morgan b Shiner	0
T Nicholls b Radcliffe	2
A Hardwick b Shiner	0
A Williams b Radcliffe	1
C Sayer b Atherton	2
J Bisder b Shiner	2
C Young b Atherton	0
H Macey b Atherton	0
W Petheran b Gage	4
J H Fowler b Gage	0
S Hurley not out	1
Extras	8
	92

YATTON

C Knowles b Luff	7
A E Clapp retired	20
E W Blew c Gill b Luff	18
H Gage retired	23
T Chamberlayne b Luff	0
W A Winter run out	3
W H Shiner not out	1
Extras	3
	75–6

A J Atherton, C R Knowles, O G Radcliffe and B Crossman did not bat.

An Innings by Jessop
Cambridge, May 1899

No book on bizarre sporting moments would be complete without the inclusion of a game influenced by an innings from Gilbert Jessop. There are plenty of candidates.

One obvious example is the final Test match of the 1902 England–Australia series, when Jessop's 104 in 75 minutes on a crumbling wicket in the second innings rescued England from 48 for five and provided the backbone for a one-wicket win. 'I was lucky enough to get a few runs,' understated Jessop in his autobiography.

Jessop was not particularly tall (5ft 7in) and he bent low in his stance, a technique which earned him the nickname of 'The Croucher'. Throwing theory to the wind, he developed a range of strokes for every ball and became probably the most consistent rapid scorer the game has ever known. Almost always he dominated partnerships. According to Gerald Brodribb, in *The Croucher*, Jessop made 72 per cent of the runs scored while he was at the wicket. On one occasion in 1907 Jessop represented a Surrey club side on a day off, scoring 200 while the batsman at the other end added 14.

Yorkshire were more than once on the receiving end of his onslaughts, such as the 63 out of 65 in less than 30 minutes he made against them in his first season for Gloucestershire (1894), the 101 out of 118 in 40 minutes in 1897, and a century in each innings at Bradford in 1900. Perhaps the most astonishing sustained spell of dominance, though, was when he captained Cambridge University against Yorkshire in 1899.

Jessop's wonderful innings came on the opening day. He came in when the third wicket fell for 40 runs and in under two hours made an unbeaten 171 out of only 206, finally running out of partners. As often was the case, he gave the bowlers some opportunity while he was adjusting to the wicket. At 24, he skied a ball towards point. Frank Mitchell took responsibility, even though Lord Hawke was probably nearer, and the catch went down. Mitchell didn't have the best of games, later being out without scoring.

Sullivan's innings was almost the obverse of that of Jessop. He made two of the first 40, then one more during the stand of 53 with Jessop. He was out with the score at 93, having made three in 80 minutes. At lunch the score was 141 for five, with Jessop unbeaten on 85. Soon after the break he completed a 55-minute century. The *Cambridge Daily News* stated that Jessop 'gave a grand explosion of hard and determined hitting'.

On this occasion Jessop's innings failed to bring success for his team. Jackson and Brown put on 194 for the second Yorkshire wicket, and the county's first-innings lead of 185 was more than enough to inflict an innings' defeat, mainly because Jessop was caught for two in the second innings.

Three years later, Jessop batted with Jackson in the stand that rallied England against Australia at the Oval, before Hirst and Rhodes knocked off the winning runs, mainly in singles, in their famous last-wicket partnership. Those three key Yorkshiremen also knew what it was like to play against Jessop.

CAMBRIDGE UNIVERSITY

L J Moon c Bairstow b Brown, jun	9	b Rhodes	15
A M Sullivan c Tunnicliffe b Rhodes	3	b Jackson	19
J H Stogdon run out	0	st Bairstow b Rhodes	10
E R Wilson b Rhodes	24	b Jackson	12
G J Jessop not out	171	c Wainwright b Jackson	2
T L Taylor b Hirst	14	c Bairstow b Rhodes	3
S H Day c Bairstow b Hirst	1	c Bairstow b Jackson	4
G E Winter b Hirst	8	c and b Rhodes	22
E F Penn c Tunnicliffe b Rhodes	3	lbw b Jackson	11
A E Hind c Bairstow b Hirst	0	not out	0
H H B Hawkins b Jackson	6	b Jackson	0
Extras	7		2
	246		**100**

Bowling: *First Innings*; Hirst 24–10–69–14, Brown, jun, 12–4–33–1, Rhodes 20–6–80–3, Jackson 10.2–3–48–1, Brown, sen, 2–1–9–0. *Second Innings*; Hirst 7–4–12–0, Brown, jun 7–3–17–0, Rhodes 15–5–18–4, Jackson 14.4–4–51–6.

YORKSHIRE

J T Brown, sen, c Sullivan b Hawkins	168
J Tunnicliffe b Hawkins	42
Mr F S Jackson c Moon b Wilson	133
Mr F Mitchell c Hawkins b Penn	0
D Denton c Sullivan b Penn	5
E Wainwright c Stogdon b Penn	11
G H Hirst c Day b Wilson	10
Lord Hawke not out	38
W Rhodes c Taylor b Wilson	1
J T Brown, jun, b Jessop	0
A L Bairstow b Jessop	1
Extras	20
	429

Bowling: Hind 22–8–49–0, Penn 35–4–122–3, Jessop 18.4–3–57–2, Wilson 34–5–103–3, Hawkins 25–6–63–2, Winter 3–0–15–0.

Cricket on Deck

The Mediterranean Sea, June 1904

There is a story about a seasick ship's passenger who endures a stormy crossing and is received at the other end by someone who asks a stupid question: 'Did you find plenty to do on the voyage?'

'Yes,' he replies, testing the intelligence of the questioner. 'In the evenings we played snooker below deck, and during the daytime we played baseball and cricket on the deck.'

The point of this story is that the idea of playing these sports on a rocking and rolling ship is beyond comprehension for the connoisseurs, but, with cricket, where there is a will there has to be a way . . . and usually a strange game is the result.

Take the crew of the HMS *Irresistible*. They invented an evening game to play at sea or in harbour. The first problem, of course, is the possibility of the ball going overboard. This was solved by hanging the seine net around the deck, suspended from the wire running along the edge of the awning. Portable wickets were then pitched on deck and creases marked with chalk. So as not to encourage big hitting with the risk of the ball clearing the top of the net, the game took on a 'tip and run' identity. Should someone put the ball in the sea, the rule was that the whole team would be given out. Not a case of six and out but nought and all out.

Playing with home-made bats and balls, or, rather, made-at-sea bats and balls, the teams were usually seven or eight a side. The fielding team were allowed to bowl from the most convenient end, which put pressure on the batsmen to complete their run before the next ball. They had to run at least one for each ball. If either batsman was run-out on the first run, then the striker was always the batsman out. He was held responsible for guaranteeing a run off each ball. Run-outs on subsequent runs would follow normal practice. The best shot, risky but rewarding, was to chip the ball down a hatchway as it wasn't easy to find and runs were there for the taking. Predictably, it was a tiring game. Teams would knock up perhaps 50 runs in only fifteen minutes' batting. It was good exercise.

When Women Met Men at Trent Bridge

Nottingham, September 1907

At the end of a season which saw Nottinghamshire crowned as County Champions, it is intriguing to note that the game described by the *Nottingham Evening Post* as 'one of the most interesting cricket matches witnessed on the Trent Bridge Ground this season' did not involve the county team. It was a charity game between Notts Crimea & Indian Mutiny Veterans and Nottinghamshire Ladies. There were about 1,500 witnesses.

The umpires were the Sheriff of Nottingham, Councillor Ball, and Mr A O Jones, captain of the Nottinghamshire champions. The Veterans won the toss and invited the ladies to bat. The ladies, incidentally, included one man, Councillor Swain, an organiser of the game, which was played for the benefit of poor children in the city. The proceeds of the match went towards a holiday home at Skegness.

Bearing in mind the dates of the Crimean War, which began in 1853, and the Indian Mutiny, which started four years later, it is understandable that the Veterans of these actions did not show too much élan in the field in 1907. Corner and Cox bowled underarm, and Alice Watts and Miss Pawlett made runs easily, in a manner that was technically correct. Miss Hickling and Councillor Swain put together a good partnership, but when both woman and man had reached their twenties they were out, Miss Hickling caught at mid-on, Councillor Swain deliberately hitting all round a ball from Cox. The consensus was that the Ladies' 106, made in an hour and a half, would take some matching.

The Ladies' team, with the exception of Councillor Swain, took to the field wearing long white skirts, white shirts and green ties. The Veterans batted more slowly than the Ladies, wary of taking a single unless there was an easy two or three. Trooper Holland, a survivor of the Charge of the Light Brigade, sent in to seal up one end, used his own bat, which was as wide as the wicket. A wicked spinning ball from Miss Hickling still did for him, and the Ladies took a commanding position, except for the resistance of the Veterans' one 'ringer', Mr Whitby, who, earlier in the day, had caught out his wife (in the context of a cricket match, that is).

Games between men and women are abundant throughout cricket history, and various rule-changes have been incorporated for such occasions. Men have batted and bowled with their unorthodox hand, or bowled underarm. Women have been allowed to catch the ball in their skirts, men have been penalised three runs for fielding the ball with their stronger hand. Men have batted with broomsticks, women have broomsticked with bats. Men have dressed in women's clothing and vice versa. But, in recent years, international women cricketers have shown themselves capable of taking on good club cricketers on equal terms.

NOTTINGHAMSHIRE LADIES

Miss A M Watts b Corner	9
Miss L Pawlett b Cox	8
Miss Hickling c Whitby b Corner	24
Miss Mutch b Corner	1
Miss Taylor b Corner	4
Councillor R H Swain b Cox	23
Miss E M Vaulkhard c Whitby b Taylor	6
Mrs H S Whitby c Whitby b Corner	5
Mrs J Gaskin b Taylor	17
Miss D Hutton c Tomlinson b Taylor	2
Miss L Simpkin not out	0
Extras	7
	106

NOTTS CRIMEA & INDIAN MUTINY VETERANS

Sergt-Major G Watson (11th Hussars) c and b Hickling	1
Private G Corner (84th Foot) run out	18
Private T Cox (34th Foot) b Pawlett	0
Trooper M Holland (11th Hussars) b Hickling	0
Sergt G Willbond (KR Rifles) b Pawlett	1
Mr H S Whitby b Watts	52
Private W Tomlinson (Land Transport Corps) b Pawlett	0
Private W Taylor (95th Foot) not out	6
Private S Baxter (81st Foot) not out	0
Extras	4
	82–8

Alletson's Innings

Hove, May 1911

One might expect the possibility of a hard-hitting sensation from an Ian Botham or a Kapil Dev, but not a Nottinghamshire nonentity at number nine. What made Ted Alletson's innings so phenomenally strange was that he had been in and out – more often out – of the Nottinghamshire team during his five years as a professional.

When Alletson went out to bat, in Nottinghamshire's second innings at Hove, his team were nine runs ahead with only three wickets left. There were 50 minutes before lunch on the third day. Sussex could reasonably expect that the game would soon be over. In the first innings the last three Notts batsmen had contributed thirteen runs, and Alletson's share had been seven.

The son of a wheelwright on the Duke of Portland's estate in the Nottinghamshire Dukeries, Ted Alletson was a strapping 27-year-old six-footer. He had played local cricket for Welbeck and then had one season as a professional in the Huddersfield Alliance before joining Nottinghamshire in 1906. He was more a bowler than a batsman, and his opportunity in the game at Sussex came mainly because Wass, the front-line Notts bowler, was injured. Alletson himself was nursing a sprained wrist and was barely passed fit.

At 185 for seven, therefore, on a grey Hove day, Alletson went out to join Lee. Alletson kept the Notts innings going until lunch, when the score was 260 for nine. He had made

47 in 50 minutes, hitting five fours, two threes, four twos and thirteen singles. It was nothing out of the ordinary, but a useful innings for his team. There were a couple of strokes of good fortune – a skier not going to hand at 25, and a difficult slip catch being put down at 42 – and Alletson was free to come out after lunch and deliver the most extraordinary display of sustained hitting ever seen in cricket. He was not a technically good batsman, but he could drive harder than anyone, using his powerful physique and the leverage of his 6ft 6in arm span.

John Arlott, in his delightful monograph *Alletson's Innings*, reconstructs (with the help of Roy Webber) the best estimates of what happened in the 40-minute period after lunch. Leach had four balls left of his interrupted wicket-taking over. Riley, the number eleven bat, survived them without scoring.

The next 65 balls brought 152 runs. Then a wicket fell, and Nottinghamshire were all out.

Edwin Boaler Alletson faced 51 balls after lunch, according to the Arlott–Webber interpretations of patchwork evidence remaining from the scorebooks. He scored 142 runs and was caught on the boundary by Smith, who was allegedly over the boundary ropes. By then Alletson was almost glad to be out, perhaps sensing that Nottinghamshire, 236 ahead, had a chance of victory.

The 51 balls brought Alletson eight sixes, 18 fours, two threes, six twos and four singles. He failed to score off twelve balls and was caught from the 51st with his score on 189. The full details of those post-lunch balls are as follows:
0 4 4 1 2 4 2 0 1 6 0 4 2 4 6 4 0 6 3 4 4 0 2 1 4 6 0 4 3 4 6 6 0
4 4 4 6 0 0 0 0 4 4 2 2 6 1 4 4 0 W.

Perhaps the most incredible spell came in the middle of the 40-minute period after lunch. In the course of five overs, three by Killick and two by Leach, Nottinghamshire picked up 100 runs, 97 to Alletson and three to Riley. One over from Killick, which included two no-balls, went for 34 runs

– 4, 6, 6, 0, 4, 4, 4, 6 – a record for an over until Gary Sobers went to work on Malcolm Nash.

Sussex were left to make 237 in three and a quarter hours. They finished 24 short with two wickets to fall.

Ted Alletson stayed with Nottinghamshire for just three more years. When his career ended he had made 3,217 runs at an average of 18.59. His 189 at Hove was his only century, although he hit Wilfred Rhodes for three consecutive sixes at Dewsbury in 1913 and there were other occasions when his powerful driving had fielders cowering for cover. During the First World War he served in the Royal Garrison Artillery and later he worked at Manton Colliery.

NOTTINGHAMSHIRE

Mr A O Jones b Cox	57	b Leach	0
J Iremonger c and b Relf (A E)	0	c Tudor b Killick	83
G Gunn st Butt b Cox	90	st Butt b Relf (R)	66
J Hardstaff b Cox	8	c Butt b Relf (A.E.)	7
J Gunn c Relf (R) b Killick	33	b Relf (R)	19
W Payton c Heygate b Killick	20	lbw Relf (A.E.)	0
W Whysall b Killick	1	c Butt b Relf (A.E.)	3
G M Lee c and b Killick	10	c Cox b Leach	26
E Alletson c Killick b Relf (A E)	7	c Smith b Cox	189
T Oates not out	3	b Leach	1
W Riley c Smith b Killick	3	not out	10
Extras	6		8
	238		**412**

Bowling: *First Innings*; Relf (A E) 19–5–40–2, Leach 11–2–53–0, Vincett 4–0–31–0, Relf (R) 11–0–36–0, Cox 25–4–58–3, Killick 10.2–4–14–5. *Second Innings*; Relf (A E) 33–13–92–3, Leach 19–2–91–3, Vincett 3–1–25–0, Relf (R) 19–6–39–2, Cox 9.4–2–27–1, Killick 20–2–130–1.

SUSSEX

R Relf b Jones	42	c Oates b Jones	71
J Vine b Jones	77	c Payton b Riley	54
Mr R B Heygate c Lee b Iremonger	32	b Gunn (J)	13
G Cox b Riley	37	st Oates b Riley	5
A E Relf c and b Jones	4	c Oates b Riley	0
Mr C L Tudor c Oates b Riley	23	b Gunn (J)	4
E H Killick c Hardstaff b Lee	81	c Lee b Riley	21
G Leach b Lee	52	b Gunn (J)	31
Mr C L A Smith not out	33	not out	12
J H Vincent c Iremonger b Lee	9	not out	1
H R Butt b Riley	13		
Extras	11		1
	414		**213–8**

Bowling: *First Innings*; Iremonger 34–7–97–1, Riley 29.4–5–102–3, Gunn (J) 29–2–87–0, Jones 22–2–69–3, Alletson 1–0–3–0, Lee 14–1–45–3. *Second Innings*; Iremonger 14–2–34–0, Riley 33–9–82–4, Gunn (J) 25–9–41–3, Jones 5–1–24–31–0, Lee 4–0–31–0.

Fifteen All Out and Then . . .

Birmingham, June 1922

Hampshire won the toss and put Warwickshire in. Thanks to a steady innings from Santall (84), who broke a tile on the pavilion roof with a six, and some lusty blows from Calthorpe (70), whose three sixes included one over the pavilion into a field, the home county reached 223 all out. Hampshire's opening bowlers, Jack Newman and Alec Kennedy, were typically united, the former penetrative and slightly erratic, the latter persistently accurate. Warwickshire's disappointments came in the middle of their batting. Reverend E F Waddy was out without scoring, and the younger Quaife also went for a duck. As it happened they were good role models for the Hampshire innings later that same day.

Hampshire lasted 53 balls and 40 minutes. The slow over rate was no fault of Warwickshire's Howell and Calthorpe. There was a lot of walking about – on and off the field. Kennedy went to the third ball of Calthorpe's first over and Hampshire were soon nought for three. Mead managed a single, and Lionel Tennyson, the Hampshire captain, streaked a four through the slips before being caught. Brown was immediately bowled, and Hampshire were five for five. Mead batted steadily and took his own score to five. With the total on nine, Newman was caught in the slips, a run later Shirley went the same way and McIntyre was leg before wicket. Ten for eight. Hampshire were in grave danger of recording the lowest score of all first-class cricket which was – and still is – twelve.

They were saved by four byes which, after Mead had notched another single, took the score to fifteen. The last two wickets then fell, leaving Mead unbeaten on six – quite an astonishing achievement considering he had lost eight partners. Eight of the team were out without scoring. Had it not been for four byes and a lucky four through the slips, Hampshire would have made only seven.

There was nothing sensational about the wicket. It was purely an accident of cricket. Hampshire batted badly, and the innings accumulated failure. They followed on, and at the close of play on the first day were 98 for three, which showed that runs could be made, although not enough.

When Mead was out early the next day (127 for four) Hampshire needed another 81 to avoid an innings defeat. Just before lunch they were 177 for six, still 31 behind. The five remaining batsmen had scored one run between them in the first innings. They evoked memories of Tennyson's comments about the late-order batting early in the season.

Observers early that Thursday afternoon, recognising that less than half the allotted time had been used, were quite pleased when Hampshire started to make a bit of a fight. Brown and Shirley put on 85 for the seventh wicket, and Brown and McIntyre cobbled together a further thirteen for the eighth. At 274 for eight, however, 66 ahead, Hampshire seemed to be showing token resistance.

The ninth-wicket stand brought together George Brown, a notable left-handed battling batsman, and wicket-keeper Walter Livsey, Tennyson's valet, who had chalked up a pair against Sussex in the first match of the season. The stand was worth 177 runs. Brown hit 18 fours in his 172, and at the end of the day Hampshire were 475 for nine, 267 ahead. Brown's century was reminiscent of his fighting effort against Essex in 1913, when his unbeaten 140 saved Hampshire from the unenviable position of 119 behind with four second-innings wickets left. In his career, Brown was to score over 25,000 runs. Livsey, however, was moving towards unknown territory, although he had shared a last-wicket stand of 192 with Bowell the previous season.

Hampshire batted for a further 40 minutes in the morning, and Livsey was able to complete his century. Boyes (29) helped him add 70 for the last wicket.

When Warwickshire batted again they needed 314 runs to win, and there was ample time to make the runs. Bates went quickly, and in came Santall, top score in the first innings. He was bowled for nought. Suddenly the game was alive, and Hampshire had control.

Wickets continued to fall – Reverend Waddy completed his 'pair' – but Quaife, senior, kept one end intact. When last-man Howell came to the wicket, Warwickshire still needed more than 150 to win. Quaife looked solid at one end, Howell picked up a few runs and was then dropped by wicket-keeper Livsey. A few more runs, and Howell was dropped at slip. Surely the course of the game could not change again? No, Newman picked up Howell's wicket, and Quaife was left unbeaten after resisting for 100 minutes.

Hampshire, fifteen all out in their first innings, had not only made a fight of the match, they had won convincingly by 155 runs. 'The victory taken as a whole,' said *Wisden*, 'must surely be without precedent in first-class cricket.'

It wasn't even the end of Hampshire's strange matches that season. Jack Newman made the news in August when he lost his temper over an umpiring decision and kicked down the stumps. Lord Tennyson ordered him off the field and, at the end of the day, sat down to help Newman compile a letter to the Nottinghamshire captain and president: 'I humbly apologise for my action on the field of play at Trent Bridge and herewith I tender my deep regret,' wrote Newman.

WARWICKSHIRE

L A Bates c Shirley b Newman	3	c Mead b Kennedy	1
E J Smith c Mead b Newman	3	c Shirley b Kennedy	41
Mr F R Santall c McIntyre b Boyes	84	b Newman	0
W G Quaife b Newman	1	not out	40
Hon F S G Calthorpe c Boyes b Kennedy	70	b Newman	30
Rev. E F Waddy c Mead b Boyes	0	b Newman	0
Mr B W Quaife b Boyes	0	c and b Kennedy	7
J Fox b Kennedy	4	b Kennedy	0
J Smart b Newman	20	b Newman	3
C Smart c Mead b Boyes	14	c and b Boyes	15
H Howell not out	1	c Kennedy b Newman	11
Extras	2		10
	223		**158**

Bowling: *First Innings*; Kennedy 24–7–74–2, Newman 12.3–0–70–4, Boyes 16–5–56–4, Shirley 3–0–21–0. *Second Innings*; Kennedy 26–12–47–4, Newman 26.3–12–53–5, Boyes 11–4–34–1, Brown 5–0–14–0.

HAMPSHIRE

A Bowell b Howell	0	c Howell b W G Quaife	45
A Kennedy c Smith b Calthorpe	0	b Calthorpe	7
Mr H L V Day b Calthorpe	0	c Bates b W G Quaife	15
C P Mead not out	6	b Howell	24
Hon. L N Tennyson c Calthorpe b Howell	4	c C Smart b Calthorpe	45
G Brown b Howell	0	b C Smart	172
J Newman c C Smart b Howell	0	c and b W G Quaife	12
Mr W R Shirley c J Smart b Calthorpe	1	lbw b Fox	30
Mr A S McIntyre lbw b Calthorpe	0	lbw b Howell	5
W H Livsey b Howell	0	not out	110
G S Boyes lbw b Howell	0	b Howell	29
Extras	4		27
	15		**521**

Bowling: *First Innings*; Howell 4.5–2–7–6, Calthorpe 4–3–4–4. *Second Innings*; Howell 63–10–156–3, Calthorpe 33–7–97–2, W G Quaife 49–8–154–3, Fox 7–0–30–1, J Smart 13–2–37–0, Santall 5–0–15–0, C Smart 1–0–5–1.

Two Against Eleven

Wittersham, Isle of Oxney, September 1936

This strange game, two men against an eleven from the Isle of Oxney on the Kent–Sussex border, had its origins in a bet made in the early 1830s, more than 100 years earlier. The landlord of Wittersham's Norton's Inn had been so disgusted with the boastings of the local village side that he wagered he could find two cricketers to beat the lot of them. The crafty publican turned up with two Kent professionals, Edward Wenman and Richard Mills, who beat the eleven from the Isle of Oxney by 66 runs in a two-innings match.

In 1936 someone had the idea of repeating the game. Different players, of course, but two professionals against a team of local lads. A two-innings game was planned, whereby the professionals would be 'all out' as soon as they lost a wicket, but they were given the concession of being able to change their bowling at will.

The two-man professional team consisted of Bert Wensley of Sussex and Bill Ashdown of Kent. The Isle of Oxney team, captained by coal-merchant S J Pridham, were mainly local workmen: three gardeners, two carpenters, one hop-dryer, two farmers, a bricklayer and a motor mechanic.

The publicity for the game was excellent. It was advertised in all the pubs, and the idea caught the imagination of people in the region. The BBC decided to broadcast a radio commentary of the game. A big crowd turned out on the day – one source says 2,000 plus, another gives it at 4,000 – and the proceeds went to charity.

The game started at 11.30 and the Isle of Oxney batted first. The two-man team of Wensley and Ashdown rotated between wicket-keeping and bowling. There were no other fielders, which meant there were only two gaps in the field – all the on side, and all the off. Not surprisingly, neither Ashdown nor Wensley managed to bowl a maiden over in the whole innings, which lasted 24.4 overs. When Bill Catt, the bricklayer, and one of the Bromham brothers took the Isle of Oxney score from 39 for one to 102, things looked really bleak for the professionals (and the onlookers who had betted on them), but the two men stuck at their task. Isle of Oxney were dismissed for 153.

Ashdown and Wensley went in knowing that one mistake would end the whole innings. In 36.4 overs they took the total to 186, an excellent first- and last-wicket stand. Wensley was the man out after hitting three sixes and thirteen fours in his 96. Ashdown, unbeaten on 83, had hit fourteen fours.

Unfortunately the rain came down, and the last two innings were never started. The professionals won on first innings, and had emulated the performance of their counterparts in the early 1830s.

ISLE OF OXNEY

F G H Pridham st Wensley b Ashdown	11
W Catt b Ashdown	68
A Bromham run out	20
G Cook b Wensley	0
C Gorman b Ashdown	0
C Bush c Ashdown b Wensley	2
A Bush b Wensley	14
P Shanbrooke lbw b Ashdown	28
F Jenner b Wensley	0
F Burt b Wensley	0
F Bromham not out	5
Extras	5
	153

Bowling: Wensley 12.4–0–66–5, Ashdown 12–0–82–4.

THE PROFESSIONALS

Ashdown not out	83
Wensley c Cook b Bush (A)	96
Extras	7
	186

Last Man 163

Chesterfield, August 1947

When Ray Smith was caught by Marsh off Pope, Essex were 199 for nine, still 24 behind Derbyshire's first-innings total of 223. On his walk back to the dressing-room Smith passed his cousin, Peter Smith, an unusual number-eleven batsman if ever there was one.

The previous season Peter Smith was one of the five *Wisden* cricketers of the year, in the distinguished company of Laurie Fishlock, Vinoo Mankad, Cyril Washbrook and Alec Bedser, but his special talent lay in bowling leg-breaks, googlies and top-spinners rather than batting. Ipswich born, Smith had had early pretensions as a batsman and quick bowler, but, when attending a trial with Essex, he bowled leg spinners by chance, just when the county were about to reject him. In his first season he played five games and picked up one wicket – a full toss landed on the top of Jupp's stumps – but one event of that season was recalled almost 20 years later. In his first county match, against Derbyshire, Peter Smith watched the opposition's opening bats, Storer and Bowden, put together a stand of 322. Whether or not he intended to pay back Derbyshire for this some day is a matter for conjecture, but he certainly did so on an August day in 1947.

Peter Smith could bat a bit, and he moved up and down the batting order. In 1936 he hit a century in 80 minutes against Hampshire, and, batting at three, he scored another century against Hampshire just after the war. In this 1947 season, however, his benefit year, Peter Smith's form had been erratic. In the last match, against Worcestershire, batting at ten, he had been bowled by Jackson for nought in both innings. On that form he deserved his place at number eleven against Derbyshire. On his form against Derbyshire, though, he made a mockery of it all.

In 140 minutes, Peter Smith scored 163 runs, surely the most devastating annihilation a number eleven has given first-class bowling. Vigar, the number-five Essex bat, offered support and steadily made his way to his own century. When Smith was finally bowled by Worthington, the two men had put on 218 for the last wicket. Peter Smith offered two hard chances while hitting three sixes and 22 fours in his scintillating innings.

In their second innings, Derbyshire lost eight wickets before they took the lead. Almost as intriguing as Essex's lower-order revival was that of Derbyshire. Cliff Gladwin, batting at ten, scored a 50 and was his county's second highest scorer for the second time in the match. Gothard, at nine, made runs for the second time. And, even more surprising was the 38 not out made by fast bowler Bill Copson, who went in last for Derbyshire. Copson was a rustic bat who swung the bat hard and was never expected to stay long. In his career he averaged 6.81 in 279 matches. There is a story of him going out to bat against Glamorgan at Swansea and simply plonking the bat down in the block-hole.

'Don't you want a guard, Bill?' the umpire asked.

'No, I had one here last year.'

In Essex's second innings, when they were set 111 to win, Peter Smith was promoted in the order. He made four. But that year he did the 'double' of 100 wickets and 1,000 runs for the first time in his career, and his cousin Ray did the same.

DERBYSHIRE

A Townsend b P Smith	86	b R Smith	1
C S Elliott b R Smith	2	run out	68
T S Worthington c P Smith b Bailey	0	b Bailey	9
D Smith run out	10	b R Smith	35
G H Pope c Insole b Bailey	5	c Dodds b Bailey	11
A E Alderman b Bailey	20	c Insole b Bailey	27
E Marsh c Crabtree b P Smith	24	c Horsfall b Bailey	4
A E Rhodes c Insole b P Smith	4	c Horsfall b R. Smith	0
E J Gothard not out	24	b R Smith	40
C Gladwin c Insole b Bailey	27	c Wilcox b Bailey	52
W H Copson b Bailey	0	not out	38
Extras	21		19
	223		**304**

Bowling: *First Innings*: Bailey 24.2–1–83–5, R Smith 18–3–50–1, T P B Smith 18–2–59–3, Vigar 2–0–10–0. *Second Innings*; Bailey 30.5–6–92–5, R Smith 49–14–122–4, T P B Smith 22–6–53–0, Vigar 5–0–18–0.

ESSEX

T C Dodds lbw b Copson	20	c Townsend b Copson	23
S J Cray b Copson	11	b Pope	9
A V Avery c Pope b Copson	0	lbw b Pope	0
H P Crabtree lbw b Pope	2	c Worthington b Gladwin	30
F H Vigar not out	114	not out	40
R Horsfall b Pope	8	not out	3
D R Wilcox b Gladwin	9		
T E Bailey b Worthington	19		
D J Insole b Copson	48		
R Smith c Marsh b Pope	21		
T P B Smith b Worthington	163	c Worthington b Copson	4
Extras	2		5
	417		**114–5**

Bowling: *First Innings*; Copson 36–8–117–4, Pope 27–8–73–3, Gladwin 13–3–54–1, Worthington 21.5–1–90–2, Rhodes 18–4–44–0, Marsh 11–3–37–0. *Second Innings*; Copson 14–3–36–2, Pope 15–5–39–2, Gladwin 3.1–0–15–1, Rhodes 5–0–19–0.

Fog at the Seaside
Scarborough, May 1951

This was not cricket weather. The air was cold and moist, and the cricket pitch was covered with a mist which had swirled in from the sea. The panorama was more akin to a Hammer horror film than the cricket match between Scarborough 'A' and Driffield.

At times the fog completely obscured the wickets and the players, but they made a game of it. Driffield's Smithson won the toss and sent in Scarborough. It was not a successful move. The bowlers had more trouble than the batsmen in adjusting to the conditions, and the ball did not move much in the ghostly atmosphere. A cricket reporter on the *Driffield Times*, who for some reason called himself 'Red Rose', was critical of the first over by Alex Oxtoby, the first-change bowler. 'Red Rose' called it a 'shining example of how not to bowl at Scarborough'. Including the bowler and the wicket-keeper, there were ten fielders on the off side, leaving Woodcock alone on the leg, and then Oxtoby bowled six balls on leg stump. The field placing was certainly mysterious. Perhaps the skipper couldn't see where everybody was.

Scarborough had 200 on the board inside 103 minutes, and George Shepherdson reached his century twelve minutes later. Driffield managed only one maiden in their allotted 48 overs. The target set was very stiff.

The weather had by this time taken a turn from bad to worse. The ball was wet and slippery, the light was bad, the fog rolled in more thickly. At a nearby game in Ravenscar, visibility was never less than the required 22 yards but the fog was so bad that the umpires had to call out the runs for the scorers.

Driffield fought on but the game was abandoned through fog, which shows what a great leveller the weather can be. Scarborough had outplayed Driffield for five hours, but, with the game abandoned, the East Yorkshire Cup game was a draw.

Professional games affected by fog include Glamorgan against Hampshire in July 1946, Warwickshire against New Zealand in August 1931 and Nottinghamshire against Surrey in 1878. But fog, rain and bad light are far from the only weather conditions to disrupt cricket. Intense heat stopped the 1868 game between Surrey and Lancashire, and, in a game between Victoria and New South Wales in 1896, the heat was so great at one time that the bowlers had to use sawdust in order to hold the ball. Extreme cold called a temporary halt to the games between Cambridge University and Essex in 1981 and Gentlemen and Players in 1903 (at Hastings), while fielders wore greatcoats and gloves for a time during a game between MCC and Oxford University in the 1890s.

SCARBOROUGH 'A'
G Shepherdson run out 108
K Hudson lbw b Oxtoby 17
J R Knowles b Yates b Gee 21
E S Alcock not out 63
L Halstead not out 24
Extras 6
239–3 (48 overs)

Bowling: Smithson 0–75, Atkinson 0–57, Berriman 0–32, Gee 1–17, Oxtoby 1–52.

DRIFFIELD
T Southwick c Atkinson b Hood 23
G J Whittington b Hood 4
W Rose c Rigby b Shepherdson 20
A Oxtoby c and b Rigby 24
H Gee not out 9
B Holmes b Shepherdson 1
J W Atkinson not out 1
Extras 4
86–5

Bowling: Hood 2–31, Lewsey, 0–15, Shepherdson 2–2, Rigby 1–34.

Politicians Against the Stage

East Grinstead, September 1955

Can you imagine the present government putting together a team of cricketers which includes the Foreign Secretary, the Home Secretary, the Lord Chancellor, the Employment Minister and an assortment of other Members of Parliament? Well, it happened in 1955, and surprisingly there was no place for Sir Alec Douglas-Home, who had once been a useful cricketer.

The team of Politicians included Harold Macmillan (Foreign Secretary) and Viscount Kilmuir (Lord Chancellor), both of whom hadn't played for 30 years. (Viscount Kilmuir cheated somewhat by using practice nets a few times before the game.) Sir Walter Monckton (Minister of Labour) had played as recently as nine years before, but Major Lloyd George (Home Secretary) was another whose cricket kit was difficult to find and even more difficult to fit into.

The Stage XI, captained by John Mills, included regular Lord's Taverner cricketers like Leo Genn, John Slater, Richard Attenborough and Mills himself, but Douglas Fairbanks and David Niven were late cry-offs. Each team was strengthened by the inclusion of county cricketers – Gerald Cogger (Sussex) and Hubert Doggart (Sussex) for the Politicians, Denis Compton, Reg Routledge and John Warr (all Middlesex) for the Stage team – and there were two strange rules. One rule was that a batsman reaching 50 would compulsorily retire. The other was that any bowler capturing a player's wicket before he had scored would be fined a guinea.

The Politicians' captain Earl De La Warr (Postmaster-General) won the toss and decided that his team would bat. Lord Hawke, nephew of the famous cricketing namesake, opened the innings with Lieutenant-Colonel Bromley-Davenport, the MP for Knutsford, Cheshire. Lord Hawke made a single before being bowled by Denis Compton's second ball. Bromley-Davenport (29) and Lloyd George (three fours in his 23) put together a substantial partnership, during which there occurred an accident. Leo Genn bowled a friendly full toss, and Bromley-Davenport hit it towards Dickie Attenborough in the deep. Attenborough ran 20 yards and misjudged the flight of the ball, which hit him on the forehead. He collapsed unconscious, blood poured out, and he was taken on a stretcher to the Queen Victoria Hospital, East Grinstead, where he stayed for two days before being discharged. The game continued in his absence.

After Hubert Doggart's quick 50, two cabinet ministers, Harold Macmillan and Sir Walter Monckton, found themselves batting together. The stand was broken during an especially strange over from Richard Hearne, well known to every child in the land as 'Mr Pastry', a man responsible for many a custard-pie war. Mr Pastry bamboozled Harold Macmillan; the future British Prime Minister played back so far that he hit his own wicket. Sir Walter Monckton was even more baffled by a ball from Rex Harrison which bounced four times and bowled him. Some good batting from the late-order peers took the total to 178 for eight, made in 100 minutes.

At the fall of the first Stage wicket, Dickie Hearne came out to bat dressed like an American football player, padded out with chest and elbow protectors. He hit two fours before being bowled.

Then came the big shock of the afternoon. Denis Compton, whom many of the crowd had come to see bat, was bowled second ball by Gerald Cogger. As Compton had yet to score, Cogger was fined a guinea. He wasn't displeased.

The absence of the hospitalised Dickie Attenborough meant the Stage XI might have to bat a man short, but they had a better idea. A make-up artist got to work on Denis Compton, who created some kind of record by batting twice in the same innings. The tannoy announcer, John Snagge of the BBC, welcomed the number seven batsman as 'Denis Pastry'. Compton did better this time, but the Stage could not match their target, the game ending in a draw.

The beneficiary, incidentally, was the Sackville College Appeal.

POLITICIANS

Lord Hawke b Compton	1
Lt-Col Bromley-Davenport b Warr	29
Major Lloyd George b Mattingly	23
Hubert Doggart retired	53
Sir Walter Monckton b Harrison	6
Harold Macmillan hit wkt b Hearne	2
Lord Kilmuir b Compton	15
Earl De La Warr b Mills	16
Viscount Gage not out	10
Gerald Cogger did not bat	
Mr J B Goudge did not bat	
Extras	23
	178–8

STAGE

Leo Genn st Sub b Lord Hawke	16
Edward Underdown c Doggart b Lloyd George	10
Richard Hearne b Lloyd George	8
Denis Compton b Cogger	0
John Mills b Doggart	6
John Slater retired	50
'Denis Pastry' b Doggart	32
Rex Harrison c Sub b Bromley-Davenport	0
John Mattingly not out	18
Reg Routledge not out	14
John Warr did not bat	
Extras	8
	162–8

Bordering on the Ridiculous

East London, South Africa,
December 1959

Border against Natal in the Currie Cup. Border, having a run of indifferent form and bad luck, hosted the game at the Jan Smuts Ground. They had a psychological lift from memories of the corresponding game the previous season, when they had forced Natal to follow-on 199 runs behind.

Natal batted first on a treacherous rain-affected wicket. Border struck immediately with the wicket of Jackie McGlew, appointed South Africa captain for the forthcoming tour to England. Had Border not dropped five catches, Natal would have been skittled out more cheaply, but they recovered from 50 for eight to reach a final total of 90, inspired by a bat-fling by Malcolm Smith which brought a six and five fours.

Border's reply was uninspired, to say the least. Only four batsmen scored runs. Trevor Goddard, bowling a good length, moving the ball both ways, did most of the damage. In eleven overs, Goddard conceded a two (in his sixth over) and a single (in his seventh), and the last three of his six wickets came in the form of a hat-trick – Griffith, Knott and During. The last, top score with nine, tried to club his team out of trouble. He achieved more than half of Border's sixteen runs.

By the close of a rain-interrupted day, 23 wickets had fallen for 145 runs in four hours' play. Natal had made 90 in 110 minutes, Border 16 in 80 minutes, Natal 39 for three in 55 minutes.

Batting was easier on the second day – for Natal. Kim Elgie's unbeaten 162 was the backbone of a big score. When Jackie McGlew declared, eight wickets down, Border were required to make 369 to win.

The Border batsmen did no better the second time around, but, with the help of a couple of extras, they forced their total up to 18 runs. Unlike the first innings, there could be no complaint about the difficulty of the wicket. Wicket-keeper Malcolm Smith took seven catches, and the bowling architect in chief was Geoff Griffin, who a few months later would find himself the central figure in a throwing controversy. John Cole finished with match figures of seven for seventeen, Goddard six for four, Griffin seven for eleven. Natal won a game of 418 runs by the margin of 350.

Kevin Commins, promoted after his first-innings duck, bagged a pair, as did Peter Muzzell and Sid Knott. Peter Tainton batted for 57 minutes for his unbeaten seven. This time the innings lasted 97 minutes. Border's aggregate score of 34, made in less than three hours' total batting, is still the record lowest aggregate for a first-class match, and Neil During's first-innings boundary was the only four they hit in the whole game. In their next game, against Western Province, Border proved that it was a fluke by making 163 and 116.

NATAL

D J McGlew c Hagemann b Knott	0	(5) c During b Schreiber	22
T Goddard lbw b Knott	4	(1) lbw b Knott	0
M K Elgie b Hagemann	11	(3) not out	162
R McLean b Knott	0	(6) c Hagemann b During	23
C Wesley c and b Hagemann	11	(7) b Schreiber	36
L Morby-Smith c Muzzell b Hagemann	0	(8) c Griffith b Schreiber	43
G Griffin c Hagemann b Knott	22	(2) st Kirsten b Schreiber	5
A Tillim c Schreiber b Hagemann	0		
M Smith c Griffith b Hagemann	33	(9) lbw b Schreiber	2
P Dodds b Knott	8	(4) c Knott b Schreiber	0
J Cole not out	1		
Extras	1		1
	90	**declared**	**294–8**

Bowling: *First Innings*; Knott 13.3–2–40–5, Hagemann 13–2–49–5, *Second Innings*; Knott 15–5–24–1, Hagemann 10–3–37–0, Schreiber 29–5–126–6, Tainton 3–0–13–0, Commins 4–1–16–0, Griffith 1–0–5–0, Muzzell 3–0–23–0, During 15–3–49–1.

Fall of wickets: *First Innings*; 0, 15, 15, 18, 21, 47, 47, 50, 90, 90. *Second Innings*; 0, 13, 13, 46, 80, 145, 267, 294.

BORDER

A Hagemann b Cole	2	c Smith b Griffin	3
P Muzzell lbw b Goddard	0	b Griffin	0
P Fenix b Goddard	0	c Smith b Cole	1
K Kirton b Elgie b Cole	4	c Smith b Griffin	3
N During b Goddard	9	(8) c Smith b Cole	1
K Commins c Tillim b Goddard	0	(5) c Smith b Griffin	0
P Tainton c Elgie b Cole	0	(6) not out	7
M Griffith lbw b Goddard	1	(7) b Griffin	0
S Knott c Cole b Goddard	0	c Smith b Griffin	0
E Schreiber c McLean b Cole	0	c Smith b Cole	1
N Kirsten not out	0	c McLean b Griffin	0
Extras	0		2
	16		**18**

Bowling: *First Innings*; Griffin 1–1–0–0, Goddard 11–9–3–6, Cole 11–4–13–4. *Second Innings*; Griffin 13–6–11–7, Goddard 4–3–1–0, Cole 9–7–4–3.

Fall of wickets: *First Innings*; 2, 2, 2, 8, 11, 11, 12, 16, 16, 16. *Second Innings*; 1, 5, 5, 5, 10, 10, 11, 12, 15, 18.

Nothing to Lose
Elgin, May 1964

In the North of Scotland League game at Elgin, the home team batted first and compiled a reasonable total of 145 for five declared. People thinking it might be a fair contest reckoned without the showing of the Ross County team, who batted a man short.

Elgin had a useful pace attack. Bernard Woolfson, from Beccles near Norwich, had twice played for Suffolk before moving to Scotland, where he worked as a Post Office sales representative. Dave Murray, employed by the Forestry Commission at Elgin, took the other end.

Up strode Woolfson for his first ball. A wicket. In came Woolfson to the new batsman. Bowled him. The number-four Ross County batsman, Oliver, survived the remaining four balls.

Now it was Murray's turn. He bowled a wicket-maiden and at the end of the second over Ross County were nought for three.

With the first ball of his new over Woolfson dismissed the stubborn Oliver. Hannant went to the fourth ball, Taylor to the sixth. Ross County were nought for six at the end of the third over.

Murray needed only one more over to finish the match. He claimed Niven's wicket with his third ball, bowled Northcliffe with his fourth and Frazer with his sixth. The ten-man Ross County team were all out for no runs. They had never really recovered from the bad start of losing two

wickets with the first balls, although observers pointed out
that they hadn't had much luck. One batsman had hit his
own wicket, two others had played on to their stumps. They
had no run of the ball . . . and no run between the wickets.

Ross County won praise for their sportsmanship. Most of
their away games involved travelling between 100 and 200
miles. The home team were glad their opponents had
turned up so they could play cricket, let alone beat the long-
standing league records for low scoring. In 1896 Kinross
had scored one against Auchtermuchty, while Arbroath
United had amassed two against Aberdeen in 1868. It
would be difficult to beat the Ross County record, although
many teams have equalled it.

A writer in the *Cricketer* (June 1923), believed there
were already about 70 instances of scores of nought at this
stage of the sport's history, the first being a game at
Hampton Green in Norfolk in 1815. 'Some years later an
extraordinary game was played in Derbyshire between
Kegworth and Diseworth,' the writer continues. 'The latter
went in first and made only a single, the hero of the innings
being the vicar's groom. An easy victory for Kegworth
seemed assured, but, to everyone's amazement, the side
collapsed without a run.' There is also mention of a game of
dubious authenticity at Chiswick in April 1899, when both
teams allegedly scored no runs.

One of the more interesting examples of a team being
dismissed for nought was that of Fitzroy in a Victorian
Scottish Cricket Association game in 1913. Replying to
Williamstown's score of 98, they lost by 98 runs, and
Davidson took ten for none. As with all such innings, the
fall of wickets proves very easy to estimate.

ELGIN
T Manley b Oliver 28
B Woolfson b Hendry 0
J Wright b Nevin 43
F Muir lbw b Nevin 8
J Leithead not out 36
W Phimister b Nevin 6
R Draggan not out 12
Extras 12
                                                            145–5 declared

Bowling: Hendry 15–0–53–1, Northcliffe 7–1–20–0, Nevin 11–2–42–3, Oliver 4–1–18–1.

ROSS COUNTY
B Kenny c Phimister b Woolfson........... 0
G Shiels c Stewardson b Murray 0
J Hendry b Woolfson 0
W Oliver b Woolfson 0
J Niven hit wkt b Murray 0
R Hannant lbw b Woolfson 0
I Taylor b Woolfson 0
S Bull not out 0
J Northcliffe b Murray 0
N Frazer b Murray 0
Extras 0
                                                                    0

Bowling: Woolfson 2–2–0–5, Murray 2–2–0–4.

All Around the Clock

Cambridge, June 1973

There was a lot of cricket in Cambridgeshire that week. The local county team were playing Lincolnshire at Wisbech, the Queen Mother was shown a cricket match when she visited Leys school and the New Zealand tourists were in Cambridge, fashioning an exciting finish with a sporting declaration against the Combined Universities. Imran Khan inspired the Universities on their last-day chase of 211 to win. They finished 207 for nine.

The most unusual game that week took place on Parker's Piece, the open stretch of city-centre Cambridge land that divides 'gown' from 'town'. The cricket game was all 'gown'.

Members of the Cambridge University cricket society took the field at five o'clock on the afternoon of 14 June. Their mission was to create a record for non-stop cricket. They were helped in their challenge by the Fire Brigade, who pumped 1,500 gallons of water on to the wicket and also provided gas lamps for evening play, and by the sponsorship of various firms, including the cricket-ball manufacturer Alfred Reader, who provided special orange cricket balls. The students brought their own whisky and coffee to help them through the night.

The two captains agreed to suspend fast bowling during the darkness hours, and it was between 1 a.m. and 4 a.m. that Roger Coates scored the only century of the game, a feat which earned him the Haig prize for best batting. The

Alfred Reader prize for best bowling went to Philip Cornes.

Each team had five innings. Altogether 1,395 runs were scored for the loss of 89 wickets in 367 overs. They played until five o'clock the following afternoon, 24 hours' cricket, non-stop apart from a lunch break. They raised £170 to help the mentally handicapped.

LANGLEY'S XI: 59, 179, 83, 200 and 161.

SUCH'S XI: 126, 254-8 dec. 121, 142-8 dec and 70-3.

LANGLEY'S XI: T Brown, A Ave, R Court, J Brett, J Chambers, D J Yeandle, T Wald, J Preston, N Peace, M Coultas, D Langley.

SUCH'S XI: R Coates, P Such, P Cornes, A Radford, M Williams, A S I Berry, J Burnett, P Kinns, M Shaw, R Henson, M Furneaux.

'G Davis Is Innocent'

Leeds, August 1975

'What does Headingley have in store this time, I wonder?' pondered John Woodcock in *The Times* on the morning of the Third Test between England and Australia. 'Almost always this corresponding match has something unusual about it, whether it is Australia scoring 404 in a day to win, as in 1948, or Underwood running through the Australian batting on a controversial pitch, as in 1972.'

Neither spectators nor cricket correspondents could have foreseen the unusual controversy that struck Headingley on the final day. Nothing remotely like it had happened in living memory.

As a game, this Test was interesting and intriguing, edging further and further towards an England victory until Australia staged an excellent recovery on the fourth day. Australia were one up and held the Ashes, a strong position for a series of only four Tests.

David Steele plodded through the first day – during one 90-minute period his score moved by only ten runs – and there was some threat from Gary Gilmour's swing. On the second day, Australia slumped to 107 for eight when faced with the two English left-arm spin bowlers, the experienced Derek Underwood and the debutant Phil Edmonds. Edmonds, the 1973 Cambridge University captain, beat Ian Chappell's ungainly swing on the second ball of his second over, trapped Edwards not playing a shot next ball and added the wicket of Greg Chappell, caught at square-leg, in his next over. At tea Edmonds had three for four from fifteen balls. At the end of the next session, cut short by rain, he had five for seventeen from twelve overs.

Another persevering innings by Steele on the third day – an unbeaten 59 in 210 minutes – provided the anchor for England's overnight lead of 337 and a match-winning position. Shortly before lunch on the fourth day, Australia went in for a second time needing 445 to win, but the ball wasn't turning as much and the wicket was more placid. At the close the game was beautifully poised. Australia needed another 225 with seven wickets remaining.

The storm broke the next morning, at 6.50, when the Headingley groundsman rolled back the covers on the wicket. During the night, unseen by the police patrol, someone had climbed the wall, run on to the pitch and crawled under the covers, pouring oil over the wicket (right on a good length) and digging three-inch holes with kitchen knives and forks. On the outside wall were slogans proclaiming that George Davis was innocent. Until that day, few people were aware that George Davis, a 34-year-old London mini-cab driver, was serving a 17-year jail sentence for his alleged part in a robbery in which a policeman was shot. Within a week the name 'George Davis' was common knowledge.

The campaign to free George Davis had already been in action a year without being able to reopen the case. It was now stepped up: slogans at the Central Criminal Court, sit-down protests, a march to Downing Street, campaigners chained to the Monument and demonstrating on the dome of St Paul's Cathedral, and naked displays at an East London boating lake. The campaign leader, Peter Chappell (no relation to Ian, Greg or Trevor), was given an eighteen-month jail sentence at Birkenhead in January 1976 for his Leeds and London graffiti prose and for topping up the Headingley pitch with oil. When cricket fans now referred to the Chappells they had to define exactly who they were talking about.

Captains, managers and umpires converged on the Headingley wicket around nine o'clock on the morning of the final day of the Third Test. The groundsman felt he could repair the holes in the wicket, but oil was a different matter. The only possible way of continuing the game was if the captains, Tony Greig and Ian Chappell, could agree on another strip of wicket of similar wear. Greig was happy to do this. Understandably, Chappell could not comply, and the game was abandoned. Loss of gate receipts and scorecard sales probably amounted to nearly £6,000, but it was unlikely that the game could have been finished anyway. At noon it rained.

Nine months later, after serving two years of his sentence, George Davis was released from jail by the Home Secretary. In July 1978 he was back in jail, sentenced to fifteen years' imprisonment for an armed raid on a bank the previous September. He pleaded guilty to this offence, which helped reduce his sentence to eleven years on appeal. In January 1987, soon after his release from the bank-raid sentence, he was sent to prison for eighteen months for an attempt to rob a mail-train. Again he pleaded guilty.

ENGLAND

J H Edrich c Mallett b Thomson	62	b Mallett	35
B Wood lbw b Gilmour	9	lbw b Walker	25
D S Steele c Walters b Thomson	73	c Chappell (G) b Gilmour	92
J H Hampshire lbw b Gilmour	14	(7) c Chappell (G) b Thomson	0
K W R Fletcher c Mallett b Lillee	8	(4) c Chappell (G) b Lillee	14
A W Greig run out	51	(5) c and b Mallett	49
A P E Knott lbw b Gilmour	14	(8) c Thomson b Lillee	31
P H Edmonds not out	13	(9) c Sub b Gilmour	8
C M Old b Gilmour	5	(6) st Marsh b Mallett	10
J A Snow c Walters b Gilmour	0	c Marsh b Gilmour	9
D L Underwood c Chappell (G) b Gilmour	0	not out	0
Extras	39		18
	288		**291**

Bowling: *First Innings*; Lillee 28–12–53–1, Thomson 22–8–53–2, Gilmour 31.2–10–85–6, Walker 18–4–54–0, Chappell (G) 2–0–4–0. *Second Innings*; Lillee 20–5–48–2, Thomson 20–6–67–1, Gilmour 20–5–72–3, Walker 15–4–36–1, Mallett 19–4–50–3.

Fall of wickets: *First Innings*; 25, 137, 159, 189, 213, 268, 269, 284, 284, 288. *Second Innings*; 55, 70, 103, 197, 209, 210, 272, 276, 285, 291.

AUSTRALIA

R B McCosker c Hampshire b Old	0	not out	95
R W Marsh b Snow	25	b Underwood	12
I M Chappell b Edmonds	35	lbw b Old	62
G S Chappell c Underwood b Edmonds	13	c Steele b Edmonds	12
R Edwards lbw b Edmonds	0		
K D Walters lbw b Edmonds	19	(5) not out	27
G J Gilmour c Greig b Underwood	6		
M H N Walker c Old b Edmonds	0		
J R Thomson c Steele b Snow	16		
D K Lillee b Snow	11		
A A Mallett not out	1		
Extras	9		12
	135		**220–3**

Bowling: *First Innings*; Snow 18.5–7–22–3, Old 11–3–30–1, Greig 3–0–14–0, Wood 5–2–10–0, Underwood 19–12–22–1, Edmonds 20–7–28–5. *Second Innings*; Snow 15–5–23–0, Old 17–5–61–1, Greig 9–3–20–0, Underwood 15–4–40–1, Edmonds 17–4–64–1.

Fall of wickets: *First Innings*; 8, 53, 78, 78, 81, 96, 104, 107, 128, 135. *Second Innings*; 51, 161, 174.

The Ten-Minute Game
Worcester, May 1979

The first thing to do, in order to understand this strange match, is to scrutinise the Benson & Hedges Group A Table on the morning of 24 May, the day of the match between Worcestershire and Somerset. Somerset captain Brian Rose and his team-mates certainly did so that Thursday morning. The table looked like this:

	Played	Won	Lost	Drawn	Points
Somerset	3	3	0	0	9
Worcestershire	3	2	1	0	6
Glamorgan	3	2	1	0	6
Gloucestershire	4	1	3	0	3
Minor Counties (South)	3	0	3	0	0

Two teams from the group would qualify for the quarter-final. Should any two teams finish level on points, the tie-breaker was their rate of wicket-taking. The statistics showed that Somerset were certain to qualify unless Worcestershire beat them that day AND Glamorgan beat the Minor Counties (South) in their final game AND both Worcester and Glamorgan significantly improved their wicket-taking rates so that they were superior to Somerset's.

The weather was poor that week. After Worcestershire's John Player Sunday League game had been washed out without a ball bowled, the groundstaff at New Road had been forced to work twelve hours a day in a bid to prepare a wicket while there was more rain. Extra work was caused by an accident with the roller damaging the first strip cut for the Cup game.

No play was possible on Wednesday 23 May, the day scheduled for the Worcestershire–Somerset Benson & Hedges game. The next morning, the weather was still unpredictable, and the start was delayed. Brian Rose was concerned about the weather. He was also concerned about guaranteeing Somerset's place in the quarter-final. The 28-year-old left-handed opening bat was a shrewd captain who had seen Somerset to a Gillette Cup Final the previous year. Somerset were on the verge of great success – in 1979 they won the Gillette Cup and the John Player League – and Rose, who had already played five Test matches, was tipped as a possible future England captain.

In this match Brian Rose 'sacrificed all known cricketing principles', to use *Wisden*'s words. With the support of his team-mates, Rose declared after the first over, which produced one no-ball, thereby deliberately putting Somerset in a losing position. Worcestershire scored the required two runs without loss. The ten-minute game (not counting the ten minutes between innings) produced three runs from seventeen balls.

Rose's decision was made to protect Somerset's wicket-taking rate in case they lost the game and all the other events worked out to their detriment. He recognised it was unusual practice, but he wasn't at fault, it was legal. There was nothing in the rules to prevent him declaring.

The 100 paying spectators were outraged, even when Worcestershire refunded their money. Some had been waiting around for a day and a half to see a game of cricket. Two farmers had travelled from Devon, a round trip of 300 miles. A teacher had brought a party of fifteen school-children to reward them for their good work at school, and another man had spent two days of his holiday on the ground. The groundstaff had worked diligently to prepare the pitch for a day's use. The only humour came from those shocked spectators who tried to work out who would receive the gold medal. Vanburn Holder's maiden over was OK, and Glenn Turner's match-winning two singles made him a strong candidate. In the event it was felt 'improper' to make a gold medal award.

Words like 'disgrace to cricket', 'farce' and 'not the spirit of the game' were bandied about, and the Test & County Cricket Board met to hold an inquiry. All the time Rose insisted his action was in accordance with the rules and his first duty was to Somerset. His committee supported him, although individuals made it clear that it wouldn't happen again.

On 1 June the Test & County Cricket Board ruled that Somerset should be expelled from that season's Benson & Hedges competition for not complying with the spirit of cricket. Worcestershire and Glamorgan, whose game with Minor Counties (South) was washed out, qualified for the quarter-final, but Essex won the trophy and the £6,500 prize money. The rules were amended to prevent declarations, and Somerset won two of the next three Benson & Hedges competitions.

SOMERSET

B C Rose not out	0
P W Denning not out	0
Extras	1
	1–0 (declared)

Bowling: Holder 1–1–0–0.

WORCESTERSHIRE

G M Turner not out	2
J A Ormrod not out	0
Extras	0
	2–0

Bowling: Dredge 1–0–1–0, Jennings 0.4–0–1–0.

The other players 'participating' were P M Roebuck, I V A Richards, I T Botham, V J Marks, D Breakwell, D J S Taylor and H R Moseley (Somerset) and P A Neale, E J O Hemsley, Younis Ahmed, D N Patel, D J Humphries, J D Inchmore, N Gifford and A P Pridgeon (Worcestershire).

Following-on at Headingley
Leeds, July 1981

England were losing one-nil to Australia, and this was the third of six Test matches in the series. Ian Botham had given way to Mike Brearley as England captain, but, at the end of the third day's play, having followed on 227 runs behind, England were staring defeat in the face, six for one in their second innings. At that point, Ladbroke's were offering 500–1 for an England victory.

On the first two days, England dropped catches, but Botham's six wickets ensured that Australia, progressing slowly, didn't get too far away. It looked far enough, especially when batting proved difficult on Saturday 18 July, the birthdate of W G Grace, Gary Sobers and Dennis Lillee, the last a key figure in the bowling out of England for 174.

The second innings was no better. The ball was still dodging about and Australia had ideal bowlers for the conditions in Lillee, Terry Alderman and Geoff Lawson. In spite of resolute resistance from Geoff Boycott – 46 in 215 minutes – England slumped to 135 for seven, still 92 behind.

The next 35 overs saw England add 216 runs. Ian Botham and Graham Dilley agreed that they saw little point in trying to hang around for a couple of days. 'Let's give it some humpty,' Botham apparently said, in a famous mid-wicket conference. Dilley held his own with Botham, making 56 of their aggressive partnership of 117. This was a bit of a surprise. In the West Indies, the previous winter, Dilley had made eleven runs in seven innings. The Botham–Dilley stand came within eight of Hendren and Larwood's eighth-wicket England partnership against Australia. At the time, Botham and Dilley were just having a bit of fun.

England's number ten, Chris Old, was known to be suspect against fast bowling, but he pluckily kept the momentum going. Botham, now in full swing, using a bat borrowed from Graham Gooch, went from 36 to 100 by means of fourteen fours, a six and two singles. When Old was out, for 29, Botham shielded Bob Willis, the last man, to the extent that Willis faced only five balls in the last 20 minutes of play that Monday. Willis made one of the 31 runs that came in that period.

The next morning, the stand ended at 37, with England 129 ahead. It had been a brave resurrection of the game – England players later confessed that they had checked out of their hotel rooms and had to rebook for Monday night – but Australia were still expected to make the 130 for victory. What shifted the mood England's way, however, was the psychological effect of Botham's innings.

An hour's play saw Australia at 56 for one. Seventy minutes later they were 75 for eight. The dramatic change had come from Bob Willis's second spell, bowled with the wind from the Kirkstall Lane end. Recognising that his England career was on the line, Willis put everything into that spell, and was rewarded with lift and life from the wicket. Chappell, Yallop and Hughes were all caught by close fielders after trying to fend off rising deliveries.

Lilley and Bright frustrated England with an eighth-wicket partnership of 35 in only four overs. Lillee hooked Willis, the ball bobbed up, Gatting ran ten yards from mid-on and dived to hold the catch close to the ground. Bright was bowled by Willis, and England had won an unbeliev-able victory by eighteen runs. It was only the second time in history that a Test had been won by a team following-on. The series was poised at one-one, and Brearley's team would recover enough to win it.

AUSTRALIA

J Dyson b Dilley	102	(2) c Taylor b Willis	34
G M Wood lbw b Botham	34	(1) c Taylor b Botham	10
T M Chappell c Taylor b Willey	27	c Taylor b Willis	8
K J Hughes c and b Botham	89	c Botham b Willis	0
R J Bright b Dilley	7	(8) b Willis	19
G N Yallop c Taylor b Botham	58	(5) c Gatting b Willis	0
A R Border lbw b Botham	8	(6) b Old	0
R W Marsh b Botham	28	(7) c Dilley b Willis	4
G F Lawson c Taylor b Botham	13	c Taylor b Willis	1
D K Lillee not out	3	c Gatting b Willis	17
T M Alderman not out	0	not out	0
Extras	32		18
	401–9 declared		**111**

Bowling: *First Innings*; Willis 30–8–72–0, Old 43–14–91–0, Dilley 27–4–78–2, Botham 39.2–11–95–6, Willey 13–2–31–1, Boycott 3–2–2–0. *Second Innings*; Botham 7–3–14–1, Dilley 2–0–11–0, Willis 15.1–3–43–8, Old 9–1–21–1, Willey 3–1–4–0.

Fall of wickets: *First Innings*; 55, 149, 196, 220, 332, 354, 357, 396, 401. *Second Innings*; 13, 56, 58, 58, 65, 68, 74, 75, 110, 111.

ENGLAND

G A Gooch lbw b Alderman	2	c Alderman b Lillee	0
G Boycott b Lawson	12	lbw b Alderman	46
J M Brearley c Marsh b Alderman	10	c Alderman b Lillee	14
D I Gower c Marsh b Lawson	24	c Border b Aderman	9
M W Gatting lbw b Lillee	15	lbw b Alderman	1
P Willey b Lawson	8	c Dyson b Lillee	33
I T Botham c Marsh b Lillee	50	not out	149
R W Taylor c Marsh b Lillee	5	c Bright b Alderman	1
G R Dilley c and b Lillee	13	b Alderman	56
C M Old c Border b Alderman	0	b Lawson	29
R G D Willis not out	1	c Border b Alderman	2
Extras	34		16
	174		**356**

Bowling: *First Innings*; Lillee 18.5–7–49–4, Alderman 19–4–59–3, Lawson 13–3–32–3. *Second Innings*; Lillee 25–6–94–3, Alderman 35.3–6–135–6, Lawson 23–4–96–1, Bright 4–0–15–0.

Fall of wickets: *First Innings*; 12, 40, 42, 84, 87, 112, 148, 166, 167, 174. *Second Innings*; 0, 18, 37, 41, 105, 133, 135, 252, 319, 356.

The Bramble Bank Game
The Solent, September 1984

Twice a year, for about an hour on each occasion, a sandbar surfaces in the middle of the Solent, the stretch of water between Hampshire and the Isle of Wight. The sandbar is Bramble Bank, which generally hides under the water and provides a treacherous navigation hazard for ocean-going vessels. Many have run aground on Bramble Bank.

At the spring equinox and autumn equinox, when the water is at its lowest, Bramble Bank appears, bubbling through, slowly exposing itself, creating an island of about two acres. Those two separate hours, one in March, one in September, are the best times of the year for a cricket game, unless someone would like to devise an underwater game between two teams of divers.

Small-island cricket games have often been played to establish British sovereignty – the Goodwin Sands has a long history of games, and, in February 1988, two boys launched a British claim for a new island of washed-up shingle off the Isle of Wight coast – but they have also been played by lovers of the absurd for a bit of fun.

The Bramble Bank game has a lengthy history, albeit intermittent, dating back to the early part of the twentieth century. When yachtsman Uffa Fox organised a game in 1954, he was reviving an idea which had been dormant for 32 years since the previous game. Fox's team, usings oars as bats, scored 29 and beat a team from Parkhurst Prison (mainly officers and their relatives) by seven runs. The winners had a slight advantage as only seven of the Parkhurst team were able to land.

In 1966 an air-cushion craft took the players to the sand-bank, and Uffa Fox's team beat Cowes Cricket Club by three runs. The venue will always be a more natural habitat for a sailor than a landlubberly fast bowler. There haven't been too many green wickets at Bramble Bank over the years, but nor have runs been very easy to come by.

After Uffa Fox's 1972 game against Colin Cowdrey's XI, there was a gap of twelve years. Then the Royal Southern Yacht Club (Hamble) challenged the Island Sailing Club (Cowes). The two teams waited around in a flotilla of small boats until the island emerged from the water. They landed and took the field wearing wellingtons and whites. The Island Sailing Club batted first and made 24 all out – good sailors, poor cricketers. The mainland club knocked off the required runs, the winning hit being a six and lost ball.

Island Sailing Club 24
Royal Southern Yacht Club 25 for two.

Abandoned After 62 Balls

Kingston, Jamaica, January 1998

The wicket at Sabina Park was cracked and uneven. England captain Mike Atherton thought it would deteriorate over the five days. He won the toss and elected to bat. Brian Lara led the West Indies team on to the field and Courtney Walsh measured his run-up. The fielders dispersed, Atherton took guard and the umpire signalled 'Play'.

Walsh's first ball was a loosener and Atherton steered it for two runs. The second ball kept low. The third was a vicious leg-cutter that speared towards Atherton's ribs. The fourth rolled along the ground.

Atherton was out to the first ball of Walsh's second over. He tried to take his bat away but was caught at gully. Mark Butcher's first ball lifted dangerously and he gloved it to third slip. England were four for two and now everybody suspected that this relaid wicket was not suitable for a Test match.

During the first hour England physiotherapist Wayne Morton was out in the middle for longer than most of the batsmen. He came on to treat injuries on six occasions – once for Nasser Hussain, twice for Graham Thorpe and three times for Alec Stewart, who was hit twice on the hands and once on the shoulder. Another time a ball from Curtly Ambrose bounced over Stewart and over the wicket-keeper's head for four byes. Stewart must have played on worse pitches, but he was probably playing football at the time.

The umpires, local-man Steve Buckner and Srini Venkataraghavan from India, became very aware that the batsmen could be seriously injured, especially when Thorpe was hit on the hand by a ball which reared up from a good length. After the umpires had conferred twice they called over the two captains. The teams went off after playing for 66 minutes and 62 balls (including one no-ball). Stewart had made a courageous nine from 26 balls.

There followed an hour's negotiation with the International Cricket Conference before the match was formally abandoned. Thankfully, no one had been seriously injured.

It was the first-ever Test match to have been abandoned for a dangerous wicket but the India–Sri Lanka one-day match, on Christmas Day 1997, was called off after eighteen balls in similar circumstances. The three previous Test match abandonments – Karachi (1968–9), Jamaica (1977–8) and Bangalore (1978–9) – had been provoked by crowd rioting.

ENGLAND
Atherton c Campbell b Walsh 2
Stewart not out 9
Butcher c S C Williams b Walsh 0
Hussain c Hooper b Ambrose 1
Thorpe not out...0
Extras 5
_____
17–3

Bowling: Walsh 5.1–1–10–2, Ambrose 5–3–3–1.